Interpret Your

# DREAMS

Interpret Your

# DREAMS

*Pierre Daco*

*Translated by Mark Daniels*

**ROBINSON**
London

Robinson Publishing
7 Kensington Church Court
London W8 4SP

First published in France by Marabout (Belgique) 1993
Copyright © (Marabout) 1993

This translated edition copyright © Robinson Publishing 1995

A copy of the British Library Cataloguing in Publication
data is available from the British Library

ISBN 1–85487–274–5

Printed and bound in the EC

10 9 8 7 6 5 4 3 2 1

# Contents

# PART I

# CHAPTER 1

## *Five Years of Parallel Life*

If you joined together a fifty-year-old man's dreams end to end, you could say he had dreamed for about five years.

For five years, then – roughly 1,800 days, or 45,000 hours – this fifty-year-old man has inhabited another universe; he has lived in a world that was radically different from everyday reality. In the dream world, however, he has dealt with people, places, objects and animals which, for him, represented actual reality. More than this, during these five years he has been totally withdrawn inside himself in a voyage of exploration. He has discovered latent forces within him. Often, indeed, he has found himself peering through a half-open door leading out into the universe.

Neither time nor space exists in this long night of dreams. Deeds, none the less are done. The dreamer flies, hovers, swims, conducts orchestras, and so on, quite naturally and "rationally". For the duration of the dream, everything makes sense, everything is real. We can dive into the churning sea of time wherever we want. We become children again, or revisit the scenes of our childhood. The dead are restored to life and speak to us. Voices are heard, and sometimes give rise to nightmares.

There is, then, a sort of second life, parallel to our daytime existence. Often, when we awake, the dreams vanish for ever from our memory – or do they? No energy can completely vanish. Where, then, have they fled?

Sleep takes up one-third of our lives. One-quarter of that third is taken up by dreams. This is no trivial subject.

## A personal adventure

Nothing is more individual than a dream. Here is no double life which can be uncovered by a prurient press or a prying spouse. This is the ultimate privacy, the nudity of the soul. The deepest secrets of our personalities bob to the surface.

The dream is not subject to our control. We abandon all power from the moment that it begins. We are reduced to passengers, responsible for neither the beauty nor the hideousness of the landscape through which we may pass. The dream will work out its own intricate course. Critical doubt and consciousness itself are inert.

Dreams, then, may be said to plumb the depths of our inner being. Ultimately they reveal, if only we can read them, ourselves, unguarded, untutored, untrammelled.

At night, in the wings of the theatre of life, the truth is told. With dawn come the spotlights, the sets, the direction, the acting, the comedy of manners, the lies.

With dawn, we lose the elementary and elemental truths.

## Delusions?

Surely, no one can still believe that dreams are no more than delusions, tricks played by the mind without significance or purpose. Even if we admit that some dreams appear to have no bearing on, nor relation to, our everyday lives, most of them unquestionably warrant serious consideration, if only because we take them absolutely seriously while actually dreaming them.

A conscious being may "waste" time, according to some arbitrary standard. An unconscious being does everything for a purpose. Everything that human beings do has meaning, and everything they do springs from, and reflects, a fundamental need. We would simply not dream if dreams served no useful end. There is no dream that does not relate to our more public lives. Dreams liberate (or condemn) our repressed desires, they manifest our hidden fears. They cause our minds to focus. They enable us to rehearse possible adventures far from our usual experience. They allow us to behave as we would never allow ourselves to behave.

A dream – though commonly an image of unreality – can assume great importance in our minds simply because it can show us what, in reality, we are: what we would be if our lives were not so circumscribed and ordered.

## *Tell me what you dream . . .*

Dreams have always fascinated mankind. It is hardly strange, then, that from the dawn of history we have sought to discover the meaning of this strange universe of dreams. Philosophers and doctors have speculated on what these images, never less than striking, and slithering into the conscious brain like hot wax, actually mean? What about those dreams that are felt to be warnings or prognostications? What kind of work takes place in these mysterious areas of the personality, producing messages that return to the shadows after dawn?

For those who still believe dreams to be mere nonsense, here is an example of a dream which, I believe, cannot fail to arouse one's curiosity and thereby demands an interpretation. The dreamer was a forty-year-old man. I shall return to it in greater depth in chapter 6.

*I was on a promontory, from which I could see a marvellous valley with infinite folds and hollows. These undulations multiplied in a regular way. It was the Valley of Eden. I saw a lot of fruit-trees there, laden with ripe fruit and flowers. Lots of apple-trees. Lots of rose-bushes. The valley itself was just thick grass; white cows grazed there, as far as the eye could see. Here and there, there were little groups of people dancing, very slowly. They danced to some music in ³/₄ time – a sort of slow-motion waltz, outside time itself. It was wonderful . . . I heard the music with perfect clarity. It sprang up from every side. It was the first movement of the Bach cantata: Wie schön leuchtet der Morgenstern. All these people, dancing hand in hand, signalled to me. I felt infinitely happy. I think*

*I would give the rest of my life for just one hour of such happiness.*

*Then there were these three jet aeroplanes with short wings which came from behind me, and suddenly I found myself in the middle one. The other two flanked me like the sides of a triangle. These planes moved very slowly and calmly; all their power was potential only. They flew in absolute silence, just a few feet above the earth. Everything flowed past beneath me, gently, smoothly: the grass, the trees, the people . . . The music could still be heard . . . I'll never forget that dream. It gave me a degree of energy and a feeling of sheer joy which was beyond belief.*

We, or course, must read this dream "cold". It is another person's dream. But what must have been the sensation of a dreamer who experienced this beautiful vision? "A flight from reality," cynics might mutter. Not at all. It is self-evident that something very real within the dreamer produced the dream, something which laboured in the depths of his being, wanted recognition and would not be denied.

After such an experience, it is hardly surprising that the dreamer sought to discover its meaning. How many dreams, after all, are so powerful as to demand that we at least describe them to our friends, even if they possess no apparent significance?

The fact that there has been so much research into sleep and dreams, so many attempts at interpretation and explanation, indicates the subject's importance. At one extreme, we have the numerous populist "key to your dreams" books; at the other, the most profound researches of psychology, undertaken by a host of prestigious names, among whom, of course, Freud and Jung remain paramount. Nowadays, no person who can lay claim to be informed can possibly deny the importance of our dreams.

We all know, in fact, that our dreams can draw out attention to our innermost problems, be they fundamental or fleeting. There are hundreds of dreams which explicitly address our enduring fears – dreams in which we find ourselves inappropriately naked, or lose our luggage, miss the train, and so on. Some dreams recur inescapably for years, even for a lifetime. If the unconscious is prepared so single-mindedly to stress one urgent message, we should surely take the time to discover just what that message is.

## From the Roman Senate to the psychiatrist's couch

The story of research into dreams is long. In ancient Rome, striking dreams were submitted to the Senate for consideration. Then there have been the priests and sorcerers in many cultures who, after their own fashion, have sought to "interpret" the dreams of the faithful. Then we have Descartes, the first man in our history to consider dreaming to be worthy of scientific exploration and analysis.

Meanwhile, today as in the distant past, simple people continue to believe that dreams convey messages from "the other side", are even, indeed, direct communications from the dead. Others maintain the primitive belief that the soul, separated from the body in sleep, communicates with the spirit world and translates such communications in dreams.

Others will tell you that dreams are caused by simple physiological factors – indigestion, heart disease, depression, aches and pains, and so on – or that they are triggered by situations in daytime life, or by a noise in the vicinity of the dreamer.

The French philosopher Henri Bergson threw in his pennyworth with the thesis that the dream is a direct link between sensation and memory. And so we come to the contentions of modern psychoanalysis.

The first psychoanalysts heard their patients recounting innumerable dreams. One can only imagine how astonished they must have been at some of the outrageous or grotesque flowerings of the unconscious to which these sessions made them privy. They stood at the gateways to the unconscious, peering into those cavernous labyrinths in which ordinary men and women were transfigured, becoming suddenly vast, potent, magnificent . . .

For, aside from the everyday, *apparently* banal dreams, there surged up the "great dreams" – giant, tortuous things like moonlit clouds, full of archaic, universal, mythical, brilliant, devilish, enchanting and often unforgettable images, interweaving time and space like two threads in the same weft . . .

So it was that not only did the interpretation of dreams become a vital component of the psychology of the unconscious and a vital tool of the therapist, but the dream itself was recognized as a vital element in the history of human thought.

## *"Keys to dreams"*

Books and articles offering "keys to dreams" are so numerous and their readers so many that we should ask whether they have any worth at all. This depends, of course, on how they are conceived and how they approach the symbols of dreams.

I have before me a "key to your dreams", not long published, in which I read: "Teeth. Falling out. Dreams about = a sign of sickness or death." Dreaming that your teeth have dropped out is not uncommon. This type of dream is probably dreamed by tens of millions of people every night on any continent. You rush to consult this authoritative text, and either you are scared out of your wits or, if of a rational bent, you wonder why your particular continent has not long since ceased to sustain human life.

This kind of "interpretation" is downright absurd. It is not that the author has simply invented the symbolism which he here propounds. Pure invention would not have the ring of truth and so would be infinitely less dangerous and insidious. In fact what the author has done is to condense the general significance of "teeth" without any reference to the real meaning of the context – the dream itself.

It is true that "death" and "teeth" are commonly associated. This happens to correspond to an ancient belief that was once more widespread. But unsophisticated readers who come upon this "key" will inevitably have their thoughts turned to *physical* death, when any number of other interpretations would be valid.

Symbols are created in the psyche, so all translation of

symbolism is, properly, psychological. The "loss of teeth" dream is, in Freudian terms, a castration dream, or, in more general terms, a dream about the diminution of personality (anxieties, feelings of inferiority, fear of being balked, and so on), just as a healthy set of teeth is a symbol of power (the open smile, the strength manifest in the jaws of acrobats suspended by their teeth).

We shall return to these subjects later.

It is not worth keeping a "key to dreams" that is merely trite and obvious, simply relating one symbol to one meaning. A dictionary which studies the various interpretations of symbols throughout all cultures and ages, however, is indispensable.

A good dictionary of symbols will cover a broad spectrum of shades of meaning. Any one symbol will be shown to refer to many meanings once its context is known. This is as it should be. No one symbol allows of one universal interpretation. You may say to me, "I dreamt about a savage horse. What does this mean?" I can only answer that it might mean any number of things. First I will have to know if you are healthy or ill, introverted or extroverted. I will have to relate that dream horse to its surroundings and to the nature of your feelings on seeing it. I will have to be aware of all the social, cultural, emotional and psychological influences which colour, as it were, this apparently straightforward image.

# HAVE DREAMS ANY USE?

Dreaming is indispensable to mental and emotional stability – as indispensable as food or sleep itself. It is the wavering pole which keeps us on the tightrope of sanity. A lack of dreams can be shown to lead to grave personality disorder and to protein deficiency.

Dreaming is like psychological breathing. It is, above all, an outlet for numerous impulses repressed during the day. It liberates cares, hostilities, grievances, hopes, aspirations and desires. It brings back to the surface those lingering problems which, for want of time or courage, we have set to one side. Often – such is the power of that extraordinary personal organizer which is our unconscious – it suggests solutions.

## Our secret agent

Dreaming is also our most precious intelligence service – precious because it gives us information about the very territory we know the least. The dream is our utmost solitude. In a dream, we are face to face with ourselves. Nothing external intrudes. Most of the characters who appear to us in dreams are frequently aspects of ourselves. Once again, then, we see how important it is that we should decode our dreams. Only here do these secret agents report back to HQ from the unknown territories.

## *The balance-sheet of life*

It is dreams which dare to tell us how dissatisfied we may have become with our lives. It is dreams which unmask our hostilities − often towards ourselves (see chapter 10). But it is dreams too which can act as a compensatory mechanism. They mock at wistfulness, regret and inadequacies.

How often in dreams do we earthbound creatures fly through the air with triumphant ease or fight without prospect of defeat? How often does the henpecked husband, at every turn hampered by his clumsiness and his false virtues, find himself transformed into a James Bond-style playboy, surrounded by pretty girls and gleaming limos? And how often, in the loneliness which is our legacy, do we find ourselves, in our dreams, loved passionately, loved infinitely?

Sometimes, of course, it is the other way about. Then we are rebuked, mocked, vilified, humiliated, ostracized. We fail in everything we try. We end up in prison. We miss every train in the world, while our luggage is scattered on deserted platforms throughout the globe . . .

So dreams show us how far we fall short of, or how far we exceed, our perceptions of ourselves − how little we are what we believe ourselves to be.

## *Keeping a "nightly record"*

With the exception of the "great dreams", we rarely remember a dream from start to finish. More usually we are struck by this or that section or aspect of our

13

dreaming. Each one of us dreams for between one and two hours every night. A record of all our dreams, if such a thing were possible, would soon make the library shelves groan. Imagine, then, the enormous quantity of data dreamed which never bubbles up to the light of consciousness. Consider too the enormous faculties of the brain which this fact demonstrates, faculties which are never used in everyday conscious thought.

It is possible, despite all this, to recall a large part of our dreams if we record them on paper or on tape as soon as we awake, keeping what might be called a night diary or "nightly record".

Freud maintained that the forgetting of a dream is, in fact, the repressing of a dream. In other words, the unconscious does its best to force us to consider matters of vital importance, but with the majority of them – the more perturbing elements – our conscious minds are quick to cram them back in the darkness and slam the lid down hard. We start to do this from the very moment that we open our eyes.

It is worth reminding ourselves, as we go to bed, that we intend to dream. It's a little bit like wiring an extra lead into the system. It seems to link neurons, forcing the residual consciousness to hold onto the fleeting image. It takes a few moments, but then, if it means that we retain several years' worth of dream messages which might otherwise be lost, the delay is well worthwhile.

# CHAPTER 2

## *Can we Interpret our own Dreams?*

In principle, we can all arrive at a reasonably accurate interpretation of our own dreams. In practice, however, the uninitiated find themselves rapidly stumbling upon certain inherent difficulties.

There are four main prerequisites for auto-interpretation.

*First*, we must accord dreams the importance they deserve. Just as in "real" life we may pass through beautiful landscapes without even noticing them, so it is possible to pass unseeing through a thousand dreams which, interpreted and assimilated, could change the course of our existence.

*Second*, we must learn, to the best of our ability, the language of dreams. This language, despite occasional appearances to the contrary, is always symbolic. Symbols are the words in this language, and it is no good attempting to translate without an adequate vocabulary. This is a fact that must not be forgotten. Dreams never employ causative or "binary" logic. This is not to say that dreams are incoherent. On the contrary, they have a grand logic all their own. It may be regrettable that dreams speak to us in a language other than our own, just as it may be regrettable that different cultures do not speak the single tongue of Babel, since that is the case there is no reason to refuse to learn languages.

Why, we may ask, should someone dream that she has entangled herself in the contents of her suitcase, which has burst open in the street, or that she is strolling along in rags, to the jeers of bystanders? It would be so much simpler if she could simply see herself, in her dreams, as the victim of feelings of inferiority, or as frustrated, or having a wretched opinion of herself.

It is not difficult to see that so blunt and explicit a dream would be impossible. Words, after all, are no more than shorthand symbols, and are necessarily inadequate. Dreams supply experience, sensation. How can the dreamer effectively envisage something so abstract, so essentially *verbal*, as an inferiority complex? Try explaining a concept like that to someone who does not know the term. You will instantly find yourself telling stories, conjuring up images not unlike those which the unconscious invents in dreams.

To interpret a dream symbol in depth will never be less than formidably difficult. You would need to be not only a psychoanalyst but a historian of religions, as well as a historian of art, mythology and symbols, both universal and particular. Such a polymorph is rare indeed. We must therefore do the best we can. This means returning to first principles.

*The third prerequisite* is that we tell ourselves and repeat to ourselves that all dreaming is projected by the dreamer to the dreamer. No one but the dreamer him or herself is involved in the dreaming process. We must understand that no dream must ever be taken at face value. We only need consider the innumerable dreams in which we kill our parents or abandon our children, or in which a woman finds herself pregnant or contributes to the death of a loved one, to realize the truth of this. The dream speaks only of what is happening in the innermost parts of the dreamer's psyche. There are no victims. The dreamer is alone. The application of this third condition raises difficulties, as will be shown later.

*Finally*, it must be recognized that the deep psyche – which is revealed in our dreams – hardly ever corresponds to its outward manifestations. In the unconscious, complexes, normal or abnormal, orbit like satellites around a planet. Some of these complexes have been laid down as giant fortifications, protecting the inner depths, wherein countless inhibitions stalk and prowl.

In our quest to see into those depths, we possess just two sources of light: psychoanalysis; and the analysis of dreams.

Our successful interpretation of our own dreams depends on two essential factors – what we are and what we seek. If, for example, a man has locked up his personality in those good manners and conventions which give him an illusion of power, intelligence and self-knowledge, he runs the risk of missing out on the significance of all his important dreams because that kind of person, more than any other, is likely to refuse

17

to reopen the debate regarding anything that concerns him. He knows who he is. He knows how to react to stimuli. He skates on the surface of things, but his skating is stylish. Why risk ridicule by seeking further?

Let us take, for the sake of argument, a woman to whom being "right" – or, at least, not being "wrong" – is of the utmost importance. She has a dream which whispers to her that behind her apparent certainty there lie innumerable infantile terrors and great anxieties which, while the adult personality has developed, have lurked, unaltered. Such a woman would rather look anywhere than at her dreams. She would rather wrap even more defensive bands of steel about her already rigid personality.

## "BINARY" PERSONALITIES

Personalities that I have labelled "binary" abound in our Western civilizations.

A binary personality resembles a pendulum. For such people, truth exists at one or other extreme of an arc. They refuse to acknowledge the infinite number of points between. Everything, for them, is black or white, true or false, right or wrong, yes or no. They refuse to conceive of shades or nuances. They cannot accept that everyone can be right and everyone wrong at the same time, depending upon criteria and points of view.

Existence for them is a series of little "absolutes", rigid, stereotyped and unassailable. They conceive of a river as existing only at its source and its mouth. The infinite confluences and meanderings of this living, ever-changing entity are beyond their comprehension. Such a person will never arrive at an interpretation of a dream, for in dream, as in life, all is flux. In general, people like this smother intelligence with their judgemental categories: this is good, this is bad; this is acceptable, that is not. How can such a person openly and honestly approach a dream, when a dream knows neither moral nor causative categories but, in its infinite fluctuations and tributaries, reflects the human character – and human life itself?

# THE SPECIALIST APPROACH

This section offers only a model. It attempts to outline a method which may help non-specialists interpret their own dreams.

A specialist – a psychoanalyst, for example – will be better equipped than most of us for this task, for two reasons. First, the specialist knows (in so far as any of us can) the workings of the human unconscious (taking his or her own as the starting-point). Second, he or she has long been versed in the language of symbols.

Nevertheless it must not be thought that a psychoanalyst can read a patient's dream like a page of text. No true analyst will ever give an immediate interpretation before having discovered, by consultation with the patient, the method which will draw from a dream its fullest value. Conventionally, the analyst's first step will be to use free association in relation to the dream or to certain parts of it.

## Free association

In itself, free association is one of the simplest of the psychoanalyst's tools. We take one element of a dream (a word, an image, an experience which seems particularly important) and we "brainstorm" – just allowing associated ideas to propagate in a train of thought. Other words, images, memories, and so on, will emerge, until one association strikes a particularly rich vein of energy. If we mine assiduously at this point, out will tumble complexes, repressions, memories, unconscious regrets, and so on.

It's a little like the miracle of transmutation wrought in Rutherford's laboratory. Just as there, through the bombardment of nuclei with others, a new form of energy was generated, so this bombardment of associations results in one fusion which can liberate enormous latent power. Of course, in any such process, many free associations will miss the mark. Bear in mind too that the more powerful the free association, the greater the chance that the walls of repression will crumble.

In this process, a considerable inner transformation can be wrought. Previously unrecognized energies are set free. New abilities, as yet unused, surge to the surface. Associations bounce off one another, creating chain reactions of sensations and memories which, if monitored in an informed way, can lead to the very depths of the soul.

## *A case in point*

I chose this dream because of its brevity. It was dreamed by Claudine (aged forty), but could have been dreamed by any one of hundreds of millions of women.

> *I was strolling in a crowded street. I was carrying a huge handbag, stuffed with things. The bag opened. Its contents were scattered on the ground. I was deeply ashamed. I tried to gather up all the things, but they slipped steadily away from me. Bystanders were laughing at me.*

Claudine started the process of free association, choosing for herself the elements which seemed important to her.

*A crowded street.* I never go to crowded streets – not through vanity, but through fear. I was brought up in suburban respectability; I lack spontaneity; I never dare to show what I'm like inside. What people call "the masses" frighten me, as children frighten me. Crowds and children somehow represent perceptiveness and mockery to me, the sort of eagle-eye which sees straight through you. I'm afraid of the genuineness of others. I think they can see through all my affectations and anxieties.

This dream, then, sets Claudine face to face with herself, but of this she is already aware, as of the problems and fears to which it relates and which she has acknowledged. Is the whole dream therefore useless?

An easy conclusion. Too easy. Let her continue to free-associate:

*A huge handbag.* Dirty handkerchieves, odds and ends, secrets, recess, hiding-place, shame. I felt this opening of my bag as an exposure, like a rape, or not far off. The contents seemed weird, outlandish, to me. I couldn't believe that I could have hidden so many things, lumbered myself with so much that was useless.

So Claudine saw her encumbrances as useless – that is to say, she has assumed manners and mannerisms which have nothing to do with her real personality. The most important element here is that she experienced this part of the dream as "exposure" or "violation".

*Ashamed.* I was ashamed at being observed in that state. I am secretive – secret – and all my "me" was scattered about on the ground. But why did I put it that way: my "me"? Am I then just this assortment of useless knick-knacks? Yes, I suppose . . . the baggage that I carry around inside me must be mostly fears and useless feelings. It's true. At home, I'm in an agony of anxiety if someone studies my furniture, my curtains – or, still worse, opens a door to peer into the room next door. Why? Because I always have this sense that my interior is in a mess.

We shall return in a moment to the importance of the "sense that my interior is in a mess".

Having got so far, could Claudine have continued to

interpret this dream for herself? Given her profound need and desire for truth, it is possible, but she ran the risk of stopping here, because the dream merely highlighted a state of affairs of which she was already well aware. She would then have tried to correct some inhibitory mannerism or other, but in a superficial way.

When Claudine was in analysis, she spontaneously returned to this dream and continued to free-associate. I reproduce here the seminal concepts which sprang from this process:

*Handbag*. It opens. It disgorges. [Claudine is French. She therefore uses the word *s'éventrer*. *Ventre* = belly or womb, so the bag is said to have disembowelled itself, or to have opened its womb.] Womb. Like a great stuffed womb. Dirty handkerchieves. Lock it all away. I would never show anyone the contents of my own handbag, no matter how clean and orderly – too orderly, in fact! It would be like – I don't know, it's strange – like lifting my skirt. I always wear trousers, not for convenience nor because I'm a masculine type. It's . . . it's something else. Yes, I suppose . . . I suppose I keep "myself" closed.

She pursues the handbag/womb association:

I'm certain now. The bag is my secret inner self, that part of me which I deny, which makes me panic if I imagine that anyone can see it, either physically or psychologically. My secret inner self . . . my womb . . . Sex has always horrified me. It's like rape to me. My mother always made women out to be the victims of male brutality. For me, a womb . . . It's an organ which has sprung a leak. There. That's it. The thought that I came out of my mother's womb makes me shudder.

We recall Claudine's remarks that "My interior is in a mess" and "I keep 'myself' closed". This latter concept sprang from her need to wear trousers. She could "close" her womb only by enclosing it. She wanted to deny the very existence of her womb, symbol of a shameful femininity, because she identified it with her mother.

Recall too the "dirty handkerchieves" which were the first items mentioned in her description of the bag's contents. The association with sanitary towels, which Claudine regarded with shame and disgust, is self-evident. She told me, "Do you know? I'd never dare to wear a top which was even slightly revealing? Sure, I'm well built; I've got nothing to be ashamed of in the aesthetic department; but even there I have this terror that someone could see 'inside me'. I tell you, if it weren't so ridiculous, I'd wear hermetically sealed clothes right up to my chin. I hate to let myself be seen. I mean, swimsuits! God, what shame I feel! Thanks for this dream. I'm going to have to do something about all this . . ."

Is this sort of dream so common? Well, of course, although many dreams have the same or similar foundations, each takes its particular form from its particular context. We shall revert to this type of dream in chapter 3. Claudine's dream has been used here merely as an illustration. It was a starting-point for her, pushing her to look beyond superficial appearances and, by means of free-association, to discover and try to correct previously unknown – or denied – problems.

To a greater or lesser extent, everyone can follow Claudine's path. All that is needed is a willingness to "let oneself go", and to ask oneself, "What does this or that element in my dream make me think of, or feel? What does it suggest to me, no matter how apparently absurd? What does it recall for me?"

But again I must insist: never, whatever the dream, must it be taken at face value. It's significance is always symbolic.

## Chain reactions

We have already seen the nature and the strengths of chain reactions. We must return and return, unceasingly if necessary, to those elements which seem important. If Claudine had "blocked" her progress at the superficial level of the handbag, for example, she would only have discovered those feelings of inferiority and guilt of which she was already well aware.

Instead, she discovered a profound identification with her mother which was preventing her from regarding herself as a separate and integral person in her own right, and which pitilessly held her back from love, friendship, maternity – in short, from life.

## Another example of interpretation by the dreamer

The following was dreamed by Luke (thirty years old). At first sight, it is considerably more complicated. I find it interesting, for four reasons.

First, Luke, from start to finish, chose the elements which warranted investigation by free association.

Second, it will be seen that his associations reached an apparent dead end along the way. This shows that, although the dream invites us to proceed further and deeper into our inner selves, we can provide our own short-circuits which impede us.

Third, this dream extends far beyond its immediately apparent meanings.

Finally, Luke made his associations without intervention of any kind from the analyst.

*I must have been eighteen in this dream. I was in my childhood home. I crossed the courtyard and opened a door. This door opened on to a staircase which descended into the gloom of a cellar. I went down it. There were several people down in that cellar. Everything was dim and blurred, but I knew that this gathering of people was watching me. I was suddenly seized by panic. I felt movements in my legs. I told myself, "I must wake up . . . I must wake up" . . . I woke up drenched in sweat.*

The following were the elements that Luke chose, and the associations that he derived from them. Luke, by the way, is an intelligent, well-read and extrovert man whose learning is not specific or restrictive.

*My childhood home.* My father. Toughness. You must make good, boy! Must prove worthy of your name! No excuses. Must obey your father. My mother. Oh, I love her all right, but barely dared show her my feelings. Not manly, that sort of thing, not worthy of a father like mine.


*Door.* Every door leads into something else, unless it's a delusion, like a stage set. Gate of heaven, gate of hell. Door of delights. Door of my father's office. Knock knock! God, it was no joke, knocking on that door. It always meant a ticking off, a reckoning – nothing to do with me, with who I was, whether I was happy, just always to do with social success or failure. Door? I could have – I should have taken the door to the fields, to the sea, to far-off places, and said, you know, like, shit to all the fathers in the world. Meanwhile, instead, there's this door in my dreams and it leads down to a cellar.


*Staircase.* Staircases. They go up, they go down. They go where? The staircases at Fontainebleau. Farewells. Farewell to love, farewell to happiness. That word – farewell – has always pursued me. Farewell, never more, *adieu, mon amour* . . . disappearing, leaving, dying, the farewell in Mahler's *Lied von der Erde*, fading away, into the blue. Love of my adolescence, goodbye, farewell, my life. I have taken the staircase to adult life and I have abandoned you. Where are you today? Golden staircases, climbing to heaven, black cellar stairs, blurred rays of light . . . the uncon-

scious, shadow, deep shadow, concealing so many
things within me . . . I want to see those things but to
be happy all the same.

*Cellar.* Shadow and twilight. Revelation? Initiation?
Who are these people who await me there?
Motionless. Silent. Are they friends, judges, an
inquisition? My father multiplied by the number of
figures down there. Yes. That's it. Is it hell or heaven
which awaits? Cellar of my childhood. Fear of the
dark, fear of someone waiting for me down there.
These people . . . a tribunal. Yes, that's it. A tribunal.

*Gathering of people.* Secret. Examination. Secret opinions. Appraisal. Being appraised. Behind me, the staircase, like a possible retreat back to the light. I don't
want to. I want to know. The accused. Me. That's
how it feels. I am the accused. Reckoning time. You
must not falter. You must not founder. I am not a man.

Luke now revisits certain elements of the dream.

*Door.* I was often summoned into my father's office.
It was like being summoned by God the Father!
Tread carefully, now, boy ! Watch it! He would say
to me, "Sit down, sit down. I have something to
discuss . . ." In fact, he was concerned only with
himself, with his success or failure through me.
    As for my father, confidant and guide – pull the
other one. When it comes down to it, that man
castrated me. He stifled my mother's personality . . .
But, yes, my mother, who was she?

*Gathering of people.* My every action has had just one end: to give others a certain image of myself – of a fake me, of course – I realize that now. I tried to correspond as closely as possible to what others expected of me. Nothing else. As a result, spontaneity never featured in my life. I've never really thought of all this; it was vague; it was too painful. To think that I've lived for nothing except not to displease others! It's as if my blessed father has been everywhere in my life. This gathering, then – these were the judges of my existence – or, to put it another way, they were the whole human race. I keep behaving as my father expected and demanded that I behave. I must succeed. Failure or weakness are sources of shame to me. If I am ill, I am tormented by anxiety and guilt because I'm aware that I'm not moving onward and upward. Same applies if I am idle, even on holiday.

*The gloom of a cellar.* Bizarre. A very strange sensation, very profound. I was almost relaxed there, in that gloom. I was out of the light, of course, but there was advantage to that. From gloom to deeper darkness . . . I was descending always towards the depths from my everyday life and that artificial, fraudulent light which floods it. Could it be here, in shadow, out of sight of myself and my father, that I would find freedom?

*Freedom.* Hippies . . . playboys . . . Flower power, not dollar power . . . Hippies – how I would love to have known some real hippies. But I would never dare to speak a word to such exotic creatures. They would scoff at my stuck-up uptight manner. Oh, if only they knew!

Gifted people: they have freedom too. They succeed without much effort. God, yes, I envy hippies and playboys, but I hate them. They are all that I am not yet would so like to be. But what made me feel that somehow my freedom was to be found in that cellar? Gloom. Of course, it's true that I am in fact the very opposite of my apparent self, the dark side of the real me. Yes, a shadow, a phantom. I, my I, exists only in shadow. I must delve deeper there, dig it out. Maybe there in the shadows I will find my soul. Maybe even the love of a woman . . .

So where have all these reflections and sensations brought Luke? To sum up his conclusions in depth would be to recapitulate his every point, which would take more pages than we have at our disposal. To boil it all down to its basic constituents, however, we find that Luke has stressed the following elements:

(a) emasculation, a sense that he has been emotionally castrated.
(b) the fact that he knew nothing of that deeper life exemplified by his mother. His life and soul were related in his mind to his mother – hidden, shadowy, waiting, deeply buried in the labyrinths of the unconscious.
(c) the fact that he considers all "letting go" to be a serious crime.
(d) above all, the ideas of *shadow* and *darkness*. We will

30

return to this image in a special chapter. I believe it to be one of the most important in our dream vocabulary. It is in shadow (in the cellar) that Luke believes he might find freedom – and his soul. We find here too the concept of anima, that immense power in man, so often watered down or openly suppressed. Another chapter will be devoted to this notion.

(e) suicidal tendencies. We only need to review the associations which he makes in relation to the word "staircase" – "farewell" or "adieu", again and again, "fading away" (in the sense of disappearing), the colour blue (the colour of the distance into which one may disappear, "dying", "abandoned", and so on.

In fact, in this dream, behind Luke's apparent extroversion, behind the extravagant stream of associations, we find a deep sense of despair and regret.

This dream tells Luke "You are not what you believe yourself to be. Your soul, the feminine part of you, is like Eurydice, imprisoned in darkness. It is there that you must seek. It is from that darkness that you must retrieve it. You must tear yourself from the false values and the false notions of life which have been bequeathed to you by your father. Descend into the dark caverns of your unconscious. There you will find your truth."

# HOW FAR CAN WE GO ALONE?

I suppose that the question really should be: what conditions must we meet if we are to plumb the depths of a dream? Obviously, in the first place, we need the theoretical knowledge – the knowledge of symbols. This, however, is worth little unless the second condition is fulfilled. Every dream (I cannot stress this too often) is a confrontation with oneself. This confrontation can reveal many aspects – both positive and negative – of a personality. We know that a strongly negative dream can encourage us to consign it to the dustbin of forgetfulness. At the same time, however, it is rare for a negative dream not to serve to prepare us for constructive stock-taking. If someone stops and doubles back in the face of an apparently negative dream, that person runs the risk of shutting out a part of his or her personality, leaving it unrecognized and unused (see, for example, chapters 7 and 10).

All interpretation of dreams must be accomplished coldly and rationally. The emotion provoked by the symbols of dream is rapidly toned down on awaking. The subsequent interpretation depends upon a rational system. The language into which we translate and with which we interpret the dream is therefore woefully inadequate.

A dreamer, then, might be compared to a painter, working on a canvas with all the inspiration and emotion that can be mustered. The interpretation of that dream is then carried out by the art critic, who, however talented, can never fully express the original motivating impulses of the artist.

As for theoretical knowledge, we may readily acquire this by reading psychoanalytical books or works devoted to symbols. Anyone deeply interested in his or her own dreams will make the effort to seek these out.

### A dream with a partial self-interpretation

*Catherine dreams that she abandons her child in order to become a prostitute. She sees herself sunk in a maelstrom of dark streets, bars and fleeting pleasures. Multitudes of men spin around her.*

Catherine's first reaction was to see this as a "horrendous" dream and to try to forget it. This in turn caused her great disquiet and anxiety. When we read what follows, we realize that, had she not placed obstacles in her way, she might never have discovered certain truths, even though those truths seem almost self-evident. On the other hand, had she maintained those obstacles, we will see how much she would have lost in terms of energy and profound perception.

Once again, I will give a brief summary of the associations which Catherine drew from this dream, without intervention from the analyst.

*I abandon my child*. Impossible. I know what's right. I know my duty. I know nothing but my duty. I'm tough on others, but I'm tough on myself. My life is predestined. It is a straight line. I must never deviate. The heart is one thing; duty is quite another. I should have been a soldier. My life is blameless.

It is quite true that Catherine's life was blameless, but it also lacked any element of fantasy or spontaneity. She was indeed like a little soldier. Duty? Certainly she did her duty, but she was uptight, stiff and rigid in the shackles of her stereotyped concept of duty. This concept had not originated within her, but had been instilled into her by parents who were probably as rigid – and as tormented – as she. She was hard on herself and, as she said, on the whole world, upon which she could not stop herself from passing judgement.

Catherine, in fact, exemplified the classic "binary" character. Everything, for her, was either good or bad, true or false, yes or no. There were no nuances for her, no transitions, no understanding of those multifarious circumstances and influences which engender – and justify – human actions. She understood such things no more in relation to others than to herself. It goes without saying that, basically, Catherine harboured a great unconscious unhappiness and at the same time a proportionate, though repressed, appetite for life. Her "shadow" (see chapter 10) was also important.

Let us look at the associations which she continued to make with this same element in her dream:

*I abandon my child.* I do everything for my child. I don't know how I could have had such a ridiculous dream. I'd give my life for my child. Yes, she will be virtuous and straight like me. She's like me. But everything that she wants, I'll make sure she gets it. This dream is absurd. I mean, how could I think, even unconsciously, that I could want to abandon her?

And another element:

> *Prostitution.* Come on. This dream is a joke. All that stuff is so completely alien to me! It's the exact opposite of everything that I am! Thank God we aren't responsible for our dreams. I hate prostitutes. I despise them. I have nothing but contempt for them. Not just prostitutes; I hate all those sort of fluttering floozies who play fast and loose with all the men. Prostitution? Bars? "Nocturnal pleasures"? I'd sooner die.

## Catherine and her "shadow"

Catherine's free associations ended here – or, rather, she stopped them here. It was obvious that she wanted to pass on to another subject and completely to forget this "ridiculous" dream. Did she consider this dream disturbing, monstrous? No. The dream did not even concern her. Not any longer.

Yet, listening to Catherine as she spoke of her daughter, it became obvious that she was in some sense blaming herself in relation to her child. She was attempting to anticipate and satisfy her child's slightest whim. To put it another way, she was the child's willing slave. The child's slightest tantrum or unhappiness plunged Catherine into deep gloom. She told me: "I would do anything, absolutely anything, to make her happy."

The little girl was, for Catherine, a sort of living reproach. The mother was perhaps incapable of spontaneity, but how could even she prevent spontaneity in a small child? The child was her accuser, the catalyst of her unspoken guilt.

After all, as we have seen, Catherine had forbidden herself happiness, spontaneity, the ability to let go and enjoy life, and the right to amusement.

And now came this dream, brutal in its simplicity, resounding through her being like a gong. It turned her values upside-down. Face became obverse; dark side became light. This dream – the absolute opposite of Catherine as she and the world saw her – represented her true self or ego (in a *symbolic* sense only).

## What is that "true self"?

The dream is telling her, "Recognize the sense of guilt which you project on to your child. Not only are you her slave, but you are going to make of her a woman as rigid and as narrow as yourself. You must vary your way of life, not enclose it once and for all within rigorous judgemental limits. Your true self, your 'I' or ego has dwelt in darkness; and your 'straight and narrow' are no more than stereotyped forms of behaviour which spring from and reflect your fear of living. Your whole system of values is a lie. The image of the prostitute represents your evaluation of that side of yourself which rejects rigidity and lack of compassion, sympathy and warmth. Again, in apparently rejecting your child, you reject all the guilt which you transfer to her."

## Conclusion

If Catherine had continued to "block" this dream, she would probably have redoubled her system of false defences, becoming even less forgiving towards herself and others on catching this deceptive glimpse of her "dark side". This dream kept coming back in her memory after a while. Catherine said, "I keep thinking of that dirty dream . . . I suppose it's my dream, after all! I would like to return there, but I'm a bit scared."

And this, for her, was the beginning of a whole series of recognitions which I will not go into here, but which led towards a happier and more constructive existence, a slow but sure blossoming of this unhappy woman who was to become, in consequence, an "ex-little soldier".

## A dream wrongly interpreted

This was dreamed by Jean, a married woman aged twenty-eight.

*I have dreamed about my mother's death. It's a dream which recurs fairly often in one guise or another. I am always watching her death agony, and I'm dancing at the same time! But I love my mother . . .!*

This type of dream is common. It falls into a large category of dreams about the "death of loved ones". Again, perhaps more than ever with a dream like this, it must be stressed that it must not be taken at face value.

Jean told me: "Dancing! I mean, it's just horrible! Am I really such a completely unfeeling creature"? Jean jumped to the wrong conclusions, confusing appearances with reality. She failed to translate the symbols. In consequence, she suffered dreadfully at this vision of herself as shameful and monstrous.

Let us look at some possible interpretations.

1 Jean could have read Freud superficially. Had she done

so, she might well have concluded that this was a "wish-fulfilment" dream and that, albeit unconsciously, she desired her mother's death (or disappearance), a death which would make her free to lead a more extrovert, externalized life, as symbolized by dancing. It is, of course, entirely possible that Jean did harbour some such desire, for any number of reasons, but, if this were the case, it is the word "death" which must be regarded here as symbolic. Jean simply wanted her mother's influence to disappear from her inner life. This is not the same as being an accessory before the fact of murder.

2 Again, Jean could have read Jung superficially. She might then have told herself that her dream signified that her "mystic participation", her "fusion" or her "identification" with her mother must cease (or was in the process of ceasing). Becoming once more her untrammelled self, she launched into a "dance of life".

3 Jean could have consulted a serious dictionary of symbols. She might then have supposed that the dream referred to the "death" of some part of herself, too closely bound to her mother. This, of course, could be related to the earlier, Jungian interpretation. Again, she might have concluded that the "death" related to the disappearance of some part of her vitality and thus to the risk of illness.

4 Of course, Jean might have believed in "premonitory" dreams. In this case, she would be stricken with anxiety as she awaited the future which, she believed, had been revealed to her.

5 And there again . . . but let's listen to what Jean had to say, after she had had time to consider:

I'm twenty-eight. I'm at a turning-point in my life. Bit by bit, I'm identifying more and more with my husband, as part of a couple. I'm not at the age to take stock yet. Not consciously, at least. I'm too young. I'm not at the age where my perspective is going to change or I'm going to adopt new values. Since my mother often appears in my dreams – and dramatically in this one – I must know my attitude deep down towards her. I reckon that it's significant that I am dancing. Yes. I think that this dream probably shows me my childish attitude towards my mum, and towards other people in general. What fixations have I got in relation to my past? It probably means that my mother dies in me, that I must free myself from her and from my anxieties about an independent existence. I'm looking at inner freedom, so I'm dancing, moving towards a new life of creating, a happy new life.

So Jean sides with the Jungian interpretation.

## A "verification" dream

A few days later, Jean had another dream which served to reconcile her to the first one.

*I was climbing straight upward, inside a sort of spiral which was broad at the base but narrowed as I climbed. It seemed to be some sort of cone, with a point at the top. I felt more and more stifled as I climbed. It was as though I were caught in some sort of trap. It seemed unrelenting. I flung myself violently at the summit, the . . . the apex of the spiral, but, try as I might, I could go no further.*

These were Jean's free associations:

*Climbing*. Well, it's going towards something higher. It's growing, getting bigger, stopping being a child. The future, tomorrow, succeeding, creating, achieving things. Heaven. Light. My climb upwards, headed for the heights.

*Spiral*. It narrowed. Trap. Cage. Like a wickerwork cage, you know? Then a dead end, a blockage. No way onward, no way upward to an adult life, I guess. Skirt. Yes. It was like a skirt. I was hemmed in by skirts. I am married, yes, but I'm still Mummy's little girl. Yes. It's true. I'll never get any higher. I'll never fly from the nest. This dream – it's a serious warning. If I relate it to the earlier one . . . What it comes down to – I've got to shed my sense of guilt towards my mother. Because it is true. I somehow feel guilty whenever I do something free and independent – I don't know, go to the cinema or on holiday or something, with my husband. If I have children, I feel that I'd never dare to bring them up on my own without asking Mum's agreement or approval all the time. I'm really going to have to work at that. It's such a major factor in my life, now I come to think of it! – so intrinsically mixed up in everything I do – so unconscious, but always there . . .

# JUST HOW DIFFICULT IS IT?

The interpretation of one's own dreams is often difficult, discouraging – and thrilling. Take it step by step.
The extent of your education can be important with
certain sorts of dream, but I believe that, in general,
goodwill towards yourself, and a sincere desire to
become what, in truth, you are; are worth more than all
the knowledge in the world.

It is essential that you feel no fear at the prospect of
discovering your true self. The "dark side" may appear
alarming, but it is a vital part of you, and, if you are
afraid, you are likely to repress or to undervalue the
most important parts of your dreams. A dream's function is to reveal the extent to which we confuse
ourselves with our ideas of ourselves and to show us
how often we take the projections of "ghosts" of
ourselves for the real thing while our real selves languish
unrecognized in darkness, desperately seeking recognition through our dreams, only, too often, to be forced
back into shadow by the conscious mind. Life-forces
need light and air. Denied them, they become distorted
and destructive (see chapter 10).

Tell yourself, then, before you start, that dreams
belong to three principal families:

(a) the dream which says, "Here is what is currently
    happening within you."
(b) the dream which says, "This is who you really are,
    deep down."
(c) the dream which says, "This is what can happen,
    given current circumstances."

# DOING THE BEST WE CAN

We can only do our best, according to our own abilities when it comes to interpretation, but I believe that anyone who bears in mind that the dream is the staircase between darkness and light, the unconscious and the conscious, will profit from the analysis. Neither Freud's works devoted to dreams nor the dictionaries of symbols are particularly inaccessible, and I hope that this book will prove as helpful and as easy to read as any. Armed with such basic knowledge, we can all usefully undertake self-interpretation.

You would be astonished, however, at the number of people – prisoners of their images and of their terrors – who reject the freedoms offered by this route. They are prisoners, it seems, who cherish their prisons because they seem safer than the fresh air of freedom.

# CHAPTER 3

## The Most Frequent Dreams

Countless symbols, whether signs or images, could be mentioned in this chapter. They are often very simple symbols and appear in the dreams of hundreds of millions of people every night all over the world.

The most common dreams are generally short, and contain a single striking image. Therefore all attention is concentrated on one symbol which becomes a kind of focal point around which secondary elements revolve.

Thousands of dreams could be reproduced here. In order to make a selection, I have begun by listing some symbols that appear very often, and have then identified the main currents of human emotions that produce this type of dream symbolism.

Here I shall deal only with dreams that have a "negative" aspect, whether by alerting the dreamer or by describing an internal situation. Obviously many of these symbols can appear in highly positive dreams, and we shall return to these later in the book.

## Some of the most common symbols

| | |
|---|---|
| Abyss | Hotels |
| Aeroplanes | Houses |
| Amputation | Insects |
| Apocalypse | Labyrinths |
| Balloons | Lifts (elevators) |
| Blood | Luggage |
| Brakes | Murders |
| Cars | Mutilation |
| Cellars | Nakedness |
| Clothing | Plains |
| Colours (specific) | Policemen |
| Corridors | Precipices |
| Courtrooms | Prisons |
| Customs officers | Public debates |
| Deaths | Pursuit |
| Disasters at sea | Railways |
| Dizzy heights | Snakes |
| Doors | Spiders |
| Examinations | Staircases |
| Falling | Teeth |
| Forests | Telephones |
| Frightening animals | Ticket collectors |
| Guards | Tickets |
| Hair | Tidal waves |
| Horses | Tyres |

We should note that these symbols can be linked to many human emotions that overlap with one another. For example, feelings of inferiority always engender feelings of castration, anxiety, guilt, impotence, rejection, abandonment, and so on.

We could add any number of other symbols to the preceding list. In fact we could all "make" a symbol which is particular to us, according to the places where we live, the objects we see every day, and our own feelings and memories. A particular symbol could then have an important meaning for a particular person and mean nothing to anyone else.

It would be impossible to take up each of the symbols listed and give a detailed explanation. I shall quote from the accounts of dreams which I have on record wherever appropriate. On every occasion, the dream will be reduced to its main elements, and, drawing on the dreamer's free associations, I shall demonstrate how these dreams can be interpreted according to the psychoanalytic approach outlined in chapter 2.

This chapter will be divided into sections on (a) inferiority dreams, (b) castration dreams, (c) anxiety dreams and (d) dreams about abandonment.

# INFERIORITY DREAMS

Feelings of inferiority are an inevitable part of the human condition, their manifestation and their nature vary according to the individual's disposition. From infancy onward, we may be assailed by a sense of weakness, impatience, ignorance or dependency. These feelings, of course, may be increased or diminished by experience: education has its effect; confidence is inspired by successes, fears are induced by betrayals. Parents, of course, play a major part, but so too do race, social position and many other factors.

These feelings of inferiority give rise to any number of compensatory mechanisms whose purpose is to establish (admittedly spurious) equilibrium, and to give the sufferer a sense of ease and strength. We therefore find many apparently paradoxical offshoots of paranoia – exaggerated aggression, pathological disdain, overbearing pride, excessive self-assurance, contempt for others, insistence on being right, and so on. It goes without saying that, the more extreme the compensation, the greater the risk that the sufferer will slip back into his or her initial sense of inferiority, and the more terrifying will such a relapse seem. The dreams which result from such a condition will be strongly marked by this fear, conscious or no.

## A holiday dream
This was dreamed by a young woman.

> *I was going on holiday in the south of France. I arrived in a hotel bedroom. The porter threw my suitcase on to an unmade bed. He just looked at me without saying a word, then went out. The walls of the bedroom were dirty, the toilets were disgusting. I slumped down on to a chair. I was desperate.*

Every reader will at once grasp the overall "feel" of this dream, which clearly indicates internal feelings of inferiority. The young woman told me: "The south of France always represented the height of elegance to me. I'd never been there, and had always imagined that no one but high society ever visited the Riviera."

Already she has professed her sense of unworthiness

for this sort of holiday. With inferiority feelings, we often find that aspirations come to a dead end. In this case, the holiday does not culminate in the hazy glamour envisaged, but in a shabby hotel room. The dreamer also feels rejected. She does not so much as earn a welcoming word from the porter. This dream could, then, represent an unconsciously desired failure, as if the dreamer were saying to herself, "I am unworthy of success and of positive achievement. I want to run aground, to progress no further, and thus to ensure the inner peace which is denied me by any sort of competition."

## A nudity dream

This man's dream belongs to the commonest type of all dreams:

> There I was, walking along a bustling street, and everyone was looking at me, laughing. I caught sight of my reflection in a shop window. I was stark naked.

This dream is as explicit as it is common. The dreamer feels that everyone can "see straight through him", that he cannot hide his real nature from others. To put it another way, he is ashamed of himself.

## A closet dream

To all intents and purposes, the following dream (by a man) is the same type as the travel dream:

> I had arrived in a hotel. I had to carry my own luggage, even though all the other guests seemed to manage to get porters. The staircase was steep and narrow. My room

47

> *turned out to be just a closet in the attic. I lay down on*
> *the bed. The strange thing was that I felt good, a sort of*
> *. . . bitter peace, I suppose you'd say. I was glad that*
> *there was no window, glad to be cut off from the crowd.*

Again there is the need for a setback, springing directly from inferiority feelings.

This is a "masochistic" dream. The sense of rejection is obvious. The dreamer must carry his own luggage, he is excluded from his community (the hotel), he feels ostracized by his society (the other guests, the porters). He engages in a regression towards childhood. The room or closet (without a window on to the outside world) becomes a little world unto itself, set apart, a sort of womb, with all the passivity which that entails, and the consequent peace and sense of security.

It is worth noting that the dreamer was barely aware of the profound masochism of the dream and of the extent of his wretchedness. He had compensated with a vengeance for his inferiority feelings, and ended up in a situation from which he could derive inordinate smugness and pride. It is easy to see that, in theory at least, he should have been tormented by his situation. Instead, he revels in it. In the end, this dream reflects "suicidal yearnings", a regression to nothingness and to total separation from the world.

## A lift dream

A man recounted the following dream about a lift or elevator:

> *I pushed the button in the lift in order to go up, but the*

*lift plummeted downwards. The more I stabbed at that button, the faster the lift descended. I woke up with my heart pounding.*

Here we have a dream of descent rather than climbing – a falling dream. The dreamer told me:

I am certain that this dream gives me an instruction. I am to go down to my inner basement, as it were, to see what is stored there. I'm always thinking about climbing the ladder, rung by rung. From the outset, that's been the direction in which I've been pointed – upward, always upward. For once, I'm being told to look downward. I must explore what's going on down there in my unconscious. But oh, that plummeting! That fall!

That plummeting? That fall? Why the concern?

It is the same fear as that which we have already encountered above. We are afraid of losing our carefully structured defences, our compensations, in that bid to rediscover our real selves. We are afraid of losing our comforting illusions and coming face to face with ourselves.

Dreams about falling are extremely common. Some recur, sometimes for years on end, such is the urgency of the unconscious mind's demand that it be acknowledged, such is our terror of shedding our façade.

We all know those dreams in which we fall from a rock, or where a precipice suddenly gapes beneath us, where we scramble to the summit only to find ourselves unable to descend again, where we fling ourselves into the void, where an aeroplane crashes on to a town, or a train plunges into a chasm, and so on.

Dreams about falling can also reveal anxiety at our inability to "stay afloat", fear of being once more engulfed by a smothering mother, unconscious fear of madness and of worry at the idea of being lost in nothingness, of ceasing to be, etc.

Dreams about giddiness, vertigo or dizzy heights are directly related to the above – although, perhaps, the dreamer's conscious fears restrain him or her still further from "taking the plunge".

## A luggage dream
The dreamer was a man.

*I bought a ticket for a town which I did not know, but which, I was somehow convinced, was very sunny, with many fountains . . . I was really happy to be leaving my home town. As I headed towards the train, I noticed that it was called "The Bluebird". Then I realized that I had somehow lost or forgotten my luggage. I started to hunt for it in a panic while the train began to move off.*

We find, then, the *unknown town*, the *sun*, the *gushing waters*, the *happiness* at moving, the *"Bluebird"*, the *lost luggage* and the *check* to a planned journey.

The predominant element in this dream is that this man is setting off on a journey towards himself, or towards the deepest parts of himself. It has to do with *anima*, of which I will write further in chapter 7.

Unfortunately, the happy traveller appears to have forgotten his luggage.

Does this matter?

You'd have said that, with happiness at the end of his journey, it was a fairly secondary consideration. It would seem, however, that the dreamer attaches disproportionate importance to the trivia of life. It would have been simpler, surely, to have hastened on to happiness – to this wonderful town which, for him, was permanently on holiday – and to worry about replacing the missing articles when he got there.

## A clothing dream

> I no longer remember exactly where I was. It could have been a street, or a room in a house . . . Anyhow, there were people there. I slowly pulled off my clothes – some sort of grey uniform – but underneath, I found a sort of one-piece outfit, a sort of jumpsuit. It was blue – the same blue as denim. I was suddenly infinitely sad. Then I was in another place, this time in sombre navy-blue. People came and went, but I felt peaceful.

This was dreamed by a very elegant young woman. Her clothes certainly bore no resemblance to any sort of uniform. She appeared happy, vivacious and gregarious, mixing with a fashionable crowd.

She was allowed to free-associate in relation to this dream:

> The strangest thing is this succession of "uniforms" – grey, dull, denim-blue . . . Like the standard dress under Mao . . . Everyone in blue, everyone in grey . . . Or was it just me? Sadness. My elegance is all front.

51

My real personality is grey, conformist. This dream told me just how much. I've spent my life hiding. I ought to take off all those uniforms like the layers of an onion until I reach my true core.

*Navy-blue suit*. Boarding-school. I hated boarding-school, but it was my refuge from my parents' eternal rows. A bitter-sweet sort of refuge.

*Navy-blue*. Behave. Obey the rules. Yes, miss. No, miss. Thank you, miss. I'll go back into line, miss . . .

It's true, I did put myself in uniform. Outside, all this coolness and elegance stuff, but inside, in here, I conform, do what others do, just so as no one has the chance to tick me off or laugh at me. I don't stand out of line because I don't want to be noticed. I don't want anyone seeing through me.

No, but this dream is good because I reckon I'm . . . I seem to want to know what's under all these uniforms. I have to take care not to step back into line, like I did at school, simply so as to find a spurious peace.

I must battle against all the easy compensations offered by the lies, but I must also be sure that I don't over-compensate by trying to be too different from everyone else. I run the risk of falling into a trap from which it'll be difficult to get out.

We can add to these associations the fact that divesting yourself of a uniform corresponds to a sense of deep disillusionment about the uselessness of false values.

This is an excellent focusing and warning dream, and in fact the young dreamer, to a large extent took notice of it and profited from it.

## A travel dream

*I'm in a train, in a first-class carriage. The inspector comes in and checks tickets. He sort of drily observes that mine is only a second-class ticket. He asks me to leave the carriage, which is full of pretty women and well-dressed young men.*

Here is a dream (by a man) which we find over and over again in one form or another. The meaning, I think, is clear enough. The inferiority feelings shout at us.

Here, condensed, are the dreamer's thoughts: "I feel myself to be an impostor. In life, in my job . . . I'm a doctor, a good doctor, but I've always had this sense that I don't deserve my qualifications or my success. A voice deep down in me keeps telling me, 'Given the paltry thing that you are, how can people place their trust in you?'"

We find in this dream that sense of unworthiness from which so many men suffer, a feeling that carries with it its own pitiless shadowland, enduring anxiety and fear. In this instance, the dreamer is "expelled" from a privileged position to which he feels he has no right (under the gaze of pretty women whom he considers himself equally unworthy of).

## A station dream

*I arrive at this big station. It is totally deserted and desolate. The solitude is . . . horrendous. There is no light. I have lost my way, mistaken my platform. I see my train on a disused track. It has no engine.*

There is little need to comment on this dream (by a woman). The sense of abandonment is overt and overpowering – the deserted station, the disused track, and so on. There is no setting off towards life, towards light, towards a future. The power (potency?) is missing. No locomotive is there to wrench the train from its immobility.

## A train dream

Again the same theme; this time in a dream by a man:

*I arrived at the station to see my train vanishing over the horizon. I ran after it along the tracks, lumbered by heavy luggage.*

Here is that sense summed up in the phrase "missing the bus" – the fumbling of chances, the sometimes apparently innate art of being in the wrong place at the wrong time.

The dreamer is carrying heavy luggage. Is it his whole existence that he finds too weighty, or are there unwieldy elements in that existence which he might profitably throw away?

## A house dream

This was dreamed by a man:

*I returned home, but my house was next to a sinister sort of factory. The house had become minuscule and the roof had caved in.*

The diminished house here reflects the dreamer's sense

of his own diminished personality. The sinister factory symbolizes the diminishing factor. This man, further-more, fears the loss of his intellectual faculties, hence the caved-in roof (see Dictionary, *house*).

Dreams like this follow hot upon one another's heels. Trains leave without the dreamer. Trains break down, or have obstacles in their way. Stations are desolate or isolated in hostile countryside. Trains rush by and do not stop. Luggage goes astray or leaves in the wrong train. The dreamer arrives late at the station or is brought to a halt by a traffic jam or a dead end. The car will not start. The car sets off backwards. The car keys are lost. Our dreams are full of situations ceaselessly signifying the inferiority and impotence which are the legacy of the human race.

# CASTRATION DREAMS

Castration, in its broadest psychological sense, attends every moment of human life.

Birth, for example, is the first great "castration". The individual is torn from the blessed peace of the maternal womb, only to be projected into frenzied activity and noise. Childbirth is, for the mother too, a significant castration: that which she carries within her – a part of her – is removed from her.

In such terms, human existence is just one long succession of castrations with varying degrees of impor-tance. They are deemed "normal" – for example, when education proceeds harmoniously; but castrations are inherent in that process none the less, in that the child is "channelled" according to imperatives which come from the outside. Meanwhile, abnormal ones also occur – all the "mutilations" of the person, physical or psychological, which occur in a lifetime.

The feeling of castration frequently manifests itself in dreams, usually accompanied by a sense of anxiety. We dream about limbs being wrenched off or teeth being pulled out or falling out. We dream about losing our hair or getting punctured tyres. We dream about a bullet slowly leaving the muzzle of a gun with hardly any sound of a shot being fired. Exams and law-courts occur frequently, as do balloons which either fail to leave the ground or are punctured, and so on.

## An examination dream

The following was dreamed by a man:

*I was taking a university finals exam. The examiners were standing, with black robes and black caps. I thought I saw one of them take my degree certificate in his hands and simply rip it up.*

An exam is a rite of passage, a transitional point internally as much as externally. If we pass the exam, not only do we progress, say, from student to graduate, but, in terms of our self-perception, we progress from aspirant to "master". We move forward a stage. Failure, on the other hand, signifies stigma, stasis and stagnation. An exam is a method of taking stock. It tests us against the standards of the world. It gives us an identity, a right to exist. In this dream, there is a "castration" in that the ripping up of the degree certificate constitutes a mutilation of the dreamer's personality, a denial of the right to move onward or to develop. But who is this examiner? Of whom is he the projection? Whom does he represent deep within the dreamer's spirit?

## A hair dream

A woman dreamed the following:

> I was looking at myself in the mirror. I saw that I had gone completely bald. When I woke up, I flung myself out of bed and rushed to the mirror to make sure. The dream was that convincing.

This is another common sort of dream related to those about losing teeth. It is a classic castration dream. In that it was dreamed by a young woman, we might suppose that it reflects a fear of losing beauty or seductive power. The dream, however, goes further than this. Hair is rich in symbolic associations. It is a universal emblem of virility and active power. As a secondary distinguishing sexual characteristic, it represents in a woman a powerful means of attraction. This dream demonstrates the extent to which the young woman dreads losing her power, her creative strength, the dynamism of youth, etc. It is an intense anxiety dream.

## A mutilation dream

> It was a short dream, but, God . . .! I don't know where I was but an enormous monster suddenly loomed up and

*tore off my father's right arm . . . It was appalling. I felt
my own right arm being ripped off too.*

The dreamer, a woman, free-associates:

I never knew my father well. My mother did everything she could to turn me against him. I think – I
feel that that monster was my mother . . .

She was surly, vindictive, always criticizing, never
loving or gentle. She prevented my father from living.
She stole any strength or power from him. By the
time she'd finished, he was as good as non-existent.

As a child of that sort of relationship, there was no
way that I could be guided by him. He was a cipher.
I get the feeling that this dream was really important.
A girl without a father-figure is locked into an endless
cycle – girl, woman, woman, girl . . . My right arm,
that's my creativity, my dynamism. I've got to try to
strengthen the bond with my father, and to hell with
my mother.

So the monster and the mother who devours personalities and prevents them from flourishing in freedom
are one and the same. The "arm" is obviously a phallic
symbol. It represents strength, power and protective-
ness. It is the arm which strikes, the arm which cuddles,
the arm upon which one leans. We speak of the long
arm of the law, and, of course, in English, the word is
ambiguous. An arm is a weapon as well as a limb. The
dreamer here stresses that it is powerful. In this dream,
then, the father is effectively castrated. His virile power
is taken from him. The dream also shows how at the

same time the girl is cut off from her "masculine" power – that is, from her creativity, her enthusiasms, her ability to "strike a blow" in life. She is also cut off from the future (symbolized by the right). For the symbolism of directions, see chapter 13.)

## Another "mutilation" dream

*I arrived at the office. I realized with dismay that my right arm had been amputated. I told my boss, "It's nothing. Give me something to do with my left hand, but keep me on.*

The dreamer, a man, free-associates:

My boss? That must be my dad. Fear of my dad. Fear of men. I play at being a man, but in reality I am yielding, submissive. What can I do without my right hand? Useless. Mutilated. Done for. My father castrated me. Those high "principles" of his! I never had the balls to rebel. You see how polite I am? Excuse me, I haven't got a right arm, but please don't worry about it. It's nothing. I'll manage with the little that remains. Keep me on, such as I am. Don't be nasty to me. Don't chuck me out, please, sir. I'll do anything that you ask, only don't be unkind to me.

Of course, I seek refuge with my mother or my wife. I would do anything just to be loved and reassured . . . not to be thrown out. Anything but that . . . The office – I know in my bones that that's my family. I do everything, anything for others, even overtime.

. . .

59

There is no point in adding commentary to these lucid free associations. Once again we find the right arm – the arm of strength and virility – cut off. It symbolizes the phallus, so here we find ourselves in the midst of the famous Oedipus complex (see Dictionary).

## A teeth dream
This was dreamed by a man:

*All my teeth were wobbling. I pulled them out one by one, and they came out easily. I woke up shaking.*

Teeth bite. They chew food. They tear (meat from bone, for example). Shown in a snarl or a smile, they indicate confidence and strength. Toothlessness is associated with malnutrition and the final frailty of age. Teeth also play their part in sexual seduction – dazzling smiles, amorous nibblings, etc.

Dreaming about rotten, ripped-out or wobbling teeth is often a sign of feelings of impotence (sexual, professional, social, etc.). This man is aware – or afraid – of diminution and powerlessness.

Women often dream about losing their teeth after childbirth. This is to be expected, in that childbirth, as we have established, is also a form of "castration" (there is a "pulling out" and mutilation of part of the mother's body).

## A dream about tyres
A man recounted the following dream:

*I left my workplace to return home. All four tyres on my*

*car were punctured. I tried to move off all the same, but the motor turned over and I couldn't get it into gear. I said to myself, "Is this because of the tyres?" I looked around for a garage. All I saw was people coming and going.*

Again, this is a dream about castration, impotence, diminution of the self. This man feels "deflated" in relation to life. The gears, furthermore, do not respond. He cannot externalize the potential forces within him. These feelings, however, are all unconscious. The dreamer was to all outward purposes efficient and organized (if deeply disturbed) in everyday life. The dream reveals his real feelings about himself. It is, again, a focusing dream and a warning.

## ANXIETY DREAMS

Whether conscious or otherwise, anxiety plays an important role in human existence. It is hardly surprising, therefore, that it is the theme of many of our dreams.

In general, anxiety is translated into negative feelings in dreams. Inescapable or frightening predicaments are commonplace. In recurring dreams, one event from the past may manifest itself again and again.

Mundane anxieties, metaphysical anxieties, cosmic anxieties – all find their outlet in our night-time life.

*Aeroplanes* crash or catch fire, people shout, *crowds* are seized by *panic*, *mazes* extend into infinity, we *wander* lost and alone, in *unknown towns*, *houses* collapse, *earth-*

*quakes* rumble, *tidal waves* sweep all before them . . .

Then there are dreams which reflect deeper, more enduring anxieties: a *son* kills his mother, a *mother* stabs her child, a *husband* sees his wife drowning in the sea, a *ship* sinks into the depths of the ocean. Immense deserts or snowy wastes have their place here. *Houses* are unoccupied, deserted, hostile, overgrown. *Sobbing* is heard as we sleep. Strange, mythical *animals* are seen, *insects* proliferate, the dead arise to menace us. We are *lost, bewildered, rejected, deserted, alone* in the world and in the whole universe. Human anxiety is almost limitless.

## Physiological factors in anxiety dreams

Anxiety dreams – even nightmares – can sometimes be provoked by physical disorders. These may be trivial or grave. Breathing difficulties and heart irregularities are among the many possible causes, and everyone knows that indigestion can bring on anxiety dreams. Whatever the physiological factors, the psychological condition of the dreamer will always determine the presentation of this or that image in a dream. The physical disorder serves merely as a trigger. It sets the dream in motion, but will not ordain its imagery.

## Anxiety dreams and sexuality

Sexual needs and desires, especially repressions, play an important part in anxiety dreams. Amongst the most prevalent are the Oedipal dreams (see Dictionary). It is very rare for these objectively to describe a situation.

Once again, symbols take on the burden of showing the prevailing desires, anxieties and repressions. In my own files, I have some twenty dreams in which, in different contexts, a son "stabs" his mother. These are dreams not of hatred, but of sexual impulses: the dagger symbolizes the phallus.

Puberty produces innumerable anxiety dreams. This is only to be expected. This, after all, is a period of enormous sexual and behavioural difficulties and readjustments, fear for the future, anxiety at moving away from the security of the family, and so on.

## Some common symbols of anxiety

Snakes frequently occur in the sexual anxiety dreams of both men and women. They are, of course, phallic symbols. Equally, reptiles, jungles, forests and bushy thickets (often symbols of the pubis, though they may also represent the unconscious) also appear. We also find crumbling *towers*. The tower again is an obvious phallic symbol, and its collapse represents fear of social or sexual impotence. *Revolvers* often do not go off, or the bullet simply plops from the muzzle. *Ships* founder, people are *engulfed* in the sea or in swamps (symbolizing fear of returning to the unconscious and to the influence of the mother).

In young girls' dreams we find more specific *male characters*, often menacing or hirsute (symbols of a dangerous animus: see chapter 8). Their dreams often reflect a fear of rape (*snakes*, *knives*, *pointed objects*, *cars* and *trains* which bear down upon them, *open wounds* on genital organs, etc.).

Nowhere more than here must it be stressed that

dreams must not be taken at face value. Many adolescents, already troubled and confused, have been thrown into panic by too literal an interpretation of their dreams.

## Distressing circumstances

Anxiety dreams often take the form of distressing and difficult situations, past or present. These dreams can often recur over several years. Here are some examples:

1 *Jim often dreams that he is still in the army, that he is recalled to the ranks or that he is accused of deserting.*

   Jim is fifty. It seems, therefore, that the army marked for him a trauma or a period of anxiety, unrelieved by demob. This sort of dream may appear superficial, but in fact it reflects a deep concern, of which the dream is just the symbolic translation.

2 *Paul frequently dreams that he is back at the office. He returns there after an unjustified absence. His boss ticks him off for some job badly executed and he nerves himself to resign but never succeeds in doing so.*

   In reality, Paul has been self-employed for several years. These "office" dreams are always marked for him by intense anxiety. To understand why, we would first need to know what the office represents for Paul and, equally, what a never fulfilled intent to resign means to him. Is this "fear of freedom"? As for these "unjustified absences", they spring surely from a general sense of guilt, projected on to the images of the office and the boss. It is undoubtedly in Paul's childhood that the key to these recurring dreams lie.

3 *Theresa often dreams that she is swotting for university exams.*

This, despite the fact that she has been a qualified doctor for many years. Could it be that life is for her a permanent exam? Is she so suffused by guilt that she feels obliged forever to assess and pay her dues?

4 *Fred often dreams that he returns to the house where his mother (dead for many years) lives. He calls, but no one answers. The darkness and silence are absolute. He wants to climb to the first floor, but is paralysed by terror. He wakes up drenched in sweat.*

Fred's anxiety while his mother lived alone was that he might find her dead. In fact, when we get down to the nitty-gritty, we discover that Fred's anxiety sprang from his unconscious desire that his mother should die, in order that he should be free from the heavy responsibility with which his mother had burdened him. The anxiety felt here is thus like an electric field between positive and negative poles. It is produced by the powerful antagonism between the conscious desire (that his mother should live) and the unconscious need (that his mother should die). There is also, in these dreams, a characteristic anxiety at the prospect of being abandoned.

5 *Jean frequently dreams that a woman is pushing her towards a great mirror from which she turns away in horror.*

A word of explanation here: Jean's mother unconsciously refused to allow her to grow up. She wanted Jean to be no more than a little clone of herself. Jean experienced anxiety whenever she made the slightest tentative move towards liberty or autonomy. This recurrent dream was saying, "My mother wants me to see her image, not my own in the mirror. I refuse. I want to become what I am, even though I am afraid of looking the situation in the face."

6 *Peter often dreams that he is leaving his parental home but that a voice calls him back. He half turns.*

Peter is forty. He is married. His parents are dead. These dreams are tied up with a feeling of culpability. Peter always felt that he had "abandoned" his parents when he married – parents who, incidentally lived in comfort and never for a moment reproached him. These are dreams of "abandonment" and "fear of freedom".

7 *Jacqueline often dreams about a great river glittering in the sun and covered with little boats, but a blanket of black birds flies over the river.*

Here is an anxiety dream if ever there was one. Jacqueline spent her childhood and adolescence in the care of her grandmother – a classic "castrator" figure, who was the very personification of mourning and sorrow at the death of Jacqueline's mother. Year after year, she continued to dress in widow's weeds and, at the last, became for Jacqueline the tangible symbol of death itself. It is scarcely to be wondered at that Jacqueline feels thus anxious, torn as she is between the sparkling life which exists within her and this constant image of death which hangs over her.

8 *John has dreamed for several years that the telephone rings during the night. He dreams that he gets up, lifts the*

*receiver and hears a woman's voice. It is a soft voice, which
says nothing other than to speak his name. Then there is
silence. Every time, John awakes in a state of anxiety.*

Who can she be, then, this woman who pursues
the dreamer yet is content merely to call him and to
speak his name? I had simply been sent an account
of this dream, so could only guess, but this could
perhaps have to do with John's anima (chapter 7)
which cannot "get through" to him. Perhaps he
cannot separate his anima from the maternal influence which encumbers him. Is there here an overpowering nostalgia for childhood? Or is the voice
that of his mother, to whom John is still bound by
current circumstances or by guilt?

9 *Virginia often dreams that she is walking along in a big
town. She asks the way or the time without ever receiving
an answer, so she begins to run towards the police station.*

This is an abandonment dream. Virginia feels cut
off from ordinary social relations. She feels rejected.
Walking within herself (the town), she finds no
helping hand, no listening ear. Alone in the world,
she rushes towards the police, who represent for her
some element of maternal security.

10 *Jim often dreams that houses are collapsing around him but
he is unable to move.*

This type of dream can indicate a potentially
dangerous state of unconscious mind. A house
could represent Jim's "me" (incidentally, Jim was a
man who frequently suffered depression). This
"me" crumbles, but, at the same time, it is the
whole vertical structure which disintegrates. These
dreams therefore translate a deep-seated feeling of

impotence in life and are, too, quite clearly castration dreams.

So it is that anxiety surges up during the night. We must *never* neglect a recurrent dream. Anxiety dreams are just symptoms warning us that we must seek out the sources of our problems. Repetition of the same images, like chronic twinges of pain, serves as a reminder that matters are still unattended to.

"*Great dreams*" indicating anxiety also occur, often accompanied by archetypes. There are *rearing horses* that threaten to unseat the dreamer. There are *menacing giants* and *mythical monsters*. *Threatening voices* are heard. We see *enormous forests* in which we are lost without hope of finding our way out. *Colours* acquire apparently disproportionate importance. *Dangerous dwarfs* and *bands of outlaws* haunt the dreams of many women. Here is a man who walks within endless *mirrors* . . .

But, dreams are as varied perhaps as anxiety itself. I can do no better than cite a few symbols in the hope that they will find echoes in the reader's dreams.

## Dreams about crime

Another commonly experienced form of anxiety dream which can plunge the dreamer into deep depression, consists of dreams about crime, prison and pursuit.

### The dreamer as a prisoner
A man aged twenty-seven reports such a dream:

*I had just been freed from a prison where I had served a long sentence for some crime or other. The road was in sunshine and was heavily populated. I started to run. I felt that I was being chased. Glancing back, I saw a whole menacing crowd running behind me.*

The dreamer began his analysis with the words: "But hold it. Was it me that they were chasing? I thought so at the time, but I have no proof". His free associations continued:

*Prison.* I am in prison. I've always been there. I am never free. What offence am I paying for? A feeling of not having a right to be. Nobody loves *me*. I must do things, make things to make them love me. I don't want to be alone. I don't want to be free. But I am freed all the same. Sun. Why do I run as though the whole world was on my heels? Always this feeling of being watched, observed, appraised. Shyness. Anxiety. And yet – there is sunshine out there. Why not for me? I even feel guilty with my wife and children . . . This sense of being a little boy in a world of grown-ups . . . No; not to be alone . . .

So the "prisoner" (of himself) experiences a certain inner relaxation. Freedom beckons (the sun-soaked street), but guilt remains (I haven't the right to be free, happy, autonomous). He refuses freedom. It horrifies him. This, of course, is another "abandonment" dream, which we shall discuss later.

In this sort of dream, *representatives of the law* often turn up: *judges, policemen, customs officers, teachers, directors, executioners*, *barristers*, etc. The dreamer is *trailed*, *interrogated*, *investigated*, *condemned*, *thrown into prison*, *decapitated*, etc. These dreams can be linked to the *Oedipus complex* (see Dictionary).

## The dreamer as a killer

A twenty-two-year-old man recounts a dream:

> *I have killed my older brother. The gun is still on the table. My brother is sprawled on the floor. He is dead, but he watches me, smiles at me, says a few words. My parents are there. The scene seems entirely natural to all of us, myself included. That's the most extraordinary thing. Afterwards, I feel a sense of liberation.*

An inner liberation, needless to say. Without going into details, important though they are, let me point out that this young man, Philip, had always thought of his brother as his superior, the one who got all the respect. The dreamer saw himself as the "junior", the "baby of the family". He believed himself to be second also in terms of his parents' love. This perception has changed. He recently realized that he had fabricated this illusion of inferiority. Why had he done so? Because, he said, of a certain "masochism", which he hoped could ensure his parents' total love and concern. He had been imagining a non-existent situation in the hope of receiving pity and solicitude. It was at the moment when he recognized this that he had this dream.

He kills with a gun, which of course, is a phallic symbol and so a symbol of virility. The important factor, which he stresses, is that the scene seems *natural*. This

70

apparent domestic harmony demonstrates Philip's inner peace and the reappraisal which he has made.

As already stated, crimes often occur in dreams. Usually they reflect the *Oedipus complex* (see Dictionary) – even if the dream seems to have nothing to do with the dreamed situation. So, for example, *an employee kills his boss* or the dreamer *hits a representative of the law.*

In another dream, a man drives his car straight at a car park attendant. Again, the car is phallic. The attendant symbolizes the father who must be killed in order to ensure the mother's total love. Many women dream about killing with a dagger; this too is a phallic weapon, which can indicate the rebirth of a masculine element that has been too long repressed.

## The causes of anxiety dreams

We have already compared anxiety to an electric field between positive and negative poles. Let us extend that comparison: in a condenser, energy concentrates in the insulator which separates the cables – that is to say, in the space between the electrons. The same is true of anxiety, whose sometimes enormous energies are accumulated and condensed between opposing emotions. In a dream, negative feelings (hatred, hostility, needs, desires, etc.) manifest themselves in floods. The unconscious, knowing no "morality", lets loose its contents without restraint.

Anxiety can also be compared to a dammed river. An important movement in the personality finds itself blocked or stopped by a barrage (of morality, for example). Powerful emotions are at play here: love, hate, sexuality, autonomy, freedom, and so on.

Let us take one example from among thousands: a mother encounters severe problems in bringing up her difficult child. The child's education takes up all her time, denies her any liberty and gives her enormous and continuous worries. It is thus *normal* for her to think (more or less consciously), "If only he were not in my life, I could be happy and enjoy personal freedom." It is normal in that it is true! So a dream appears, such as the following (dreamed by a woman of thirty-two):

> *I was setting off on a trip with my fiancé. We had aban-doned our little dog. It was horrible, but there I was just talking to my fiancé about Venice.*

Examining the dreamer's free associations, we note that she is travelling with her fiancé (now her husband). She travels backward in time to the period of freedom, the period of holidays, the period of high hopes. She leaves the present and refuses, in her dream, to be married (i.e. not free). The little dog, of course, symbol-izes her child, but, even in her dream, an inner censure – a taboo, even – prohibits her real desire. The monstrous nature of her inclination is too great, and the dream softens or sweetens it. This mother, after this dream, judged herself to be a wicked woman, and rapidly turned her thoughts to other subjects, but the anxiety, as usual, remained, like a sort of building-up of pressure against the dam. Only when she recognized that her unconscious was showing her a very real and natural desire (to have no obstacles to her freedom) in

72

direct contravention to her equally real and natural desire (to raise her difficult but beloved child), only then did she feel peace restored to her.

# DREAMS ABOUT ABANDONMENT

The fear of being abandoned is one of the most fundamental and universal. It is the anxiety of the little child who, deprived of her mother for whatever reason, feels absolutely alone in a world suddenly become dissociated and terrifying. It was the fear which cropped up in the dream previously cited in which Virginia, left bewildered in a town, ran to the police station.

It is also the anxiety of the child whose mother sulks – the worst thing that she can do. Sulkiness and silence are felt as a rejection. A "wall" is set up between mother and child. The bond is broken. Guilt and the need for forgiveness, no matter what the cost, appear in the infant mind.

In adults, anxiety at the prospect of abandonment generally manifests itself in three principal ways:

1 Sufferers feel an exaggerated need to have friends "on whom they can count". This is often manifested in affectionate tyranny, a need for complete exclusivity. The desire *to be loved* far outweighs the need *to love*. The loved one must always be around, always at the lover's disposal. In general, the loved one represents the mother, the archetypal slave to our slightest whimper, and, as with a child, the most important thing is "not to be alone, never to be

alone, no matter what the cost". This sort of person will invite people in, no matter who they are and no matter what the circumstances. When they say "I hate being alone", what they really mean is: "I feel ceaseless fear of being abandoned by my mother, by God and by mankind . . ." It must be reiterated that this fear is both fundamental and profoundly human, but that it increases considerably as soon as the individual feels deprived or incapacitated, as soon as one believes oneself to be merely tolerated, or even ostracized by others.

2 Sufferers try to forestall rejection by anticipating it. They reject all possible bonds, they shy away from all attachments. They refuse overtures of love, friendship and affection. Their subtext is always the same: "Why bother? Nothing lasts. Everything ends, and one way, or another, I'll finish up abandoned in the end". These kinds of people are often negative, critical and aggressive. In attacking others, they justify, in their own eyes, their rejection of bonds with others.

3 The fear of being abandoned is transformed into a fear of abandoning others. This type of anxiety often occurs between people who are very close. It is easily explained. In this sort of person, all autonomy or independence is checked by the thought that "If I act freely – say, by going to the cinema alone – I suffer anxiety at the notion that I am somehow abandoning my wife/husband" (subtext: "abandoning my mother"). This sort of thinking is particularly common among young people going out together or preparing to marry. Here it can be translated as "If I become autonomous and adult, I abandon my parents

and they will then be alone in the world". This apparent solicitousness for others, needless to say, is often a reflection of the sufferer's own fear of autonomy.

## An abandonment dream

*I often dream that I am walking in open countryside at night. I call out. No one answers me. I start to cry. I wake up with the shivers – shivers which seem to shake me from top to toe.*

This dream, recorded by a young woman, reflects a permanent anxiety. As a child, this young woman was effectively abandoned by her mother. An aunt reared her and brought her up strictly. The dreamer lived among a host of friends of both sexes (or, at least, she described her associates as such!). She hoped, no doubt, that one at least of these "friends" would become so close that he or she would never abandon her.

Might this fear perhaps also be the reason for the proliferation of societies and support groups?

### *The causes of fear of abandonment*

Instances of "abandonment" in childhood abound. As often as not, these abandonments are occasional and short and due to perfectly normal pressures and circumstances. The child has little sense of time. "I'll be back in five minutes" and "I'll be back in ten years" are often barely distinguishable. There is therefore only a narrow line (which also varies according to the child's

75

personality) between the acceptable frustration at Mummy's short-term absence (when she goes to work, say) and the sensation of a permanent abandonment and desolation, which rapidly becomes a profound neurotic anxiety. In the latter instance, the child grown to adulthood can never regard human relations other than in terms of ultimate abandonment. This is a ceaseless, agonizing torment, as often as not buried in the unconscious.

An intense inferiority complex emerges. Sadism may be a side-effect – I suffer, so others must pay. People of this personality type do not allow us to take them at face value. We are expected somehow to guess at their feelings and intentions. When these sorts of anxiety sufferers abandon a friend, for example, they will make out that it is the friend who has abandoned them. Many symptoms may signal this abandonment neurosis. Some people, for example, can never be happy or relaxed unless they always have to hand a list of important telephone numbers (those of hospitals, doctors, police, etc.). Others are seized by anxiety if, in the car, we take minor roads and thus risk getting stranded. Their arguments may be apparently cogent – "But if we break down, we might have to wait for hours before we get help. Better stick to the main roads" – but this is no more than rationalization. The real terror is not of missed engagements but of those moments spent alone and waiting for help. The policeman in his Panda car on the motorway, then, represents the mother.

Abandonment neurosis, masochism and sadism are frequently related. It is unsurprising too, considering the ubiquitousness of this neurosis, that literature abounds in situations where abandonment is the central theme.

Among the causes of this type of neurosis, the following are common:

(a) Too early weaning – though here much depends on the atmosphere of continued caring created by the mother and on the personality of the infant.

(b) An upbringing in which the mother does not pay enough attention to her child. The child in consequence feels "non-existent" and unworthy of interest. He or she feels abandoned – which is scarcely surprising, since to all intents and purposes, that is just what has happened.

(c) A child who is raised by the mother alone (the father, for example being dead) has only one support. A sense of abandonment, perhaps partial, is experienced as a speechless anxiety which sometimes instigates uncontrollable panic attacks.

## Some abandonment dreams

### Alone in a forest

*Julie dreams that she is walking in the forest with some friends when suddenly, without warning, they vanish. Terror seizes her. She calls out, but no one answers. The silence seems endless. Night falls.*

This is a classic case of the dreamer feeling all alone in the world, in blank silence, and in total darkness: Absolute isolation.

## A frosty welcome

> *Mary dreams that, arriving at the home of some close friends, she meets with a frosty, indifferent welcome. In desperation she rushes out of the house again. She finds herself in the midst of a great waste. Snow falls. She turns back, to find that the lights of her friends' house have been extinguished. She awakes in tears.*

Mary was a young woman who was "abandoned" in so far as her mother never paid attention to her, never asked for any help from her, never took interest in her studies, never read or reacted to school reports and never doled out punishments or rewards. Given that her father too seemed never even to notice her presence, Mary was a classic case of a girl wedged between a father and mother who might as well not have existed for all the response that she evoked. She was, to all intents and purposes, alone in the world. She spent her whole life rejecting any bonds so as not to be abandoned one day. Ultimately she abandoned others so as not to be abandoned herself.

There are countless abandonment dreams of one sort or another in my files. The dreamers go about their business without being deigned so much as a glance by others. Or, at a party, they see themselves *alone in a corner*. They speak into telephones, but no answer comes. They find themselves begging in the street (begging affection). Others will dream of houses where there are no women (without a mother), where only a towering man is to be found on the doorstep. Sometimes a young woman saunters naked in the street, but nobody sees her.

# CHAPTER 4

# *What is Known as "Neurosis"*

Human personality is like an architectural structure. From childhood onward, structural "beams" are set in place, supporting or laying pressure upon others, settling, shifting, seeing the best accommodation of the growing weight of experience in order to attain overall equilibrium.

## WHAT IS NEUROSIS?

We could assert that human beings are made up of a whole mass of buttressing neuroses, but first of all we must forget the generally accepted meaning of the term "neurosis" in the sense of "sickness".

Neurosis, in its most general sense, occurs whenever a human personality – a system in constant flux – adapts to restraints or "norms" imposed from without. Every child, from birth onward, must adapt to these norms, to values, and so on, which are never his or her own, since the child never ordains them at the onset.

Pushing things to their limits, then, life can be seen as an immense series of adaptations to others which, in turn, set up thousands of neuroses, localized in time. Some of these endure, some disappear, some are normal, some grotesquely abnormal.

Every human being is a tightrope walker. At any given moment, the whole organism is striving to maintain its balance. At any given moment, equally, we may attain such equilibrium, but it cannot endure, for, as living beings, we are under a compulsion to move forward.

Our unconscious minds, therefore, like giant computers stuffed full of information, ceaselessly work for the system's equilibrium, but often can only achieve this end to the detriment of this or that constituent part.

It is extremely important that the would-be interpreter of dreams should understand this. Imagine a great central computer in a vast factory. Suppose that, for the sake of argument, a hundred thousand people work there, from the chairman down to the tea-lady, each having a defined position and function.

Let us further suppose that this computer possesses all the information about everything which happens in that factory, down to the whereabouts of the smallest paperclip and the movements of the tiniest molecule of the employees.

That computer continues to work, day and night. But now here we find an employee – one of a hundred thousand – working in his office on the twenty-fifth floor. He obviously knows only a bare fraction of what goes on in the "bowels" of the computer. The computer on the other hand, works only for the whole factory and knows nothing of that employee except in so far as he is a constituent of the whole. As an isolated element, he has no meaning.

The computer, ceaselessly maintaining only the equilibrium of the whole, will replace this piece of a machine, remove a supplier or an employee, promote or demote this or that director. Each of these elements is *personally* affected by such decisions, but, no matter what the personal cost, the equilibrium of the whole is maintained. The computer has performed its function.

These personal reactions within the factory are our neuroses, normal or otherwise. An abnormal neurosis, then, is like our employee, who is desperate to perform his own job and no other, although the computer has ordained that he move on to another department. He becomes, as it were, a fixation; his work is stereotyped. He works for himself, apart from the whole vast mechanism, clinging on for dear life to a fixed point long after all else has changed.

Great tension will inevitably arise, then, between this rogue employee and the dynamic computer, between one man and his fellow workers, etc. This tension, in the mind, is manifest as anxiety.

In the factory of the human brain, every neurosis, normal or otherwise, is an attempt to adapt to perceived pressures. In the case of an abnormal neurosis, it is as though one small part of the whole by some stimulus or "trauma", is working just for itself (like our employee on the twenty-fifth floor). "Complexes" appear: These are like foreign bodies in the personality.

Now, rigid forms of the "super-ego" are put in place. The organism as a whole imposes several rigid protective mechanisms while, in turn, those foreign bodies attract to themselves, like magnets, a whole series of reactions which, left to themselves, would have remained normal. The personality becomes polarized. Tension grows between the "healthy" (that is, simple, or evolutionarily functional) organism and the no less committed rebel and its by now many associates. Power is imposed. It subdues the rebel, but still it works silently in the shadows, and, as with all rebellion, the greater the repression, the greater the growth and the vigour of the repressed element. Meanwhile, however, the great central computer works on without cease in pursuit of one thing only – overall equilibrium, no matter which part of the personality, to that end, must "go to the wall".

## My mania is my security

Let's start with a reiteration: everything we do corresponds to a need, be it conscious or unconscious.

Here is a dream by a thirty-year-old woman:

*I was a charlady. I was in this vast, glittering hall, scrubbing the floor. I was on my hands and knees. I had the impression that I had been there for a long time. People came and went. This was some sort of reception, I reckon. I saw a pile of dirty crockery which needed washing and polishing. It was – I don't know – as if I was at a culminating point in my life, summing up – a feeling I can't describe. I was sad, alone, outside everything.*

First, let me say that this woman suffers from various well-known compulsive "manias" or "obsessional neuroses", the passion for order, dusting, examining everything for blemishes, and so on. As we have already seen, this type of mania springs from an anxious need to be always in the right in face of an authority – an inner authority, of course, or a previously external authority (a parent, a given morality, etc.) now become an artificial satellite of the personality. The person afflicted no longer obeys the edicts of the outside world, but obeys an internal police force. This is a form of "super-ego".

Since, however, in the nature of things, there will always be something to tidy or to order, such a person can easily pass, in a lifetime, from one obsessive mania to another (constantly checking doors, gas, water, lining up ornaments, shoes, etc. etc.). This sort of obsession is extremely draining and can end up taking up the afflicted person's complete life. It is impossible, however, to abandon such behaviour, because it has become an essential mechanism for security (to be in the right, and so at peace).

In these cases, we can only treat the cause, which is inevitably a feeling of guilt and the dreadful anxious need for "perfectionism".

In this dream, then, we find in equal measure the concepts of destitution and reversal of fortune (she has become a charlady and works on her hands and knees). To this is added an additional sense of indignity (the passers-by do not even see her).

This dream proved very useful to the subject. She was able to recognize that she had always hidden, beneath her compensatory mechanisms, the fact that she believed herself unworthy to exist. These compensatory mechanisms were the usual ones: arrogance, contempt for others, overweaning pride, insistence on being right etc. – in short, characteristic paranoiac behaviour. Above all, she recognized her need for a halt, a reversal.

# BLAME AND GUILT IN DREAMS

A sense of guilt appeared, for example, in one dream recounted by a forty-year-old man:

> *I was in a park. I was watching two lovers through a gap in the hedge. People were watching me and gathering all the time.*

After hearing the dreamer's free associations, we found that the "gap in the hedge" is related to the keyhole through which children try to see what is happening in their parents' bedroom, with the feelings of shame and guilt which such voyeurism engenders. People watch and assemble – society sees through him and condemns.

## *The need for failure*

The fact that one believes oneself to be inferior and blameworthy simply for existing automatically engenders an unconscious need to fail. This is easy enough to understand. Such a person cannot believe in any sort of success (even if he or she enjoys "social success") because a non-existent person cannot succeed. Success is thus a contradiction of the fundamental tenet that it is better not to exist.

Failure signifies "rediscovering peace" – without

combat or competition with others or with oneself. The layman would be staggered to know just how many people – even at the height of social success – nurture within themselves this unconscious need to fail.

This was illustrated by a "hotel dream" recounted by a forty-three-year-old man:

> *I was coming back from a long trip abroad – to India, I think. I was worn out. I don't know how I got there, but I suddenly found myself in a smoky little bar-room. The hotel was in the slums. Urchins were bawling and flinging stones at one another. People were drinking beer. Someone said to me, "Ah, you're back with us, then?" I had no more money – not even my passport.*

The dreamer was a very rich businessman, apparently happy and self-possessed. It would take too long to detail his psychological problems here. Suffice it to say that he found a sense of tranquillity in places frequented by the poorer classes.

In this dream, we encounter the *return from a long journey* (life itself), India (for so many, the country of "inner liberation" and truth), fatigue (with life again). The *smoky little bar-room*, the *urchins* or *slum-kids*, the *beer*, the "*you're back*", all indicate a return to nothing (as far as the dreamer was concerned). The *lack of money and passport* completes the failure.

This man, furthermore, had often spoken to me of his desire to set off for distant places alone and penniless, and he had once related to me his bitter picture of himself never returning but dying abandoned by the world.

## Clans and fellowships

This section deals with an important class of symbolism in the dreams of people who blame themselves, who feel the need to fail and suffer from anxiety at the prospect of abandonment.

We tend to find "clans" or "brotherhoods" in such dreams in the form of travelling people, actors, gypsies, circus folk, mafia gangs, bands of outlaws, etc. What is their significance in real life, and what in dreams?

Fellowships – whether high or lower class – consist of a kind of family existing on the margins of conventional society. They have their own codes of honour which are strictly imposed. Members of such fellowships are frequently linked by ties which exist beyond death itself. To penetrate such a "clan" one must first be tested and adjudged worthy of admission, and must be able to show one's credentials. These groups are fiercely loyal to their own.

It is logical enough that groups of this type should appear in the dreams of the guilt-ridden, those who feel themselves to be isolated or who need failure or desertion. The feeling afforded by such a "family" is that members, once acknowledged, are totally accepted and will be welcome for as long as they live. The security of this family becomes symbolically enormous. Constantly threatening society fades away. The dreamer has the feeling of assigning responsibility to a greater force. It is a return to the security of childhood.

**A clan dream**
A woman, aged twenty, described the following dream:

*There was this group with hoods covering their faces. I had committed some sort of transgression. I did not know whom I had hurt. A judge got up and unmasked his face. He was a really handsome gypsy. I knew that he would be just. I was going to pay for my transgression – perhaps even die – but I knew that I would receive the badge allowing me to go to the great gypsy fair.*

This young woman suffered from classic guilt symptoms – the constant sense that she was not accepted by others, that she was not recognized, that she was mistrusted and unloved.

Here were the dreamer's free associations:

*Hoods.* Secrecy, anonymity, black, punishment, implacable law . . .

*Transgression.* But I always feel that I've done wrong. I always have done!

*Judge.* Overseeing, all-seeing, evaluating everything . . . childhood.

*Gypsy.* God, it must be good to be one of them, to blot out the rest of the world . . . Poverty . . .

*Justice.* I have never been recognized for myself, so how can I find the right place for myself in life?

*Perhaps even die.* Rubbish! For God's sake. After all . . .

*Badge.* A badge means I'm recognized. I can participate in the fair. Yes, I must find friends. I must attend to these fears. I must find my own family, my chosen family. Above all I must get round to acknowledging myself.

# GUILT AND MASOCHISM

The term "masochism" is today so degraded that it has lost its true, profound significance. It is used casually and inaccurately. What, then, does it really mean?

We usually define masochism as the pursuit of "pleasure through pain". This pain may be physical (suffering oneself or making another suffer) or it may be emotional: the need to ensure that one is always "under" others; the need to devalue and to denigrate oneself, to be ground down, to fail, to punish oneself, to be punished – not through a feeling of justice but in order eventually to be pardoned (once more acknowledged, loved, etc.).

In fact, masochism possesses an entirely different face; but, given the term's unpleasant connotations in current usage, we should perhaps look for a different word.

## The essential masochism or the agony of unification

The most intense human need is to feel "connected" to everything around us: other people, nature, the universe, God. Consciously or otherwise, we all possess this "religiosity" (in its etymological sense: *religare* = to bind together or unify) and ceaselessly seek to satisfy it –

or to repress it, as is the case with most of us. Earthly paradise, then, has become Paradise Lost, with all the enduring nostalgia and regret which that concept holds. We are separated from our origins and from peace. We yearn to retrieve them.

Religiosity is the basis of masochism, in the most positive meaning of that term. It consists in melding with God, nature, music, love, etc. But the melding means the abnegation of the individual ego. The masochism thus consists in reaching out towards oblivion, the denial of self, in order to attain oneness with the infinite or the absolute. This is true not just of religion *per se* but also of moral and artistic endeavour of this kind.

## A religious dream of masochism
Here is the dream of a man, aged fifty.

> *The night was reddish-pink. I was in a desert. I was sprawled out with my stomach against the sand. I had the feeling that this was a great dream – the feeling of something titanic. The earth was like a lover. I clung to it. I melted into it. All my life passed at high speed before my eyes, but it all seemed superfluous, unimportant . . . I find it difficult to explain . . . I was no longer anything, but I had become everything. I participated in something huge, something universal, but not as "me", if you see what I mean. I was – oh, how should I explain it? – I was just a molecule moving according to a universal law.*

This is a "religious" dream of fusion of the self with the universe as a whole. It is, in the broadest sense, a masochistic dream. It could be thought that the dreamer sought to return to the refuge of his mother's breast, but in fact, according to his free associations, it seems that here he became reunited with the earth mother and laws of the universe. This dream gave its dreamer (a writer) a new lease of life. The knowledge which informed this dream, and which might have prevented a sense of alienation, had been always in him. It took the dream, however, to bring the good news up to the level of his conscious mind.

This dream surely illustrates that we must separate the term "masochism" from its more restricted connotations.

## Martyrdom and masochism

Religious martyrs were once considered to be mystics or saints. Today, "science" would define them rather as masochists (in the word's negative or pathological sense). At the same time, most of them sought total fusion with the divine. In order to attain this, they knew they must no longer be separate from the divine and so must suppress their individual personalities.

Could we not say, then, that masochism — that is, the desire to negate oneself in order to be part of everything — is the basis of all human existence? Freud himself placed masochism at the cornerstone of the whole construct of the psyche.

And is not death, considered by many to be an ecstatic liberation, again the ultimate masochism?

But common usage — scientific and otherwise — has reduced the application of the term. It can now be applied only to pathological phenomena and to sexual fantasies which are no more than sickly degradations of a sometimes great, impressive phenomenon.

Perhaps, then, in the wider-reaching sense, we should substitute for "masochism" the term "agony of unification".

# THE ORGY

The term "orgy" should also be considered in its broader sense. The concept of the orgy is derived from the greater masochism – the loss of self in uniting with the whole.

## Candles and chanting
The following dream was recounted by a woman, aged fifty-five:

*I was stretched out on a blue bed. There was chanting – a crescendo. Hundreds of candles were flickering. I shouted out. "But I'm young! I'm young!" My grandmother appeared to me. She was smiling at me. There was a great crowd all about us, a calm, serene crowd. I was happy.*

This is an "orgiastic" dream. Here are some of the dreamer's free associations:

*Lights, chanting, crowd.* Mysticism, black mass, incense . . . participation. Instinct. High mass . . . Youth . . . Happiness. It just made me so happy, that dream!

*Blue bed*. I don't know if it really was blue. Maybe it was just my feeling of happiness which made me think it. Blue is my favourite colour. It's the colour of the endless sky. Bed? Lying down, horizontal . . . like water . . . defenceless, without aggression. Floating on this blue mass, on the music, in this crowd . . . Lost in infinity . . . non-existence . . .

*Young*. I felt regenerated after this dream!

*Grandmother*. The past. All the distant past . . . Roots. Continuance. Goodness. Beyond death. Eternity.

This dream demonstrates a sort of mystical participation in an eternal vastness. It is a powerful dream, a source of new energy and self renewal. It marks – and engenders – a new start in the dreamer's inner being. We have here at the same time the elements of *orgy* and of *masochism* – in the sense, of course, of "unification", as discussed above.

## A carnival dream
Here is the dream of a fifty-year-old man:

*I was taking part in a huge carnival, which was frenzied with dancing, music, shouting. But it was all in perfect order. Everyone was singing and dancing and there was harmony, beauty . . . These splendid majorettes passed by and children threw flowers . . . It was a terrific dream!*

A terrific dream indeed. We shall understand its terms better in a while.

## A hippy commune

This was dreamed by a man aged forty.

> *I was living in a commune, but it was a platonic community – hippy, you could say – all flowers and kisses and organ music. It was powerful and very peaceful. There was general, deep understanding. There were no words. We allowed ourselves just to be outside time, in a boundless climate, as if the sky and the waters were present . . . It was a miracle of heavenly peace.*

The dreamer remembers in particular "the incredible social harmony" which he encountered in this dream. He speaks of a unified spirituality in which no one person opposed another. It was, he says, "like one single soul"!

This man was a civil servant, fairly stereotypical in appearance. This dream demonstrates that you cannot tell a book by its cover. I believe that this might be a "shadow" dream (see chapter 10), and that this man is dreaming of something he most profoundly desires and has never attained. In all events, this is, in the highest sense of the term, an orgy dream. Individuals disappear. The community has become one soul. Everyone melts into everyone else.

## *What does an orgy mean?*

This term embraces a large number of phenomena. It is usually taken to be a pejorative word referring to collective debauchery, unrestrained licentiousness, mass drunkenness, wild dancing and so on. In this context, however, we should also include carnivals, discos and other such events where we abandon restraint.

Orgy, then, is excess, lack of moderation. Every form of orgy is "religious" (like masochism, in the sense of "unification"). Orgy is a term which can be applied to everything that bursts open, exploding into immensity, everything that gushes out in a storm, everything that breaks down the barriers and inhibitions of everyday life, everything that offers the sensation of being part of a greater entity and of melting into it or losing oneself in it.

The orgy can crop up in many guises, but it is always "religious". This religiousness can appear elevated and positive (an "over-indulgence" of fine music, for example) or regressive and even rotten (collective sexual or alcoholic debauchery).

## Back to source

We know of the great mass orgies of primitive civilizations. They are habitually related to Agriculture and take place at harvest-time, spring, etc. Their purpose is for man to meld with the great universal unity. In certain primitive rites, the priest couples in public with his wife. All the participants imitate them. The orgy becomes huge, gargantuan, boundless. It's purpose is to multiply the earth's riches, to instil vigour into the soil. As has been written. "Everything which is isolated ceases to be so; the union is total and individuals melt into the great Universal Matrix."

## Carnivals and rock music

We read earlier of the dream about a carnival which was "huge" and "frenzied". Orgies can be large or small, a rock concert or the spiritual immersion in music thundering from great organs. In addition to the dances and the freedoms granted in the carnival the masks represent an unconscious search for unification (they provide anonymity and suppress individuality). As for the lower variety of orgy (sexual or drunken) there too the participants seek to melt into something other than themselves — a suicide of their individual personalities, the death of the "I" or ego. It is an inverse religious experience, an orgy in reverse.

## A rock music dream

A young man had this dream:

> *The music was coming from all sides — the singers, the crowd, in a great enclosure just for rock music. I was on a stage. I was in charge of everything, and it all swept over me. I was happy as never before. There were flowers, there were fountains, there were girls . . . I was the master of it all. It was a deliriously happy event.*

This brings me to the subject of rock concerts and festivals, which often attain such a fever-pitch that reason seems to fly out the window. How is it that all those separate individuals can thus be annihilated?

First of all, the crowd is bound together in a sort of primary emotion. A more or less homogeneous mass becomes an emotional "whole", and seems to react as if manipulated like puppets.

Second, instinctive impulses brought into play recall primitive ceremonies. The atmosphere is, in effect, that of religious "mass" sometimes almost a huge collective throbbing. The individual becomes the crowd. People writhe, shout and go into ecstatic trances.

Like it or not, the religious nature of these events cannot be denied. These musical "orgies" (which have strong sexual overtones) suppress the individual and liberate, in its place, a whole community united in an overwhelming fervour.

These musical orgies, then, are no more than one amongst thousands of possible manifestations of "regeneration" and "fusion" rituals which have always existed throughout the world.

## SUPER-EGO DREAMS

The super-ego can be defined as everything that is "above" or "placed upon" the ego, everything that prevents the individual from being totally free. There are forms of the super-ego that one can call normal, and others that are pathological.

The *normal* forms of the super-ego are abundant. They range from traffic lights to all the various regulations, including all possible laws and prohibitions. Licences and permits are also aspects of the super-ego, since they imply a prohibition. Our nationality too is a form of super-ego since it presupposes civic and legal respect. Even education represents super-ego, because it is imposed by external elements of the educated ego. It is evident that no child truly corresponds to the education which he or she receives, because every child is essentially different. Social rules, fashions, trends in opinions and thought, ideology, organized religion, morals, and so on, are all aspects of the super-ego.

These normal types – particularly the educational – can rapidly take on a *pathological* aspect. If feelings of guilt or inferiority creep into the psychological machinery, that is enough for the super-ego to turn into the enemy within. It resembles a brutal and repressive police force. Inner freedom is destroyed. An ordinary red traffic light becomes a symbol of obligation which must be obeyed on pain of guilt and anxiety. The normal super-ego command, "stop your car" becomes abnormal: "I shall come to a stop perfectly so that the others can see just how much I respect the rules or because I always have the feeling that I am annoying others, that I'm not in the right place, etc." This is just one example.

Education is responsible for developing the most important forms of pathological super-ego. It is then that we experience those well-known feelings of guilt, anxiety, inferiority, non-existence, feelings that we have no right to exist, and fears, such as castration anxiety and so on.

This is where the super-ego intervenes in dreams, either to inform us of an unconscious element and so put us on our guard, or to warn us of the likelihood of some future behaviour (always via the intermediary of that unconscious computer which is infinitely better informed than the conscious).

Dreams about the super-ego often feature people in authority. *Policemen* and *customs officers* are common, (often representing not merely order but also the mother). Then we have to show our credentials. We are "in order" or "out of order". Either way, we must account for ourselves. *Lawyers* appear, *barristers* and *judges*, *schoolteachers* and *supervisors*.

As for inanimate objects, we find *barriers*, *traffic diversions*, "Keep Off" signs. Anything which checks, brakes, blocks, punishes, accuses, questions or makes us change our route − in short, any shackle on freedom − will be found in such dreams.

## A classic super-ego dream
This came from a thirty-year-old man.

> *My car was going pretty fast, but something odd was going on. Smoke was coming out from underneath. I realized that the brakes were on, and that the engine was overheating. I stopped. I saw a policeman in the distance. He came and went on the horizon, but never came towards me.*

This man's life has been "braked". The brakes are internal, of course. His personality "overheating", split, as it were, between the desire for freedom and the imperatives of the super-ego.

The policeman on the horizon is here a symbol of the mother from whom the dreamer awaits help but who, in this dream, seems not to respond to his appeal.

Given the incalculable number of normal forms of our super-ego, it is clear that a human personality is always an entity enveloped in social conditioning. Can we say, then, that our individual characters are no more than fabrications? And if everyone could get rid of the super-ego from their ego, would all individuals be the same all over the world?

# CHAPTER 5

## *The Language of Dreams*

Why is our nocturnal thinking so different from our daytime reasoning. Why do we not use the same language in both circumstances? And again, why does our dream language seem perfectly natural while we are dreaming?

Can we assert, that our dream language is likely to be our most authentic language? Perhaps it is our true mode of expression, since children and primitive people express themselves above all by means of symbols.

## WHAT IS A SYMBOL?

Let us imagine a photographer who shows us an image. He says that he wanted in this image to represent a particular emotion, or state of mind. For him, *his* image has a meaning and this same image will always evoke in him the same emotion. It may revive memories of childhood, of happiness or of sadness; it may symbolize, for him, loneliness, life or death, the passing of time, or other situations that are personal to him.

As for us, it is highly unlikely that this image will evoke exactly the same emotion, as long as the image illustrates a personal one. Obviously everything would be different, if this image could arouse in thousands of different people the same type and intensity of feeling.

It follows, then, that true symbols (or universally evocative images) are rare. Despite this, we employ this term for just about anything. A trademark is termed a "symbol". I have even heard film stars referred to as an "archetype". However, the photographer's image is a *real* symbol for him. For us, it can be no more than a sign or an allegory.

It seems, then, that a symbol is a representation that is charged with emotion. Without that emotion, a symbol ceases so to be and becomes a sign or allegory.

So, with our photographer, we could only fully understand "his" symbol if we knew the man himself very well indeed.

But this is the same principle as we have already established in relation to the analysis of dreams. Each symbol can be truly understood only if subjected to a truly personal interpretation.

## A distant expression of oneself

Many examples could be cited. Why, for instance, does a collector amass, say, weapons, swords, stamps, even matchboxes or cigar-bands? And why does another one need a collection of pencils, shoes or clothes? What can such accumulation represent? After all, there is no question of need for these things. They are symbols then, for the collector, though they leave the rest of us cold, at first sight at least. Plainly, these objects evoke something profoundly buried in the unconscious. They are signs, but the collectors know nothing of their real significance. When, however, these objects appear in a dream, they summon up the distant memories which, unbeknownst to the individual, control his or her personality.

## Symbols spring from sensation

I believe this to be an important rule: we never know anything of beings or objects other than the *sensation* we have of them. We never know their objective reality whatever it may be.

At the same time, everything becomes symbolic: a word, an image, a colour, an object, a piece of music, a gesture, etc. The true symbol always implies something more than the meaning we immediately perceive.

So we use innumerable symbols in the course of our lives, without knowing it. Better still – a whole universe of symbols exists within us. They make us act and react. They control our sensations and our emotions. If defining a symbol is so difficult, it is surely because the symbol springs from the domain of sensation, never from that of reason. The best example of this is given to us by our dreams.

## How is a symbol "made"?

As soon as we are confronted by an abstraction we try to represent it with a sign. When, therefore, we seek to evoke an idea, a feeling or a sensation, we try to do so by means of signs – images, objects, marks etc.

Every symbol possesses, then, a *subjective* meaning. For a symbol to become common to many, the sign

103

must recall immediately to everyone the abstraction which it represents. We say, then, that ∞ is the mathematical symbol for the infinite. For most people, in fact, it is only a sign evoking no emotion whatever. For others who have the *sensation*, of the infinite or of numbers, it will be a real symbol.

We see, then, once again, just how hard it is to translate a symbol by use of rational words. As Bachofen writes:

> A symbol awakens intuition; language can only explain. The symbol strikes simultaneously all the strings in the human spirit; language can do no more than plonk out one note at a time. The symbol has its roots deep in the most secret depths of the psyche; language, like a soft breeze, only scuffs the surface of understanding. The symbol turns inward; language outward. Only the symbol is capable of blending the most diverse entities in an apparently homogeneous ensemble. Words render the infinite finite; symbols enable the spirit to leap over the boundaries of the finite world.

## Symbol = religion

Every true symbol is "religious" in that it seeks to unite in a whole our ego, the world and the universe. For our primitive ancestor no less than the child, most actions are "religious" in themselves. These actions are seen as founded upon an unconscious which has remained in close and immediate contact with the surrounding world.

But the true symbol is above all experienced in the

realm of dreams. There it finds its true home and speaks its own language again. When humans gather together to descend into the depths of their dreams, perhaps they sometimes find rising up in them ancient images which have held sway in countless human brains before our own.

## Freud, Jung and symbolism

*Freud*, who has been accused of seeing all symbols as translations of sexual repression, none the less wrote: "Symbols often have numerous and multiple meanings which, as in Chinese script, allow correct interpretation in each individual case only when considered in relation to one another. To this ambiguity of the symbols themselves, we must add the dream's susceptibility to hyper-interpretation, its ability to represent structures of thought and flights of desire often distinct in their content and alien by their nature." He continues: "It is important to bear in mind the philosophical, religious and moral convictions which inform the conscious."

As for *Jung* he attempted to classify the formation of symbols.

1 *Comparison made by analogy*. For example: the sun is life-giving. It is thus comparable to love, whose "heat" is emotionally life-giving. The *sun shines* and *beams* like God or a father. The sun is *high* in the sky, which produces the symbol of *rising*. We *rise* towards light. (It would be odd to consider "descending towards light".) *Light* is associated with "glory": we rise towards glory, honours and success. (Again, we

would never speak of "descending to glory".) So it is that a simple analogous symbol can ordain the language. We can continue making these analogies as far as the eye can see, until we reach those great universal symbols which we shall consider later on.

Take another example: the *moon* is pale and mysterious. She belongs to the realm of darkness. Note that the moon is automatically feminine, and has long been a symbol of femininity, of gentleness, of mystery, of hidden love, of the mother, and so on.

Or another: *water* is without distinct parts. It is supple. It can be welcoming, or attractive and lethal. It is a symbol of femininity.

And so on – though it is worth noticing that, while the majority of languages confirm this gender symbolism (*solus, le soleil, il sole* etc., and *luna, la lune, la luna,* etc.), the German language gives the sun the feminine gender (*die Sonne*) and the moon the masculine (*der Mond*)!

2  *Symbols derived from the most powerful and universally encountered feelings.* Here the great natural phenomena occupy the first rank: water, rain, storms, day, night, the rising and setting of the sun on the horizon, the fertilization of the soil, life, death, power, God . . . These become symbols as they represent or reflect the profound sensations of humankind. Remember the sun in its glory, symbolizing God, the father, brilliance, success, whatever? We can move onward. Human life depends upon the fertility of the soil. The tools which work the earth become important symbols. So the earth (fertilized) becomes a symbol of womanhood. The sun and rain (which fertilize it)

marry to give that fertility. The ploughshare becomes a phallic symbol (it "pierces" the Earth Mother, etc.)

The sun, which each dawn rises from the horizon, becomes a symbol of rebirth after death. Its brilliance, its heat, its glory, its invincibility, are reflected in the great universal symbol of "solar" heroes whom we find in the great epics. (Cuchulain in Irish mythology, for example, and Gawain in Arthurian legend both grew stronger as the sun rose and weakened as it set).

## Cutting your coat according to your cloth

Take a poor, ill-educated person who surrounds herself with worthless objects which, for her, are absolutely priceless. These paltry things become symbols to her, evoking her childhood, perhaps, or sorrows or joys which words cannot express. Maybe they symbolize a great love, now blurred by time, or harmony with nature, or any number of other vitally important emotions. For her, such an object, brooded over and cherished like a fetish, symbolizes her union with the Absolute in so far as she is able to perceive it, and so renders her vast as her universe.

Take another person, who has an intense inner life, and for whom everything becomes a symbol: the tree and the wind, day and night, the valley and the bell, the sea and the tides, work and rest. Such a person is infinitely rich.

Take yet another person who suffers from an excess of rationality. Her inner life seems arid. For her, symbols are only archaic objects of curiosity and have no emotive context.

But night falls, and with it come dreams. And these

three people see identical images arising in their mind's eye. These are the great universal symbols.

They are to be found everywhere – among the ignorant and the educated, the young and the old, men and women, the child and the primitive. They know no boundaries of race, religion or morality. They have traversed the centuries. They have given rise to innumerable myths and legends. They have fed the universal hunger for a vision of heaven and of hell.

It is these which constitute the "great dreams", whose roots are embedded in archetypes.

## WHAT IS AN ARCHETYPE?

If it is difficult to define a symbol, it is almost impossible to explain what an archetype is. Archetypes, in fact, exist in that they are the source of symbols. Yet they cannot be "captured" in the form of tangible reality. What does this mean?

An archetype springs from *pure sensation*. It is pure *potentiality*. No more. It is, as it were, a psychic depository.

If we try to represent an archetype, we find ourselves talking of symbols. The symbol might relate to the archetype, but, if spoken or visualized, it will none the less be a symbol. The archetype is to symbols what a vocabulary is to words; or, again, the archetype can be represented as pure energy, whilst the symbol is the manifestation of that energy in light, heat, etc.

A painter who wanted to represent an archetype could only depict symbols. But there are some that are so close to archetypes that they almost cling to them. These are the great symbols which move human beings the world over in the same fashion.

These great symbols that are close to the archetype assume great potency when they appear in our dreams. They can change our lives.

# CHAPTER 6

# *The Great Dreams*

In certain dreams, individual symbols disappear. This may seem in direct contradiction with what has already been asserted – that is, that all symbols are individual and draw their significance from the particular personality of the dreamer.

But "great" dreams summon up symbols that emanate directly from profound sensations common to all humanity. These dreams, which speak to us from the depths of humanity's collective unconscious, are dazzling – often unforgettable. They can make human beings shift from a negative to a positive phase of their lives – or vice versa.

## HOW TO RECOGNIZE A "GREAT DREAM"

A great dream can be recognized, first of all, by the intensity of the atmosphere which it engenders. This is the sort of dream you feel you must tell somebody

111

about, even a bored neighbour. You must "get it off your chest", even if there is no prospect of interpretation.

- *The symbols* which characterize great dreams almost always bear upon the great subjects: life and death, happiness and unhappiness, passionate love, the unification or fragmentation of the self, the great hopes of childhood, and so on.

  They evoke, sometimes in extravagant imagery, nature itself with its forces and dangers, the fusion of the human being with other creatures and the whole universe. Often, an intense and moving poetry (positive or negative) emerges in these visions; music can be heard, and staggering landscapes seen by the dazzled eyes of the dreamer. These are the dreams of brightness or darkness, of suns and moons, and of waters of every variety. They are "elemental" in their symbolism as in their psychological significance. We will find "directions" here too (see chapter 13), and infinite ascents, infinite descents. Here too are the intensely emotive colours, (see chapter 11); or numbers and geometric forms (whose significance we shall study later).

- *Great myths* appear in such dreams. We find kings and queens, sorcerers and sorceresses, immortal or legendary women who haunt men's minds (the Anima – chapter 7), giants, princesses, labyrinths, crossroads, tunnels, enchanted or evil caves, fairies, etc.

  Fire, wind, storms, plains, valleys and mountains similarly take their place here. We find ourselves flying by magical means; we control the earth and sky. Other elements of our soul come into play, dimensions totally unknown in day-to-day life. Unknown they may be, yet they lurked deep within us, or else how could we dream about them?

Here too are the figures and faces sublimated in memory yet still ardently desired – mothers, fathers, sisters, brothers.

At the beginning of this book I reproduced the following dream:

*I was on a promontory, from which I could see a marvellous valley with infinite folds and hollows. These undulations multiplied in a regular way. It was the Valley of Eden. I saw a lot of fruit-trees, laden with ripe fruit and flowers. Lots of apple-trees. Lots of rose-bushes. The valley itself was just thick grass; white cows grazed there, as far as the eye could see. Here and there, there were little groups of people dancing, very slowly. They danced to some music in ³/4 time – a sort of slow-motion waltz outside time itself. It was wonderful . . . I heard the music with perfect clarity. It sprang up from every side. It was the first movement of the Bach Cantata: Wie schön leuchtet der Morgenstern. All these people, dancing hand in hand, signalled to me. I felt infinitely happy. I think I would give the rest of my life for just one hour of such happiness.*

*Then there were these three jet aeroplanes which came from behind me, and suddenly I found myself in the middle of one. The other two flanked me like the sides of a triangle. These planes moved very slowly and calmly;*

*all their power was potential only. They flew in absolute silence, just a few feet above the earth. Everything flowed past beneath me, gently, smoothly; the grass, the trees, the people . . . The music could still be heard . . . I'll never forget that dream. It gave me a degree of energy and a feeling of sheer joy which was beyond belief.*

This is a marvellous dream – simply wonderful. It filled the dreamer with energy and enthusiasm; the images in this dream touch directly on the great sensations of the human soul.

Here we find:

- *The anima.* This is symbolized by the immense and gentle *valley* which the dreamer takes in in a single look, since he is on a promontory. He seems to be "outside time": he is an unmoving witness. When we know that the anima is probably the most powerful unconscious sensation in the human male, and that only the realization and harmonization of the anima permit a man to be what he is, we must already be aware of the stature of such a dream.
- *Music.* This movement of a Bach cantata (No. 1) is indeed a sort of waltz before the waltz existed. It is very slow and very tranquil. One could dance to this music, as the people in the valley are seen to do. Here again, the atmosphere is "outside time". The knowledge that the title of the cantata means "How brightly shines the morning star" contributes to the beauty of the whole. This is a dawn in the dreamer's soul.
- *Vegetation and cows.* Again, the great theme is that of *fertility* (of the soul). The *fruit-trees* symbolize the *Earth*

*Mother.* A carpet of thick grass covers the ground in the valley. *White cows* graze as far as the eye can see. The cow is obviously a major agrarian symbol. Her own fertility depends in turn upon that of the soil. The cow is also, of course, a symbol of *maternity*. She gives milk and so recalls childhood and the mother's breast. The cow represents in equal measure the Earth Mother and gentle patience. She is an almost universal symbol; and, of course, venerated by Hindus.

- *The aeroplanes.* These are jets, and thus charged with enormous power, yet that *power*, remains *potential* only; it is kept in reserve since they fly slowly and in total silence, just above the ground. The three of them, furthermore, form a *triangle*, an important geometric form (see chapter 13). Here again, the dreamer is detached. He flies over the valley, a witness of the valley and himself.

- *Dancing people.* Hand in hand, they tread their stately measure. It is a sort of *ritual dance*, with overtones of the sacred. In fact, it is an *orgy* in the higher sense of the term, as previously outlined. It indicates a *sharing* in the Earth and its fertility. It establishes a *rapport* between the Earth Mother and the anima of the dreamer. It marks a *spiritual watershed* in his life. It is also a symbol of *integration* and *unification* (the dancers are hand in hand). The dance is a movement with a direction. Here we are reminded of Balinese dances, where the slightest gesture reveals a sacred meaning, a sense of religious participation, and Western dances are only pale imitations of this having long since lost their religious significance.

To sum up, then, this dream leads the dreamer towards the essential in himself and enables him to participate in all things, thanks to a harmonious and reconciled anima.

## A strange "great dream"
The dreamer was an engineer, aged forty and married.

> *I was on some sort of infinite plateau or stage, like a gigantic circular pancake. It revolved about an invisible central axis, but I didn't feel any centrifugal force. Horizons passed by, clouds, lights . . . but suddenly the stage stopped turning. Then I heard this powerful voice singing. It was the voice of a man, but in a very high register – a counter-tenor. A cold piercing voice without vibration. I did not recognize the tune. This voice was, I repeat, extraordinarily powerful, but as cold as a snow-field sparkling in the sun. Then, I don't know . . . I suppose I must just have woken up.*

This is how the dreamer talked about it:

That was the strangest dream of my life. I can still hear that voice. I think . . . that infinite plateau . . . it was like being absolutely alone . . . It was me up against myself, me seeking my place in the universe . . . It is true that I'm at a turning-point in my life; I'm not happy with my engineering job – or, rather, I'm not happy with the specializations into which I've been forced. I would like to have done astro-nomical research with a metaphysical aim . . . I'd like to give up my job, but I can't see how. I knew that the plateau or stage was revolving, much as I know that the earth revolves, without actually feeling any centrifugal force. But I just can't tell you how alluring those horizons were as they passed by. It was as if I were motionless in time, eternal. Then it stopped revolving, and everything stopped. Then that voice . . . You know the voice of a counter-tenor? Well, it's always fascinated me, that sort of voice. It's an androgynous sort of voice. It goes as high as a woman's voice, but it has no vibrations. It could be an angel's voice, or Lucifer's, shade and light both, as if announcing the last judgement! But what did that voice mean to me? It seemed to be outside me – outside everything. It was like a sword which pierced through everything . . . Yes, a magnificently beautiful voice . . . a blade, a laser beam, perfect purity . . . but lacking a woman's warmth . . . In fact, basically, everything in that dream was cold . . . I was so alone. If only a woman could have appeared . . . !

I did not see this man again, so was unable to pursue an interpretation of this great dream with him. What did it mean?

Everything, certainly seemed glacial there. Whatever the dreamer might say, we can surmise that the dream was an expression of the state of his soul at that moment of his life. The voice of the counter-tenor, which is indeed without vibration, is, of course an alto voice in a full-grown man. It is largely found in ancient music. J. S. Bach, unable to call upon female singers, who were forbidden in churches, used boys as sopranos and counter-tenors for alto. Bach often used the alto when the music was intended to represent the "fall" and consequent contrition. This makes sense. The alto is, in effect a "fallen" soprano, incapable of attaining the heights (the *tessitura*) of the soprano. But in this dream? Might it be the dreamer's anima which was lost in infinite icy wastes? Did the voice accuse him or warn him? Did it announce a "judgement", a punishment, a "castration" of his personality? Is there an indication here of latent homosexuality in the dreamer – recalling that the voice of the counter-tenor was formerly that of the *castrato* (though now specially developed by training). Whatever, this dream is obviously very curious. The main thing would have been to know what message was transmitted by that powerful, icy counter-tenor's song.

## A labyrinth dream
This was experienced by a 35-year-old woman who was a journalist:

> *I am in a vast labyrinth, but I've worked my way up to ground level. I feel pleased, proud! It's daytime. I head for the way out. Ahead of me there's a closed door. I open it, but a beam of orange-yellow light shoots down at me, pushing me back into the labyrinth. I make desperate efforts to get out, but that beam keeps driving me back. I feel no worry. I just say to myself: "What's going on? What does this beam want with me?"*

This woman was *too* sociable, *too* extrovert, living a switchback existence of highs and lows. She was celibate. She had no centre to her life. It was plain from the outset that this sort of unentailed existence allowed her

118

to run away from something (presumably herself).

The principal elements of this dream are obviously the labyrinth, the exit from the labyrinth and the beam which forces her back. We'll look at each of them separately.

- *Labyrinth*. Labyrinths or mazes, instantly summon up images of getting lost, trying to find the way out, problems of orientation, paths leading to dead ends, and so on. It is obvious that for the dreamer this is the labyrinth of her own life.

  The labyrinth can be related to crossroads, where numerous different directions are possible. The wayfinder therefore hesitates as to which way to go and then makes a choice.

  In any labyrinth, it is essential that we obtain and hold on to the "key", as did Theseus in the Cretan palace of the Minotaur by means of the thread given to him by Ariadne.

  Above all, however, the maze or labyrinth can symbolize *the search for the centre*. The function of the labyrinth is thus to *delay* the traveller in the search for his or her own inner self or "ego", which is a spiritual guest.

  Symbolically, the journey through the labyrinth is a voyage of initiation. Non-initiates cannot find the centre. *Tests* must be undergone and passed before that power is granted. A labyrinth is *concentric*. It is a magic symbol. It signifies concentration upon oneself, the overcoming of inner obstacles, not being fooled by false routes which come to dead ends, and not being deceived by appearances, etc.

119

As a symbol of inner renewal, the labyrinth is similar to the mandala (see p. 125)

- *The orange-yellow beam.* Instantly, in its concentration and power, this makes one think of the laser beam, which cuts, slices, pierces and kills (the death-ray).

All in all, what we have here is a fine dream. It's "message" is simple: this journalist must stop her headlong flight. She must no longer attempt to escape the labyrinths of her inner self. It is at the centre of her self or ego that she will find the solution to her difficulties. She must rediscover the introverted part of herself, which until now she has relentlessly shunned.

The need for such a change is pressing. The power of that beam which keeps pushing her back is proof of that. It also warns her of the danger which threatens. Society itself will reject her if she continues her game of false and aggressive assumed personalities, forcing her back on — and into — herself, willy-nilly. Thinking about this laser beam, she told me:

I've become a copy of a man. A beam like that is phallic, I reckon. And it makes sense, because I can't count the number of men who have shoved me back, saying, or just letting me know, "Become a woman, damn you. Just become capable of welcoming others in, just find a centre, and you'll be lovable."

## A town dream
This was a nightmare, experienced by a man of forty-two.

*God, I could never really describe it. It was so terrifying, so powerful . . .*

*I was in this town. It was sprawling, super-modern, Kafkaesque. I felt the place breathe! It was a living, panting, moving town! Not just living, but conscious too. It was full of these huge, grotesque noises, but then everything was huge and grotesque in this nightmare. A conscious town, which knew what it was doing. That was what frightened me most. I felt alone, isolated, lost, even though there were enormous crowds, split into bunches, all round. I was at the centre of one of these groups, which breathed as one, a living organism within a living organism.*

*The sea was on the horizon. It was breathing too! The waves rose and fell with this great raucous sound like a pair of bellows. It was horrible! That sea looked as if it was ready to rush down and devour the town.*

*In a corner of the town — actually inside the town — there was this boat, set up on blocks.*

*It was strange, that; a boat right there in the middle of town. Strange and terrible. On board this boat was its crew, in summer uniform. They watched the town, which was moving more and more, but the crew didn't move. It was as though it had nothing to do with them. I turned away from the boat, and then the whole town started to whirl faster and faster. Everything was sucked in as though inhaled towards the centre of an enormous funnel. I woke up shouting. "I don't want any more! No more!"*

Here, without going into excessive detail, is the meaning of this dream, established, of course, with the dreamer.

He, in fact, was a "director" of an important business located somewhere in France. This was the world of traditional middle-class values. Wealth, appearances and efficiency were the watchwords. The significant factor, however, was that the business, and the properties which that business had engendered, *were managed by the women*. The ownership had passed from the grandmother to the wife, by way of the dreamer's mother. To put it in psychoanalytical terms, the women were "phallic" and the men "emasculated". In effect, the "female" part of this man's soul, his "anima", had been embedded in the women who had surrounded him since childhood. He had no soul of his own – only that of his mother and, still more, that of his grandmother, of whom his mother had been the carbon copy. Added to this was the engulfing dominance of his wife. As for his father, he did not exist, since he too had been swallowed up by his wife. The dreamer himself worked for fourteen hours a day in order to escape this unbearable female environment, but also to ensure that no one could give him the slightest reproof (which would cause him intense anguish). So this was a man whose soul had been devoured and engulfed by women, who, for him, possessed a negative and dangerous image.

The dream, then, readily becomes clear.

- *The breathing town.* The town can be considered here as a symbol of maternity. A town offers protection to its inhabitants. It possesses, symbolically, surrounding walls, fortifications, gates. It is the symbol of a mother protecting her children.

  But if a town is related to the female principle, the

pitiful state of the dreamer's anima becomes all the more apparent. Instead of affording him protection, this dream town gives him only a nightmare of destruction.

This town *breathes*, *pants* and is "as though *conscious*". It represents a formidable threat: it will engulf and devour. In the face of this town, the dreamer is defenceless. Sound and fury reign. Crowds are clustered together, suffocating, isolating the dreamer from any possibility of help or support.

Since yoga was introduced to the West, we have become more aware of the importance of breathing. Air is a symbol of the spirit and of breath. Breath, in turn, is the principle of life and of creation, but does this apply to the breathing town in this dream?

For this is not a town of life but of death, and it is a fact that the dreamer has always (unconsciously) considered his own life to be the death of his individuality, his freedom and his autonomy, smothered as they are by the power of women.

If a town can be a symbol of the mother, it equally represents life *and, in consequence, its opposite: death and destruction*. The anonymity and isolation experienced in certain towns are, again, perhaps, a "death" of themselves.

Every town has a "centre", actual or symbolic (the market square, for example), from which streets radiate out (the symbol of the mandala, see p. 125). The town in the dream has no visible centre. Everything is upset and awry. The town may breathe, but the breathing is a threatening panting – that of an anima which is ready to swallow up and engulf everything.

- *The boat and its crew.* The boat is found not in the water but *in the town.* Yet it does not belong to the town: it is in waiting, and its crew stands by in summer uniform. This, then, is a boat ready to sail for sunny shores, far from this ghastly town. But the dreamer turns away from it, without according it the importance which it deserves. By turning his eyes away from that which could have saved him, he is lost. The ocean itself threatens to engulf everything.

And so to the climax: a wild gyration, together with an inhalation sucking everything in towards a "centre" – that of his sick "anima", completely overrun by the perilous image of Woman.

This dream was a grave warning. This engulfing "centre" would have been that of a deep depression or even, psychosis. This poor creature had already lost contact with the reality of all life's joys and freedoms. There was a way out, to sunnier shores, but dare he take it before he was destroyed?

I am glad to relate that he did. Alerted by the dream, the dreamer, who was in analysis, has already, at the time of writing, recovered much of the autonomy which had been taken from him.

## A "mandala" dream

The dreamer was a fifty-year-old writer.

*I was sitting in a big park. Nearby there was another park, or rather a garden. It was entirely circular, and circumscribed without being limited by flowers which grew at the level of the soil. Pathways ran in all directions from this garden, as though the garden were the hub of a*

*wheel. Four children were drinking water from a fountain*
*– two boys, two little girls. I wanted to sing, and I have*
*to say that I surprised myself throughout the following*
*morning by whistling.*

- *What is a mandala?* A mandala is composed of a centre
  about which are drawn a circle, a square or various
  other geometric forms. In certain dreams, a town may
  take the form of a mandala – especially towns with
  walls. The Place de l'Etoile in Paris is a classic
  mandala. The streets fan out from the centre like rays
  of the sun. A square is a mandala, with its four equal
  sections taken from the centre. In certain dreams, a
  wheel symbolizes the mandala, with its hub and
  spokes and enclosing circumference (as here evoked).

  In oriental symbolism, the mandala often represents
  the world. Oriental carpets feature some remarkable
  mandalas, which are used as the foci for meditation
  and are supposed to help the contemplative on their
  paths to illumination.

  Gold or silver lockets containing tiny yellowing
  photographs, or locks of hair, for example, are types
  of circular mandala, where the eye is inevitably drawn
  towards the centre.

  The great dreams featuring mandalas are fairly rare.
  They tend to appear at times of psychological renewal
  (at the end of a course of psychoanalysis, for example).
  These dreams generally mark the culmination of a
  gradual ripening of the soul, of a slow progress
  towards psychological harmony.

  This was the case the writer mentioned above. It is
  barely necessary to analyse this dream. The mandala

here is a circular garden whose circumference is decoratively marked but creates no restrictions, and from which many paths fan out in every possible direction. Here there is no anxiety about which path should be taken, as in a labyrinth dream. Here, all is peace and order. We find too the number 4 (two boys and two girls; see chapter 13). The fountain, the sign of youth, represents the dreamer's anima (chapter 7). The masculine and feminine poles are reunited. Contentment is here.

# THE GREAT DREAMS AND
# THE AGE FACTOR

"Great dreams" may be experienced by people of all ages. Children often have great dreams. This does not mean that they are undergoing precocious processes of inner renewal, but only that children are closer than most adults to the world of great symbols. Children are not yet alienated from their deep conscious.

Many great dreams also occur towards the end of adolescence — one of life's great "crossroads" where paths must be chosen, often irrevocably.

But if one such "great dream" can lead an adolescent towards a broad highroad, so another can seduce him into darker alleyways.

Great dreams tend to occur at decisive moments in our lives (adolescence, old age, spiritual transformation, career choices, etc.). They also come to us at times of psychological crisis of which we may, consciously at least, be unaware, but which demand resolution if we are to obviate any damage to our personalities. Great dreams, then, are a purging of a whole mass of tensions which otherwise would poison our innermost being.

## A balloon
The dreamer was a woman, aged fifty.

*I was going up in a balloon, being carried on my own. I had this very powerful feeling of becoming at one with my destiny, of adapting to it, giving myself willingly up to it. I felt that everything in my life had had a reason, and that everything now converged in this one moment. The balloon stopped moving. Then I saw with delight a huge expanse of earth below. That expanse was my entire life, a unified whole, without a break.*

In free association, it emerged that the most powerful sensation in this dream was the discovery of an apparently infinite expanse of the earth in all directions. The balloon was thus the centre of a gigantic circumference – a massive mandala.

She went on: "It was like a crossroads but with no need to choose a direction. Any direction was OK. There was neither past nor future. Everything fitted. Everything was right in itself. As I said, it was a representation of the whole of my destiny, from birth to death. There were no more hours and minutes, no little bits of time, just one unbroken duration of endless time."

There could be, in the broadest sense, a sexual aspect to this dream (rising, the swollen balloon, etc.). In that case, we would have to translate it in terms of "affec-tive" or emotional sublimation, of a regrouping of energies, all working towards a common goal.

# THE GREAT IMAGES OF TWO IMPORTANT SYMBOLS

As already outlined, every symbol spawns a profusion of dream images. It is worthwhile running through those symbols that appear most frequently in great dreams. Once more I must reiterate: a symbol has no value in itself. The whole person must be taken into account if we are to arrive at a serious and useful interpretation. Furthermore, every symbol has its positive and its negative aspects. Which of these is relevant depends on the context and on the inner life of the dreamer at that exact moment.

One of the most important symbols is, of course, that of the mother. Inevitably, many dream images spring from this source, Here are some of the positive images:

## The positive mother

1 *Everything which welcomes, protects, warms, reassures, envelops, etc. For example:*

| | | |
|---|---|---|
| Houses | Grottos | Barns |
| Inns | Villages | Towns |
| Enclosed gardens | Chests or safes | Cupboards |

2 *Everything which suckles, nourishes, gives life, etc. For example:*

| | | |
|---|---|---|
| The earth | Fields | Orchards |
| Farms | Gardens | Cows |
| Springs | The sea | Rivers |
| Eggs | | |

3 *Everything which is spread out or horizontal (as opposed to the masculine, which is upright and vertical), etc. For example:*

| | | |
|---|---|---|
| Lakes | Snow | Roads |
| Plains | Horizons | |

4 *Everything "mysterious", as women are conceived to be, etc. For example:*

| | | |
|---|---|---|
| Night | The moon | Marshes |
| Silence | Darkness | The underground |
| Snowy mountains | Forests | Undergrowth |
| The feline | | |

5 *Everything which encloses, contains, comprehends (like the womb) etc. For example:*

| | | |
|---|---|---|
| Ships | Submarines | Lifts |
| Suitcases | Cupboards | The underground |
| Houses | Cups | |

6 *Everything which can be thought of which claims to possess the secrets of life. For example:*

| | |
|---|---|
| Gypsies | Witches |
| Sybils | Fortune-tellers |

We move on, then, to the symbols generally felt to be negative in relation to the mother. Remember that many of the "positive" images, in a different context, will occur with a negative significance.

## The negative mother

1 *Everything which recalls the past; everything which symbolizes childhood; everything which "descends" into the depths of the past or the unconscious (see the symbolism of directions, chapter 13). For example:*

| | |
|---|---|
| Childhood | Slopes (downward) |
| Staircases (downward) | Descent below ground |
| Cellars | The depths of the sea |
| Wilted flowers | Deserted gardens |

2 *Everything which is turned in upon itself, etc. For example:*

| | |
|---|---|
| Sleep | Certain music |
| Introspection | Immobility |
| Dancing | Certain paintings |
| Night | (e.g. impressionist) |
| Enclosed gardens | Solitude |

3 *Everything which inhibits growth or advance and "imprisons" in childhood, etc. For example:*

| | | |
|---|---|---|
| Walls | Fortifications | Towns |
| Prison | Closed doors | Tentacles |

4 *Anything which can curse or cast a spell, etc. For example:*

Fortune-tellers

"Magical" animals (owls, toads, snakes, hares, etc.)
Witches

5 *All that threatens or casts into solitude, etc. For example:*

| | |
|---|---|
| Stagnant waters | Dark nights |
| Silent vigils | Deserted streets |
| Caverns | Labyrinths |
| Tunnels | Towns by night |
| Deserted towns | Deserts |

6 *Anything which demands that we show our credentials before proceeding further or before crossing a frontier (of adulthood), etc. For example:*

Customs Officers
Judges
Policemen

7 *Whatever crushes, tramples, devours, suffocates, lies in wait, carries toward nothingness, etc. For example:*

| | | |
|---|---|---|
| Avalanches | Drowning | The apocalypse |
| Earthquakes | Tidal waves | Spiders |
| Seaweed | Octopuses | Nets |
| Crocodiles | Runaway horses | Falls |
| Traps | Precipices | The sea-bed |
| Vertigo | Sinking ships | Floods |
| Fish (sometimes) | Jungles | Glue |
| Spirals. | | |

## The hotel-keeper dream

The dreamer was a thirty-year-old man.

> *I'm getting ready to leave the place where I've been on holiday, but the hotelier (a man) holds me back. He shows me a table which is already set. All the best dishes are laid out there. I object. I've got to get going. I show him my train ticket.*

This is not a "great dream", but I cite it here because we find a man (the hotelier) symbolizing the mother. This dream is neither positive nor negative. It merely points out a psychological state of affairs. The hotelier (mother) tries to keep the dreamer with him (her), while the dreamer wants to get out into life (the train ticket). This dream demonstrates that the dreamer retains a residual "hang up" in relation to his mother – a commonplace problem.

## A apocalyptic dream

This, however, is a "great dream", recounted by a woman aged twenty-seven:

> *The sky was blood-red. The earth shook. The silence was absolute; no sound; non-existence. People were running in all directions. Their screams – if they were screaming – were inaudible. The silence remained thick. It was like a silent apocalypse movie in real life. I ran too, towards an opening – a cave? A clearing? I don't know.*

Apocalyptic dreams are plentiful, and there is little purpose in giving this dream an in-depth analysis here.

The dreamer's associations will tell us most of what we wish to know.

*Blood-red.* I once saw a modern painting. It showed this part of the dream. The sky there was curved, infinite, uniformly red. The distances seemed pinkish. The picture was very beautiful but I wouldn't have had it around me for all the money in the world. That red was nothingness, death in an infinite waste without prospect of return. It's the womb.

*Earthquake.* I think earthquakes terrify me more than any other natural phenomenon. The whole idea of the earth opening up . . . to disappear, still living, as though munched up by giant jaws. Earth Mother, OK, but what a monster she must be at that moment. An evil earth, one minute a foster-mother, the next, suddenly, cursing and devouring. She sticks to you, she digests you, she corners you . . . you run, but there's nowhere to go. She'll always get you in the end . . .

*Silence.* That was the worst thing in the dream. It was an indescribable silence. Powerlessness on a cosmic scale. What can you say or do in response to a mother's silences? You'd do anything, *anything*, just to get her to come out of that silence. You'd bash your head against a wall. You'd kill yourself even, just to stop it. Vindictive, sullen, threatening silence. A mother's silence is like death itself . . . It's . . . you're relegated to an absolute sense of abandonment. Apocalypse . . . silence . . . to be horribly

133

alone . . . I went towards that opening all the same . . .

*Opening, clearing*. Hope, Luminous hope. Might this not be a new trap? With my mother, I never knew where I was. One moment, snarling and sulky, the next suddenly kind . . . I've always tried to be accepted by her. I always went through the charade of admiring submissiveness. Nevertheless I didn't get married. How could I have gone off and lived on my own in a flat instead of staying with her? But I phone her every day – more often twice than once. I can't not phone her I'd just get too distressed . . . I don't know why.

So what purpose does this dream serve? Could this young woman, *without being aware of it*, harbour such a powerfully negative image of her mother? She had proceeded no further than to manifest some superficial symptoms (not to marry, to telephone every day). In fact, had it not been for this dream and the association which it triggered she would have remained in a "larval", ageless state, a little girl constantly afraid of the opinions of others, terrified of taking the slightest liberty (she had never taken a holiday for fear of her mother's sulks and moans – "oh, so you're abandoning me again, I see . . ."), and so on. This woman was *suffering* her inner condition, but she was not *aware* of it.

The dream was, obviously enough, a shock for her. It was the safety-valve which, not before time, opened to release excessive pressure. At the same time, the increased awareness which it gave her opened up such broad new horizons that she undertook analysis and has since progressed in leaps and bounds.

We will return, by the way, to the "blood-red sky". It symbolized the womb from which the dreamer refused (unconsciously) to come out (a refusal which restricts so many people's lives, and for the same reasons). And, as with many people again, this young woman would actually cross the road if she saw a pregnant woman approaching, since the sight recalled her own birth. It is not, perhaps, so surprising after all that she remained unmarried, not only because of her fear of "abandoning" her mother, but also because of her own fear of becoming pregnant, an anxiety which had consistently caused her to reject the slightest overture from a man.

Today, the dreamer is happily married and is the mother of two children, in large part thanks to the message contained in this dream.

N.B. The various symbols which represent the mother can also, obviously, represent woman, depending on the dreamer. These same symbols may serve for the dreamer's wife, if he projects the mother figure on to her, which is common enough. How many men, after all, marry a copy of their mother?

Let us move on now to the symbols for the father, an important figure in the adolescent mind. Similarly these symbols too can be applied to a husband, brother or to men in general, depending on the individual dreamer.

The idea of the father and the concept of masculinity are inextricably confused. Masculinity, in turn, often takes on the symbolism of the phallus.

Already, therefore, by analogy, we have a series of symbols in everything which is *vertical*, *upright*, *arrogant*, *aggressive*, everything which *pierces* and *punctures*, everything which tends towards the *future*.

## The positive father

1 *Whatever evokes the future. For example:*

| | | |
|---|---|---|
| Maps | The boss | Active life |
| Plans | Targets | Driving, piloting |
| Slopes (rising) | Mountaineering | |
| Staircases (rising) | Ladders | |
| Mountain faces | Climbing | |
| Spirals | | |
| Right turns (at a crossroads, for example) | | |

2 *Everything associated with the "social". For example:*

| | | |
|---|---|---|
| Self-expression | Action | Conflict |
| Creativity | Duty | Honour |
| Success | | |

These "images" may seem abstract, but they are in fact no more than the foundation of other dream images. Self-expression, in a dream, may be represented by some sort of creativity or other; the dreamer is painting, drawing, plotting courses, conducting orchestras, etc. The notions of duty or conflict can present themselves as specific actions (the dreamer harangues crowds, for example). Or the dreamer may be starting up a steam-engine (a sign of self-expression and of the future, in that the engine converts its power into movement).

136

3 *Anything which speaks of adventure. For example:*

| | | |
|---|---|---|
| Journeys | Exploration | Research |
| Discovery | Combat | Armed services |

4 *All that is "brilliant" literally or socially; everything which recalls the sun; everything which rises (like the sun in the sky), etc. For example:*

| | | |
|---|---|---|
| Radiance | Glory | Fire |
| Light | Lightning | Burning |
| Honours | Royalty | Success |
| Heroism | | |

5 *Everything that advances, pierces, is vertical or linear, etc. For example:*

| | | |
|---|---|---|
| Arrows | Weapons | Masts |
| Columns | Towers | Trains |
| Mountain ridges | Squares | Roads |
| | | Cars |

6 *Anything that recalls the law and paternal utterances, etc. For example:*

| | | |
|---|---|---|
| Noise | Thunder | Wind |
| Breath | Storms | Voices |
| Strident sounds | Justice | |

7 *Anything that evokes initiation, activation, apprenticeship, etc.*

| | | |
|---|---|---|
| Guides | Gurus | Masters of arts/ |
| Teachers | Religious leaders | crafts |

## The negative father

*Everything which represents castration, destruction, repressive law and justice, etc. For example:*

Authority and its representatives

Customs                          Police

Weapons                          Firepower

Brutal and noisy catastrophes


# HEROIC DREAMS

These dreams earn their own section in this book because they occur so frequently. They are based on the symbol of the hero, a symbol found, with innumerable variations, in every civilization. The variants range from the great religious themes to cinema heroes, from sporting champions to the cultures of juvenile criminal gangs.

## *An eternally recurring story*

The theme of the hero is nearly always found in the same scenario. Death is the fundamental human predicament. It is logical, therefore, that we should seek something which transcends death (eternal life, immortal glory, leaving behind an impression by means of a great work, or through our children, passing on our names, etc.) In this way we look towards something that symbolizes our need for eternal life. Since it is the lot of every human being to feel frail and defenceless, the hero must be strong, brave and powerful, even if he requires the protection of invisible instructive forces.

Such may be the basis of the heroic theme, but this is how it is usually manifest.

1 Generally we know little or nothing of a hero's origins. He emerges, as it were, from a fog. His birth is obscure, and he is inclined to vanish back into that fog again. Already, we discern the eternal theme. The hero does not begin or end. He is eternal because he occupies no single historical period but rather a "golden" age or a continuation in time.

2 The hero is a solitary. He is beyond ordinary mortals. His moral and physical strength are enormous. He is precocious, and rapidly proves his intelligence. He is a being at once of knowledge and of power. Already we think of certain categories of hero from Tarzan to various religious or military leaders.

3 The hero is generally betrayed or tricked. This is inevitable. Given his inner or outer strength, it is inconceivable that he should otherwise fall or die. He is, however, capable of "heroically" sacrificing himself.

4 The hero does not vanish forever. He is invincible. He can come back to life. He can leave an indelible impression in human memories. The exception is the hero who vanishes in flames without leaving a trace of his body (Hitler, for example).

5 The hero "dies" young, whether his death be actual or symbolic (the sporting hero who "retires" after betrayal or persecution is a case in point).

## A biker's dream

The dreamer was a young man of eighteen:

> *I was riding a big bike, a Harley-Davidson. I was trick-riding in the middle of a crowd. The people were stupe-fied. I did wheelies, rising and falling. Other young people on bikes came along and joined me. The crowd made way for us. I think we had just decided to do a bank-raid when I woke up.*

This is a characteristic dream. Here we find:

(a) The bike, instrument of individual freedom. The dreamer is trick-riding. He is a *virtuoso*, and virtuosity in no matter what field is part of the hero's apparatus. Some of these virtuoso skills (on a motor bike, in cars, etc.) can conceal suicidal tendencies or, at least, the secret hope of a fatal accident.

(b) The bike is powerful in itself and in its status/associations (a Harley-Davidson). It already bears the kudos of association with other heroes. It could therefore represent an actual inner power or the *need* for a power to compensate for feelings of inferiority and impotence.

(c) The "hero" attracts "disciples". Others are drawn to his flag and join in.

(d) The theme of *delinquency* enters (the planned bank-raid). Delinquency can play a part in the heroic theme, in that it affords the impression that one is "bigger" or "stronger" than others. The "gangs" of youngsters form a mafia or clan (see chapter 4) which again is common in this type of dream as in the heroic myths (the twelve disciples, the Knights of the Round Table, etc.). These groups are isolated from society; they share secrets, and so on.

Compensatory or no, this dream indicates an "inner transformation" for the young dreamer. Transformation dreams are a category in themselves.

# DREAMS OF INNER TRANSFORMATION

All human life is flux. It is therefore subject to constant changes of varying importance. Certain staging-posts which are essential for the inner life – and therefore for life itself – are signposted by dreams, of which the following are the principal themes.

## *The crossing*

All dreams featuring a crossing mark a change of state – generally for the good . . . Such a dream can sometimes be followed by a veritable inner rebirth, accompanied by feelings of dynamism, enthusiasm and *joie de vivre*.

Crossing dreams can take many forms, for example:

(a) *fording* a river
(b) *swimming* across a river, or crossing it in a *boat*; travelling thus from one *bank* to another
(c) entering a *tunnel* to re-emerge in *light*
(d) crossing a *dark forest* to end up in a *clearing*
(e) making a crossing in a *submarine*

(f)  the theme of the tale of Jonah *in the belly of a whale*; symbolically, this can be seen as a return to the mother's breast, where new strengths are sucked in; after the journey in darkness (the darkness of the unconscious) another bank hoves into view.

(g)  travelling *by night*, in a train, a car, etc.; the journey may end at say, a road, but, at any rate, at a new place, a new starting-point.

## A dream about crossing to a town

I shall take the liberty of summarizing this fairly long dream, recounted by a forty-year-old man, in order to demonstrate the symbolism of the crossing.

*A man dreams that he is seeking a town, the town of his childhood. He gets lost. He retraces his steps to regain his bearings. He meets a gypsy woman, who shows him the way. At last he sees the town ahead. It is night. He is separated from the town by water. He is working out just how he can get across to that "promised land" when he awakes.*

A great dream. Look at what we can dig out of it:

(a)  the dreamer's desire to resume contact with the values of his childhood (the town of his birth)

(b)  the tentative gropings of the inner life (the dreamer loses his way)

(c)  the gypsy woman, who here represents the mother, she who knows the secrets of life's road, and who points to the future

(d)  the end of the journey within reach of the town –

142

within reach, that is, of the dreamer's true identity. One obstacle only remains: water. He must make one more crossing in order to arrive at the other bank – himself. Otherwise it is night (again darkness in the dreamer's mind). But we can be sure of one thing, if one thing only: the dreamer is still looking for the means to make that final crossing which will be his new starting-point, his "rebirth".

## A dream about crossing through a tunnel

Again the dreamer was a forty-year-old man:

> *A train bore me into a very long, very dark tunnel. The noise was deafening. My anxiety just kept on growing bit by bit as we went. The guard appeared. I had my ticket and everything was in order. Then suddenly the train burst out of the blackness; it trundled along mountain-tracks. Down there in the valley, a beautiful valley, I saw a little Austrian village. I was happy.*

The dreamer free-associates:

It's been a long time since I was in total darkness like that tunnel. This journey is to do with me. It's why I volunteered for analysis with you. The train was powerful. It's course was irreversible, irresistible. And what a hell of a tunnel! But I have to say that, over the past few months, my anxiety has largely evaporated. You see, despite everything, there I was, feeling somehow at fault, but the guard assured me that I was OK! As for that town in Austria, it was in Austria that I met and fell in love with a young

German girl, a long time ago. I love her still, like . . .
like a sort of faceless entity . . . She left her mark on
my soul for ever. For me, I suppose, she has become
a symbol of a deeper life, a sharing life. She's like my
"double", yet I'll never see her again. I know,
though, that somewhere there is a second me, my
other side, my other half, to use a well-worn expression. I wonder if the end of the dream would have
been a triumphant arrival?

After the crossing through that dark tunnel, then, the
dreamer emerges, overlooking a valley and the Austrian
town where he once knew a timeless love. So he arrives
at his anima, that "feminine" part of a man's soul. A fine
dream.

## The bridge

The symbol is straightforward: a bridge links two places.
A bridge enables us to move from one bank to another.
In dreams, we throw bridges between different spiritual
states or conditions, between often apparently contradictory psychological tendencies, inclinations or
compulsions. A bridge thus belongs in two categories of
symbol – that of *crossing* and that of *passage*.

Crossing a bridge signifies, in certain great dreams,
the establishment of alliances, linkage, reunion with
something vaster than ourselves.

The context therefore is all-important. Between what
points and above what does the dream bridge stretch.
What sort of bridge is it? What is it made of? What are
its dimensions? What is its condition?

## Jacqueline's dream about flyovers

*I was driving in a car. I drew up in front of lots of huge bridges like motorway flyovers, one above the other. I hesitated. I was scared. To my right, I saw a little wooden footbridge overhanging a precipice. I started to cross it on foot. I wasn't frightened, not at all, despite the void beneath, I knew that this footbridge was solid. There was a flat expanse on the other side. It could have been a plain. There were no landmarks, no trees, nothing, just a few scrubby plants, like a pampas or something. As I went over, I felt so happy.*

Jacqueline's commentary was as follows:

I don't like the car. It encloses me. It makes me anonymous. I just find it so ridiculous to pass a friend at speed and just to flash your headlights as a sort of substitute for "hello".

Those flyovers or whatever they were, they were optical illusions. Fine things, sure, well designed and so on, but cold, impersonal, and leading nowhere but from one motorway to another. Nowhere, in other words. Get on a motorway and you don't ever know exactly where you are. For me, then, those bridges were just overwhelming delusions.

But the wooden bridge, that spoke to me, it represented my freedom, since it took me to that immense expanse. Those motorway bridges, I think, represented my temptation to aim too high, to do what everyone else does, to become brilliantly anonymous on those inhuman roads . . . I've often been tempted to give up my traditional woman's role and to try to make my mark in the world of business, all that. I don't know if this dream was a warning, or simply described my decision to stay just what I am. Anyhow, I'm glad to have had it.

## Other bridge dreams

I shall summarize these without commentary. They speak for themselves:

- *Paul* dreams that he arrives at a bridge illuminated like a rainbow, running from a grey, rainy landscape to a river full of pleasure-boats.
- *Steve* dreams that, after crossing a bridge, he arrives in front of a railway station bedecked with flowers. The rails seem to stretch into infinity.
- *Fred* dreams that he is walking on a bridge enclosed in a narrow passage which tapers to a dead end.
- *Julie* dreams that she is at the exact centre of four bridges which intersect at right angles. She feels that she must make a choice (this is also a "crossroads" dream).
- *Arnold* dreams that, after having started to cross a bridge, he comes upon a huge hole. The bridge has collapsed. He turns round and wakes up sobbing.
- *Jane* dreams that she is building a little bridge above a little stream which it would have been far easier simply to ford.
- *Helen* dreams that she is climbing up a bridge which stretches almost vertically up into the sky. All her efforts are in vain. Each step makes her slip back towards the bottom.
- *Michelle* dreams that she sees her father walking on a bridge. He beckons to her. She finds herself in a park.

She cannot manage to get near to the bridge. She looks back all the time. (She cannot break free of her mother.)

- *John* dreams that the bridge he is crossing comes out into a crowd. He knows he has to take an exam.

## *The door*

Again, this is a fairly self-explanatory symbol. A closed door (or gate) makes us want to open it to see what lies beyond. It signifies possible adventure, eventual discovery, mystery, secrets.

An open door marks a *passage* from one spot to another. It is a "crossing" of sorts. If it appears in a dream, it can indicate that the dreamer is undergoing a psychological transition or change.

A door, of course, also *protects*. It ensures intimacy. It prevents entry, like the gates of a city closed against assailants.

Linked to the symbolism of the door or gate, of course, is that of the *key*. When the keys of the city are given up, it is a great ceremony. Legend is full of keys to secret rooms and secret worlds, keys to chests filled with memories or treasures.

Therefore wooden doors, golden gates, porches and porticos are worth little without the keys that go with them.

Here are a few characteristic dreams on this subject.

- *Peter* dreams that he is pushing at a half-open door. It opens on to a dark room, which he feels to be dangerous.

- *Anne* dreams that she is standing in front of a locked door. She knows that there is a garden on the other side. She feverishly hunts for the key, but cannot find it.
- *James* dreams that he is searching in the mud of a stream for the key to his house.
- *Marianne* dreams that a door opens out on to emptiness – the void. She leaps back.
- *Celia* dreams that a man leads her up to a glittering gate. He offers her the key and signals her to open it.
- *Sandra* dreams that the door to her flat has been battered down. All the rooms are visible at a glance.

Some doors, then, can open upon scenes of high promise, others on dangerous situations or on congested or terrified unconscious. We might hesitate to open a door, because it could give access to many repressions which we have carefully kept locked in. Sometimes we deliberately "lose" a particular key, so that we cannot open the door which will cast light on parts of ourselves which lurk in the darkness.

But doors also open on to enchanted gardens and on glittering rooms. At all events, however, a door always marks the possibility of an inner change or development. Similarly we should note that a key is also a phallic symbol. The symbolism of its insertion is clear enough.

### The threshold

The symbolism of the threshold is linked to that of *steps* and the *staircase*. Generally, *crossing the threshold* indicates a transition from the profane to the sacred. In dreams, it indicates passage from the exterior life, the life of "seeming", to the interior life – that of "being". Particularly in women's dreams, the threshold is frequently guarded. Why particularly women? Because the woman, traditionally, is guardian of the house. It is she who welcomes (or turns away) someone on the doorstep. To cross the threshold, visitors must show their credentials. They must abide by the rules of the person who guards the hearth and home.

The threshold is made up of one or more steps, generally rising higher, stage by stage. There are, therefore, two separate symbolisms here:

(a) *To cross the threshold* is to be accepted and admitted. It also means to pass from the exterior to the interior life, symbolized by a house or any other "secret" place.

(b) *To climb the steps* is to rise higher in one's inner life.

Here are some typical examples:

- *Suzanne* dreams that she arrives at a *downward* threshold – a sort of staircase ending up in a cellar. She none the less feels a sort of hope. (She must "descend" into her unconscious in order to emerge into her new life.)
- *Patrick* dreams that the doorstep of his house is dirty.
- *Maureen* dreams that her mother is on the doorstep. Maureen sets off on holiday. Her mother gives her blessing.

## *The wind*

The wind is synonymous with *breath* – creative, life-giving breath. Christians maintain, for example, that God breathed life into Adam.

In certain dreams, the wind can be destructive, an overwhelming force. The dreamer is sometimes carried away, a straw in the wind, or can be shattered by its force, or tossed up into the sky, and so on.

The wind is generally a symbol of masculinity, power, extroversion and creativity. It is one of the symbols of paternal authority, as we have already seen.

The appearance of the wind in a dream often indicates that a change is under way (whether positive or negative).

## *Children*

"Expecting a child" probably often occurs in women's dreams. It usually means an impending "birth" in the mind, an important development in the dreamer's emotional life.

## *Precious stones*

Precious stones in dreams sometimes indicate that a "jewel" is forming in the unconscious as the personality acquires a new centre or spiritual energies crystallize. This is notably the case when the *anima* harmoniously finds its rightful place in the soul of men or the *animus* in women, and when the *shadow* arises in its negative or positive forms (see chapters 7, 8 and 10).

Every passion for a precious stone is, obviously a projection of the individual. In dreams, a stone is precious only in so far as we give it emotional value. The financial element rarely enters, unless symbolically.

Here is a typical dream.

*John dreams that he places his whole fortune in a huge diamond. He places the stone in a casket and buries it in the garden.*

The "fortune" here symbolizes the dreamer's *energy* while the diamond represents (in this case) the "vital core" – that is, the *anima* of the dreamer. As for the garden, it indicates excessive introspection. This, then, was not a positive dream. John was hiding and repressing his inner life (*anima*) instead of trying to free it and exploit it. It would have been much better had he dreamed that he had sold this diamond for hard cash, which would have meant that he was transforming his excessively crystallized inner energy (the diamond) into money (extroverted, "circulating" energy).

Precious stones are in dreams usually being bought or sold, as presents offered or received, or as discovered, long hidden, in an attic. Occasionally, dreamers find themselves following ancient scrawled maps showing how to discover the buried treasure (the map symbolizes the labyrinth; we would therefore have to examine the nature of the stone representing the very core of the dreamer).

These are the most frequently found stones, together with the symbolism:

# Diamond

Pure crystallized carbon, the diamond is principally noted for clarity, transparency and hardness. The brilliance of the diamond marks a kind of "summit", a natural outcome of one's endeavours.

Obviously, then, the diamond can represent spirituality, the durability of the soul, and inner clarity and purity. It represents the anima in men and emotional strength in women. Diamonds also symbolize incorruptibility and spiritual freedom from restraint.

Where *coloured* diamonds occur, the interpretation must take into account the symbolism of the colour along with that of the diamond.

Here is an example:

*Noel (aged thirty) dreams of a pale-blue, absolutely clear diamond which hangs immobile in space, far from the dreamer's grasp. Noel wakes crying.*

A bachelor, Noel was one of those men whose spirit had been "consumed" by the woman who brought him up. He dreamed, of course, of an ideal love, but such a relationship was impossible for him because of this inner frailty. His "anima" had remained indistinct and powerless. Given this information, the meaning of this dream is at once clear. Noel is now working hard to overcome his affliction and may one day cease to gaze platonically at this diamond woman, distant as the colour blue, which symbolizes the inaccessible horizon.

## Emerald

The superstitious have long credited emeralds with the power to induce fertility. For others, they are unlucky and betoken danger. The alchemists referred to emeralds as "May dewdrops". According to tradition, an emerald tumbled from Lucifer's brow as he fell from grace.

Green is the colour of vegetation and of water. The emerald is clear and springlike. That is doubtless why the emerald is often seen as beneficial in dreams. Its symbolism is linked to that of water and of the colour green. At the same time, there is something mysterious about that shade of sea-green. In certain dreams, therefore, the emerald assumes the connotations of dangerous, deep, still waters.

Because of these associations, the emerald can also symbolize woman.

## Moonstone

Although of little commercial value, the moonstone is a favourite with many women, who love it for its "dreamy" simplicity. Its colour evokes the tranquillity of moonlit nights. This is a stone not of "appearances" but of the depths of the soul. It is highly feminine, "yin" as opposed to "yang". It therefore symbolizes peaceful inner life, spirituality and introversion.

## Ruby

The stone of love and of lovers. It glows red. The first lasers used rubies, projecting a beam of red light.

It is the ruby's warm glow which clinches its symbolism. In superstition, it is a good-luck token and possesses medicinal virtues. In dreams, it often indicates a transition in the dreamer's inner life; something significant is happening. This symbolism is due to the soft inner glow deep within the ruby, its discreetly ardent colour which seems to radiate from the centre of the stone.

## Amethyst

The amethyst's symbolism is linked to that of its violet hue – the colour of wisdom and of temperance (the word "amethyst" is derived from a Greek word meaning "preventing intoxication"). It is the stone of true humility and of spiritual responsibility.

## Turquoise

With the colour of blue sky or blue-green water, the turquoise symbolizes much the same as these colours. The turquoise can equally represent spiritual evolution, the secret centre of the personality, and emotional fertility. In men it can symbolize the anima.

## Jade

Jade is heavily charged with universal symbolism. It is a stone of great beauty and represents the highest virtues, goodness and transparency of soul. In China it was the symbol of royalty. Because of its greenness, it is associated with nature, water, vegetation and fertility. It seems, none the less, to appear only rarely in dreams.

## Opal

This is the superstitious stone, generally credited with bringing bad luck, and having evil influences. It is not surprising, therefore, that, when an opal appears in a woman's dreams, those dreams take on a negative or menacing aspect. All this is no doubt due to the stone's constantly shifting colours (blues, yellows, reds, browns, etc.).

## Sapphire

The sapphire's symbolism is linked to that of the colour blue (cornflower-blue and midnight-blue).

It may be objected that it is not always possible to know precisely which precious stone occurs in a dream (with the sole exception of the diamond). In my files, I have the testimony of some dreamers who knew their gemstones and thus had no problems. Others have dreamed that a stone has been given or offered to them, and that it has been mentioned by name by its donor. Others have simply seen a colour and, from this, deduced the stone, particularly when it comes to sapphires and rubies – "I dreamed of a blue stone – a sapphire, I guess", or "A red stone was set in it. It must have been a ruby", or even "I dreamed that my father slipped a marvellous ring on my finger. The stone was like water. I think it must have been a turquoise, or a transparent green diamond . . . " In general, this type of after-the-event definition does not assist in interpretation.

## The pearl

The symbolism of the pearl is unsurprising. The pearl comes from the sea and belongs to the maritime world. It has been said to have been born of the sea and the moon. It is symbolically linked to woman, to the yin, to the hidden inner life and to sexuality. It represents treasure sunk deep in the sea, awaiting discovery.

Traditionally, pearls are thought to have aphrodisiac and regenerative qualities.

The pearl is an emblem of love and of giving. It has a deep spiritual significance. It is, after all, the perfect culmination of a natural evolution. It is spherical. It is rare, pure, and its conquest is dangerous. So it is that the pearl comes to possess, throughout the world and throughout time, an almost erotic significance.

## A dream about pearls

*He sees himself offering a cluster of pearls to a young woman in the street. Then, suddenly he's back at home; the cluster of pearls has become a beautiful cluster of grapes, in a chalice.*

The dreamer, a man aged twenty-eight, made the following associations (much abridged here): "Wealth. Loading with presents. Giving pleasure, seducing. Maybe the woman will come home with me. Fear of women, bunch of juicy grapes, food, maternal, children . . ."

This dream, then, swings from one point to another. The cluster of pearls is a sexual symbol; the bunch of grapes is a maternal symbol – the breast which feeds and the earth's fertility. In this dream, the need to seduce while afraid gives way to the need for a woman who is maternal and understanding. This last need (for a mother) is a regression.

For many women, a string of pearls is part of respectable appearances and also of sexual seduction. In

dreams the pearl can take on any one of the innumerable meanings described above. But the pearl's highest
and greatest meaning is its spiritual one. It symbolizes a
step towards inner harmony and the uniting of the
conscious and the unconscious.

Next to some of these great dreams, day-to-day life can
seem flat and dull indeed, for these dreams reveal ener-
getic, passionate dimensions of the human being, which
we know exist within us. These dreams are like an eye
that can see through opaque objects.

There are other symbols of inner "mutation".
*Tempests* blow, *tornadoes* are unleashed, *storms* rage. We
dream that we *die* or that someone with whom we identify *disappears*. Gardens burst into *flower*, *mists* lift to
reveal a landscape . . . We pass through narrow *corridors*.
We climb *staircases* which go on for ever. *Trees* bend
under the weight of their fruit. We *swim*, we *soar*. There
are *geometric figures* too, and *colours* (see chapters 11 and
13). *Mandalas* appear in *flowers*, *wheels*, *circles*, *crossroads*
and *crosses*. *Suns* and *waters* suffuse the dreams with their
great symbolism.

And, as a culmination, to the very privileged there
appear the symbols of the *anima* and *animus*, those spiritual elements without which no self-awareness and no
true joy can be experienced.

## CHAPTER 7

# The Anima:
# Power and Creativity in Man

Dreams of anima and animus are among the most important of all. But the two terms, which seem to be mere psychological "jargon", must be clearly defined – no easy task. Let us start, however, with the simplest statement that the anima pertains to men and the animus to women.

## WHAT IS THE ANIMA?

Anima is, quite simply, the Latin word for soul. In classical psychology, however, it is defined as the "feminine" component of a man, or even as "the woman within the man". This is a poor definition, if only because so many men, disliking what seems to be a suggestion of effeminacy, reject it out of hand. This would be a grave error, as we shall see, since that rejection would be founded upon a misunderstanding.

Let us say rather that the anima is the "feminine pole" in man. This has nothing at all to do with effeminacy, effeteness or weakness: on the contrary. We could draw an analogy with the steam-engine. The feminine pole would be the boiler and the pressurized steam which it contains. The masculine pole would be the turbine which drives the wheels. Without the boiler and the power it contains, the turbine would serve no purpose.

In the same way, without a *well-ordered* anima, without the *exploited potential* of his anima, a man's intelligence and reason would serve him little, however admirable in themselves.

The anima is inner potential. It is present in every man from childhood onward and everything depends upon what it becomes in the course of a life. The anima arranges the whole network of sensations. It is a man's radar. It is through his anima that a man experiences life, positively or negatively (though he is frequently unconscious of the negative aspect).

But, more than all this, it is by means of his anima that a man creates or destroys himself. Yet nine times out of ten he knows nothing of this – or, rather, he does not know why it is happening.

## THE MAN WITH A NEGATIVE ANIMA

Let's go back to the analogy of the steam-engine, and let's suppose that the boiler is punctured, that the pressure is too low, or that the pressure is constantly varying. Now we find the turbine functioning jerkily, stopping and starting, slipping – generally working capriciously, if at all.

This is like a man with a negative anima. When we see such a man, we observe that he has long since lost his temperamental equilibrium. His "boiler" is malfunctioning. He is capricious, like a child in a tantrum. The whole unbalanced personality is sometimes covered by a tough carapace of hyper-virility which serves to trick him and others. He is irritable, brutal, vindictive – but tears spring to his eyes for precious little reason. He may tyrannize his wife and children, but then suddenly he is all sweetness and light. He is suspicious of everything and everyone. He is often a first-rate businessman, thanks to his acquired ability to get the better of others, which is in fact no more than a projection of his own fear that someone might get the better of him. He is a charmer, but he is not pleasing. He is effeminate in the worst sense of the word – even in his false posturing as virile. He is often paranoiac. He is the sworn enemy of women because he fears them so much, but he charms them by flattery, gallantry and other courtesies. He will seek out pliable women (of whom he has less fear) but takes to his heels when confronted by a beautiful or accomplished woman.

In brief, the boiler has broken down. This man has lost genuine contact with the central generative powers of life and love.

## A dream of negative anima
The dreamer was a man aged forty.

*I was rowing on icy water. The channel was narrow. There were icebergs as far as I could see. The sky was metallic blue. I was on my own. I steered my boat straight onward, towards the infinity of ice and sky.*

161

This dream translates a tragic situation in the dreamer's soul. It is also a grave warning. We perceive the *glacial desolation* of his soul. His life is canalized to a dramatic extent (the narrow channel). The colour *blue* is here the colour of *death*, of loss of self. The boat goes *straight onward* (see the symbolism of directions, chapter 13) – irreversibly. This is a *suicidal* dream. And this terrifying world exerts the same "neurasthenic" fascination as the sirens' song which drew sailors to their death.

This man corresponded exactly with the description of a man with a negative anima. He had founded a flourishing small business. He was rich and married, but he was tyrannical – petty, that is – towards his wife and his three children. His rare moments of impulsiveness demonstrated a deep-seated sadness. He forgot himself in business trips, receptions and relentless work, but basically he lived in absolute inner solitude

A negative anima separates a man from the most essential of his survival mechanisms and the key to his dynamism: hope.

Anima is, then, at the outset, pure spiritual potentiality – wax awaiting shape and detail. Then the people and the objects of life will intervene. The first hands to be laid upon it will be those of the mother. She, as the primary female figure, will inevitably influence the feminine pole of the infant boy. Her deep-seated attitude towards life will be inveigled out of her by the child. Equally, the anima will be profoundly influenced by the boy's attitude towards his mother. Does he feel her to be a beneficent or a maleficent force? Positive or negative? Strong or weak?

In this way the anima of the boy whose soul overlaps with his mother's is rapidly distorted. Life goes on. Other female faces will come and go, some of them close, some of them mere passing glimpses – fascinating actresses and other celebrities on television or in the cinema, for example. Then there are the little girls for whom boys conceive their early passions, the favourite desired teachers, sisters, relatives, cousins . . . In this way the anima becomes an entity with numerous resonances, but the main influence remains and will always remain that of the mother or mother-figure.

A man's whole disposition towards life, women and love depends upon the healthy, or unhealthy development of the anima. Sometimes the anima and the shadow are intertwined, as we will see later.

The anima not only ordains a man's deep inner attitude but is also projected outward towards women, things, places, and so on. And, of course, it crops up in dreams in many guises.

## Projection

It is important that we should understand this concept before we proceed to examine anima dreams. Here is the dream of a man aged fifty:

*I was climbing. It was as long a climb as Everest. Whiteness, but above all stillness, silence. Menace was everywhere. The sky was fantastic, huge, blue, almost black. The snow was so calm that I expected to be engulfed at any moment. I clung to the snow and couldn't move any further. I waited for the worst.*

This is an anima dream. The anima is *projected* on to this mountain, on to the snow and the threat of being engulfed by an avalanche. Now, we know already that snowy mountains and deep snow are symbols of woman and, in this case, with the dangerous avalanche, symbolize the negative mother. We conclude, then, that the dreamer's anima is strongly influenced by his mother. It is interesting, moreover, to observe once again the symbolic workings of the dream. He could, after all, have dreamed that his real mother was threatening him while he could only stay mute, but the dream takes a broader view and describes the entire psychological climate of the dreamer. It reflects his attitude towards himself and towards existence in general.

The dreamer is *climbing*. He "ascends". He wants to go *higher*, to improve his lot. His climb is almost vertical, and therefore male, phallic, adventurous. He aspires to liberate his masculinity, to be a man, despite the snow which threatens to engulf him. The sky is *blue-black*. The snow is *too calm*. The dreamer cannot foresee what is going to happen. At the end, he *stops climbing*, and gives up the struggle.

This man was the victim of a suffocating, domineering intrusive mother. His unconscious mind projects all this on to snow. He wants to free himself by climbing, but there he is powerless. Fear and anxiety paralyse him. His anima is engulfed by the image of his mother. Life, for him, was a constant threat. His fear of others was enormous. He therefore projected his mother on to others, while with her he behaved like a guilty child.

The word *projection* is appropriate here. Put coloured films over the light in a lighthouse, and those colours will be projected on to everything which that light touches. Anyone unaware of this would thus swear blind that an object seen in this light was a colour which, in fact, it was not.

So it is with psychological projection – the attribution to people and things of characteristics which they don't really possess but which are in fact projections of the individual's own unconscious. Take a man who has never been able to rid himself of his fear of his father – but he does not know this; he has repressed it all. He thinks of himself as a grown man, his own man. In fact, he has remained and will remain a son. He projects, therefore. All men are experienced as dangerous fathers. All men are threats. All men are potential castrators. Without even realizing it, towards other men he assumes the attitude of a son. He therefore attributes to men characteristics that they don't in fact possess. Thus he will never be able to establish a meaningful relationship with a man, because he always sees men through the deceptive film of his own unconscious projection.

Most human relationships are made through a complex network of projections. One person projects on to the second, who in turn projects on to the first. Therefore they never know each other. They are in a "phantom" relationship although they believe in the truth of their mutual behaviour. Imagine then some twenty people each projecting a stack of unconscious traits on to the other. The number of mutual projections in such a gathering would be astronomical. Each one of them speaks, argues, loves, admires, scorns, hates or criticizes, but nine out of ten of these emotions will be founded upon projection rather than fact.

Any unconscious emotion can be projected on to anything at all. You can project your mother or your father, say, not only on men and women respectively, but on the opposite sex, on places, food, objects, works of art and so on.

Equally, the anima can be projected on to anything, both in dreams and in waking life.

It must again be stressed that our only knowledge of people and things springs from the sensations which we experience in relation to them. It is vital, therefore, that we purge our souls of distorting projections. Only thus can we attain liberty and a true understanding of ourselves and others. Only thus can we form relationships founded upon reality rather than fiction.

## Anima (negative) in dreams

### Some dream projections on to women

It should be borne in mind that it is easy to confuse some negative images of the anima with negative images of the mother.

• *Robert dreams that a prostitute beckons to him. The street is dark, just barely lit by old-fashioned torches. He follows the prostitute.*

*The prostitute* is a classic image of the negative or destructive anima. She degrades man; she welcomes and allows total licence provided that she is paid.

*The street* represents the darkness of Robert's unconscious. Only a few feeble lights *from the past* flicker there.

- *Maurice dreams that a woman seems to be waiting for him. He does not know where he is. The woman just stands there, immobile. He feels paralysed. The woman is wearing a very long black cloak. She sits down and Maurice moves towards her.*

  This woman *fascinates* the dreamer by her immobility. She recalls in this the Lorelei and other female destroyers who lure men to their doom.

  She is wearing a *black cloak*, which reinforces her mystery and the attraction she exerts.

- *Jack dreams about a very beautiful, very young sorceress. She is telling his fortune. Suddenly, Jack finds himself in a car going like the clappers along a twisting road on the edge of a precipice.*

  The symbolism is the same.

- *Dominic dreams about a dishevelled woman who is throwing him money.*

  Again the same symbolism. The negative anima turns on the dreamer and diverts his energies from their usual goals.

- *Simon dreams that he is dancing with a drunken woman.*

  Again the same symbolism of a negative anima, degrading the man.

- *Jim dreams about a black-haired woman who is walking alone in a park. He watches her from afar, fascinated.*

  Again the fascination theme, the dark colouring. Here is the symbolism of sirens, of Lorelei, alluring and deadly.

- *Paul dreams about pornographic scenes and gross orgies. He feels at once happy and sad.*

    The negative anima here, but also, of course, the orgy symbolism outlined earlier.

Often, then, we find these negative faces of women in dreams. We also find *statues* (the anima frozen, grown stiff and paralysed), *dirty or ugly witches, cabaret singers, vamps, striptease artists, sphinx women*, the whole gamut of mysterious women, *femmes fatales* and women as objects.

## The negative anima projected on to places and objects

We have already encountered some examples of this during the course of this book. We often find:

- *Valleys*, which are generally feminine by reason of their shape, their gentleness and their harmonious undulations. As negative animas, however, they appear as desolate, burnt or snowbound. They are without hope. No food is found there. These are valleys of solitude where the traveller gets lost. All hope is dead.
- *Plains* are again bare and arid, sometimes bathed in mysterious moonlight. There are no landmarks. As with valleys, they are places of solitude and loss of self.
- *Boats* can (negatively) symbolize the mother's womb, where we can take refuge from life. In some dreams they are in poor condition, or their rigging is in tatters. The interiors are wretched, with flaking paint. The hull is holed. The sails are ripped. There are also

*ghost-ships* or boats forever anchored, without hope of setting sail. Or, as in the first dream in this chapter, they set sail without hope of return.

• *Houses* are an important symbol. The different storeys represent the levels of the personality (see the Dictionary). A house is, conventionally, the realm of women and mothers. As a negative anima, the house is seen as possessing malign attributes. It can be stuck in the past or archaically respectable. It can be shrouded in dust and cobwebs or surrounded by a barren, abandoned garden. The attic and the cellar are causes of acute anxiety. The stairs are dirty and decayed or they lead nowhere.

## A house dream

This dream was recounted by a man aged twenty-eight:

> *I have just bought a house. I see it from a distance. It is in a sort of landscape of corrugated iron. I can see my children planting plastic fir-trees.*

The strangest thing in this dream is the corrugated iron. It recalls the valley mentioned above but here definitively stripped of any vital substance, any charm or attractiveness. It seems then that the dreamer's "self" (the house) is at the centre of an anima which is as good as dead (or repressed). To top it all, the dreamer's children, images of life itself and of the future, are planting artificial fir-trees. As the fir is a symbol of eternity, we see how distant is all prospect of hope.

• *Towns* are usually symbols of either the mother or the

anima. To reiterate, a town contains inhabitants (children) as does a pregnant mother. As negative anima, a town is felt to be hostile, corrupt, bewitching. In the dreams recorded in my files, Las Vegas, a town corrupted by gambling, frequently appears.

## A town dream

This was dreamed by a man aged fifty:

> *I am wandering in a town that I don't recognize. I'm looking for a friend's house. I ask some policewomen the way. They direct me to this place, a long way off, where I find myself wandering through all these buildings. They're buildings in Brasilia. I know, because I saw them in a film.*

It is not Las Vegas this time, yet Brasilia too is sun-baked and set in the middle of the desert, a town fixed in a sort of hopeless, futurist time-warp. The dreamer is looking for the reassuring centre of his own personality (the friend's house). The policewomen represent an anima ("uniform" – unbending, rigid authority-figures of the super-ego).

- *Gardens* are secret places for meditation, central to the inner life. When it represents a negative anima, the garden appears as icy, deserted, wintry or misty.
- *Statues* are symbols of an anima in suspended animation, frozen since childhood. They can come in all the shapes we would expect – sirens, gargoyles, sorceresses, etc.
- *Water* is a symbol of potential sinking and drowning

170

(at least in the case of a negative anima). Again we find it in the form of swamps, ponds, snow and fog, together with its derivative images: boats, water-lilies, frozen waterfalls, polluted wells, dried-up springs or fountains, sick or dead fish, the singing of women in dangerous waters or in mist . . .

# THE RECUPERATING ANIMA

We usually find that there are two distinct stages: (a) the anima which is positive but not integrated into the personality; (b) the anima which is positive and is stealing back into the personality and becoming integrated there. I know that all this is difficult to understand on a rational level, but the anima can cause such devastation and provoke such dramas (thunderbolts which end in bitterness and hatred, absurd love affairs, eternal triangles, destructive and crazed passions, etc.) that we are forced to spend time attending to it.

## *The first stage of the positive anima*

As the anima recuperates and grows positive, the image of woman is no longer threatening or dark. She is bathed in her own light. She becomes nostalgic, gentle, mysterious, romantic, but the man's increasingly positive anima remains unconscious, like a hidden block in his personality. Since it is unconscious, the anima, then, expresses itself through projection. Here are some examples of dreams which have come to men at this stage:

- *I dreamed about a young girl. She was gazing at me very sweetly. I had a feeling of infinity.*
- *I dreamed that I was reading a poem in a deep voice, while a young woman waited for me.*
- *I dreamed of a woman in white, in the park.*
- *I dreamed that I was waiting for a liner. Up on the bridge there was a very beautiful, very sad girl. I couldn't see anything but her.*
- *I dreamed about a garden. It was autumn. Two women were walking slowly there. One of them was watching me. I had the impression of a deep love within me.*
- *I dreamed about a great lady.*
- *I dreamed about a young girl, an invalid. I looked after her and loved her passionately.*
- *I dreamed that I held an unknown woman in my arms. I was entranced.*

This type of dream reflects the desire of the individual man for happiness. This is the waiting stage, the stage of unconscious exploration of the self. The man seeks himself, and runs the risk of finding himself not within but outside himself, in a person on whom the anima has been projected. It is a dangerous time.

"I know that my one great love is somewhere out there," one man told me. Surely every man on earth could say the same. This nostalgic concept is fundamental, and usually reflects nostalgia for the lost anima which men hope to find personified.

When the anima revives, this "great love" lies in wait. The two are inextricably linked, like a planet and its satellite. But what is real and what fraudulent? How much of this love is projection? At what point does a certain woman resemble the man's anima so much that he confuses her with his anima? What happens to a relationship between a man and the projection of his own anima? There are great successes but also disasters in relationships involving a man, a woman and the man's anima.

First of all, the anima will idealize the woman on whom it is projected. If this woman matches the ideal, well and good. She will be the woman whom "he has always been waiting for" and for whom "he always knew existed somewhere". It has to be said, however, that this is as rare as snow in June.

"Recognition" is a commonplace of "great loves". "It was as though I had known her all my life". "I just knew that we belonged together". "We were made for one another": these are the familiar phrases. Such a sense of recognition is hardly surprising if the man in question is projecting his own anima on to a woman. He has known the object of his passion all his life. They do belong together.

However, when the real woman turns out not to correspond to the projection, the great love rapidly crumbles, with all the inner torments which that entails.

At all events, the revival of the anima gives a man a whole new way of seeing his world. He becomes acutely sensitive and perceptive. Good fortune attends him quite simply because, experiencing a thousand times more things, he has a thousand times better chance of seizing opportunity. He feels that he has had 180-degree vision restored to him after years in blinkers, and his energy increases enormously. And this is just during the recovery. His anima has yet to reclaim its rightful place and to be totally integrated.

## The second stage of the positive anima

Here too it is very difficult to explain the process in words. By way of assistance, I reproduce the dream of a man who had attained this stage. You will see that it appears, at first sight at least, positively banal. It is, none the less, an anima dream of the highest order.

> I was in a garden, sprawled on the grass. A little girl (about nine or ten) was sitting astride me. She said three times, rhythmically, as if to music, "I love you, I love you, I love you", and I answered her in the same pitch and the same rhythm, "I love you, I love you, I love you." It was divine, marvellous, unforgettable . . . It was universal happiness . . . I only have to remember this dream – which I had more than a year ago – to feel the same energy, the same happiness that I felt then!

The anima is here projected not on to a woman but on to a little girl. The dreamer renews relations with the fundamental values, with life's promise and its joys. He has built a bridge to his childhood feelings. Note too the rhythm in three-time (see chapter 13) which recalls the "$^3/_4$ time" and the "three aeroplanes" in the dream quoted at the beginning of this book. It is a dream which wallows – without sentimentality – in love.

174

## Other symbols of the recovered anima

Inevitably we find here the same symbols as those which stand for a negative anima, but they are turned around now.

- *Valleys* are enchanted, fertile, burgeoning with life and promise. True earthly paradises, they represent femininity in all its power and its universal, eternal creativity.
- *Towns* are harmonious, spring-like, symbols of the comforts of life.
- *Plains* are infinite and without obstacles, often bathed in gentle sunlight.
- *Water* springs up or sparkles. Pleasure-boats float on rivers, springs burble and chuckle. Fountains spurt out multicoloured jets.
- *Houses* are beneficent and welcoming, *birds* and *fish* are gleaming, *landscapes* calm, *snows* and *mountains* bright and full of life.

Sometimes too we find *swords* flashing and *statues* coming to life and *dancing*.

These and other images are all that one would expect to gush forth from a renewed, revitalized soul that has been made whole once again.

# CHAPTER 8

# The Animus:
## Power and Creativity in Woman

The animus is the masculine pole in a woman, the extrovert, creative and socially structured element. It is the pole of reason and of thought. It is, in her, the dimension of the future. Here, as with the anima, everything depends upon the authenticity of the animus and its acknowledgement.

## HOW IS THE ANIMUS FORMED?

The formation – or deformation – of the animus depends on the father or, rather, on the sensations experienced by a girl towards her father.

For the young girl, her father is the first great symbolic male. He is a symbol before he is a flesh-and-blood person: The symbol of power, infallibility, knowledge of the art of "self-destruction" and social skills.

The externalized life of the daughter thus depends on who or what her father really is, on the way in which she perceives him and, above all, on the deep knowledge which she has of him. If the young girl misses her opportunity, her animus will crystallize and remain purely potential. No further exploitation of it will be possible.

This is not to say that she cannot run a business or even a country in the certainty that it is she who is responsible, when in fact she is driven from start to finish by a stereotyped animus derived from a bad relationship with her father. Such a woman does things; she does not create anything.

# THE WOMAN WITH A NEGATIVE ANIMUS

A negative animus is usually manifested in one of two ways.

## An inside-out man

In this type of woman, femininity seems to have disappeared. Sensibility and intuition seem dead. The warmth of the female spirit appears to have evanesced. An authoritarian, almost sadistic demon rules the soul of a woman devoured by her animus.

Such a woman is apparently cold, aggressive, pigheaded, obstinate, ruthless, cerebral, sulky and agitated. She is frequently dogmatic and reduces all subtle shades of argument to nothingness, preferring to assert the rightness or wrongness of extremes.

For her, the future does not exist, despite all appearance to the contrary.

Since the animus has been formed and informed by the father, it contains a strong social dimension and, in consequence, social ideas and opinions. These ideas and opinions must inevitably be turned towards the future. The woman who is afflicted with a negative animus will express dogmatic opinions, but they are all fixed. Talk of the future will evoke little profound from her. She blocks her opinions in the present.

So, essentially at a loss, she will utter views that she has read or heard somewhere. These will almost always be the opinions of men. "My husband always says . . ." or "I read in the paper . . ." are common prefaces to these expressed doctrines, but often she will present them as her own, with a force which defies contradiction.

## Whimsical creativity

In the second type of woman, femininity and its characteristics are visible but creativity remains impotent, embryonic and merely impulsive or whimsical. Such a woman stagnates. She wanders through life. She is outside time. To refer back to the steam-engine analogy, the boiler is relatively efficient, the steam is under sufficient pressure, but there is a fault in the transmission before the power can reach the turbine. Nine times out of ten, such a woman is the product of a difficult mother and an absent father.

## The negative animus in dreams

The negative animus speaks in dreams through "castration" images – that is, images of impotence in any action oriented towards the future:

179

- the classic dreams of *trains* without engines, of *cars* without steering-wheels or drivers, or of *boats* without compass or rudder, etc.
- dreams of action interrupted or thwarted: *journeys* which are cancelled, *work* which is destroyed or crumbles into dust, *streets* which come to dead-ends, *searches* or *explorations* which lead nowhere.
- dreams of general impotence in life: *revolver* bullets are feebly ejected, *fireworks* do not go off, etc. (we find the same images in men's dreams).
- symbols representing something *vertical*, *linear*, *creative*, *brilliant* and *powerful*; but *columns* are cracked, *ladders* are broken, the *sun* is obscured, *masts* are fallen, etc.

N.B. The father, of course, is never the only figure responsible for the development of a negative animus. Aside from other male figures, the mother often – perhaps *always* – plays a seminal role.

## Some negative animus dreams

The first great animus image is man, but here is a curious fact. Since the animus (created by the father) has a social dimension, it also contains a *collective* element.

So we frequently find the negative animus manifesting itself in *groups of men*, perceived by the dreamer as dangerous or threatening:

- gangs of *bandits*, *Hells' Angels* or *outlaws* attack or form on the horizon.
- *gypsies* or *travellers* menace the dreamer.
- *sadistic* or *diabolical* men (*vampires*, for example), *killers*,

*pirates*, *terrorists*, *wreckers* and *looters*, *military dictators*, etc., appear.

All these are projections of the destructive animus of a woman, of course, and these dreams are always of some significance.

## More "normal" negative animus dreams

Here, the animus does not declare its hostility by threats, danger or sadism, but by elemental men – rough, instinctive, primeval, but generally well-meaning. So we find:

• *tarzans* and other ape-men and primitives
• *great apes*
• *men of the woods*, *sharpshooters*, benevolent *outlaws* (Robin Hood, for example)
• *film actors* who appear stupid but full of goodwill
• protective *gypsies*, etc.

This kind of dream is commonly experienced by women of the "whimsical creativity" type described above.

# THE POSITIVE ANIMUS

The woman with a positive animus is autonomous, creative, active without frenzy, capable of independent reasoning. Here, boiler, steam, transmission and turbine are all in good working order. Her social interactions are easy, her position secure, though she does not need, like her less fortunate sister, constantly to stake her claim. She is a woman of considerable wit, and receptiveness to great ideas. Her animus has ceased to be a copy of a man but has become a balanced personal objectivity.

## The positive animus in dreams

As with the anima in men, the animus can appear in different guises according to the different stages of its integration, progressing from its reawakening to its complete integration and acknowledgement.

Dreams no longer feature dangerous men. Masculine groups and gangs disappear. An individual man takes their place. These are often:

- *knights*, *aristocrats*, *princes* and *kings*
- *film stars* renowned for their intelligence and character
- *heroes*, sometimes romantic heroes of legend, sometimes contemporary
- *astronauts*, *air pilots*, etc.

But the woman with a positive animus also sees herself in her dreams.

- She *pilots* aircraft, boats, etc.
- She does jobs traditionally associated with men.

It is important to establish whether we are looking at an animus growing into freedom and balanced integration, or a "penis envy" or compensatory dream.

## A recovering animus dream
The dreamer was Paula, aged thirty-five

> *I was acting in the theatre. I was on stage. There was a
> lot of light. I was improvising beautifully, perfectly, and
> speaking with absolute fluency. My husband was in the
> house. I noticed that the house was also fully lit. I felt
> very happy, very calm . . .*

Paula is no longer just watching but is an actress in her
own life. More than that, she is a "social" being (the
theatre here represents society). She improvises: she
speaks the *right words*, and they are hers, not someone
else's. She is fluent and relaxed. Her husband is a spectator, but neither is in the other's shadow. The light is
evenly distributed everywhere.

In the evolution of Paula's inner life this was a fine
dream which demonstrated that her animus was in sight
of realization.

## Other positive animus dreams
The positive animus produces dreams involving "high-
up" people such as *heads of state*, *philosophers*, *writers* and
*religious leaders*, or masculine personalities renowned for
their spirituality.

If men themselves do not appear in the dreams, then
the animus is represented by masculine symbols such as
wind and breath, or by linear or vertical objects such as
roads, towers, swords or trees, etc.

The following dream was recounted by Lucy aged
forty:

*I saw a great, flat expanse of land. A white tower stood quite a long way away, but very close to me — to my "me" or ego. What astonished me was the number of windows in that tower. Many people came and went in and out of the tower. Brightly coloured flags fluttered at the windows.*

First, note the *carnival* atmosphere, the *flags* at the windows. Obviously, the second important element is the *tower*, a *vertical, erect, phallic* object. But this tower is in no way aggressive. It is *white* – the colour of spirituality and calm. It stands like a centre of activity, a rallying point, a guardian. It is a landmark in the vast plain. It is also a secure place towards which and from which people come and go (the *social* element). In addition, it has many windows, which look out on the outside world and allow light to stream in.

In Lucy's case, and at this stage in the development of her animus, this was an exceptional dream, speaking of the reunion between her masculine pole (animus) and her feminine (the horizontal plain). It should be noted that she says that the tower was close to her "me" or ego.

## A woman meets her animus

Women encounter the same problems as men when they meet their animus. If a woman forms a relationship with the projection of her animus, she forms it with a component of herself. Here, as with men, the danger is great. When she re-encounters her true animus, how can the human simulacrum compare? How much will be left when the human being stands there, no longer clothed in her projections?

If the animus remains unconscious and a woman, say, marries her substitute projection, we can expect a passionate relationship (provided, of course, that the projection does not cease). But in these circumstances the woman falls into total emotional dependence on that man. Since the functions of the animus (creativity, goals, plans, achievements, extroversion, social role, etc.) spring from him alone. The woman will remain a devoted and adoring little girl, but a little girl none the less. One woman, considering this, said to me, "After all, it's happiness that counts, isn't it?"

# CHAPTER 9

## *Differences in Interpretation*

Is it really worth the trouble, the work and sometimes the pain entailed in the interpretation of dreams – which, after all, according to some, are no more than thoughts in fancy-dress?

As with everything, exaggeration does not help. Dreams are not the only keys to self-knowledge, nor our only means of making the most of out latent possibilities.

Let's stick to facts. As we have already established, the dreams which matter are those which we feel to be important or to have some meaning. Dreams must be thought of as privileged insights, especially since there is no moral responsibility in them. To be detached from the controlling self while coming face to face with the self proper is the privilege granted to us by dreams.

Dreams contain very intricate and complex images. Some have the power to break down barriers which would have prevented any encroachment on the conscience in daytime life. Being totally "honest", dreams also afford a playful battlefield for the noblest and the basest of human traits. They provide, therefore, a rich and fertile field of research for those who wish to become what, in depth, they truly are: free, capable of loving and of being loved, of giving and receiving with as little fear as possible.

Given too the insight into the animus, the anima and the "shadow" which dreams afford, it is plain that they constitute a vitally important tool.

If dreams – when they are interpreted and "digested" stubbornly and persistently – maximize our information about ourselves, isn't it worth going to a little trouble?

# THE VALUE OF AN INTERPRETATION

A work of music can be interpreted in many ways. As the subject of performances under different conductors, it is given different colorations, moods and paces, according to the personal feelings of its interpreter. Ideally we might think the only possible interpretation would be that of the composer, but in practice every expert interpretation has much to offer.

With a dream too there can be different interpretations. It is tempting, therefore, to suppose that one must be right and the other wrong.

## Teamwork

A psychoanalyst, sent a dream by an unknown person, could not simply "make" a complete and accurate interpretation. That dream constitutes a part of the dreamer's personality and can never be considered in isolation.

Accepted modern practice is therefore to make interpretations only with the dreamer's help. As we have established, the meaning of a symbol will vary according to the person who dreams it. This is where interpretations can diverge, according to – among others – the Freudian and the Jungian schools.

Here is a short dream. It was dreamed by a thirty-year-old man, and is susceptible to two apparently different but, in fact, complementary interpretations. The first interpretation is made according to the Freudian approach, the second according to the Jungian (each with the assistance of the dreamer).

*I had wonderful, delirious sex with a beautiful young woman. I attained heights of ecstasy which are certainly beyond anything you can attain in real life. But gradually I realized that she was a prostitute.*

## Interpretation 1: the Freudian approach

This dream seems to translate the externalization of sexual and emotional *repressions*. There is also a *compensation* factor here, in that the dreamer finds it impossible, in real life, to achieve similar relationships (sexual or emotional?) in real life. But the most important element is that this dream symbolizes the *realization* of the Oedipus complex (see the Dictionary). As for the prostitute (again see the Dictionary), here she is a maternal symbol. She represents the dreamer's mother. He is saying "I want my mother's total, absolute and devoted love. If I had that love all to myself, I could attain an almost cosmic union with her. But my mother's just a whore, because she 'deceives' me with my father. She 'gives herself' to my rival." This dream is a classic manifestation of the intense nostalgia which marks all unresolved Oedipus complexes.

It is therefore a "repressing desire" dream. The desire is repressed in waking life, but comes to the surface in a confrontation, in the night.

## Interpretation 2: the Jungian approach
The Freudian viewpoint *reduced* the dream to its essential component – the Oedipus complex.

The Jungian viewpoint would *expand* rather than reduce. This does not mean that the first reading is not valid. The second takes that as its starting-point and extends its horizons.

To start with, we note that the dreamer himself spoke of a "cosmic union" – a phrase which already leads us to consider factors beyond the strictly Freudian framework. We should leave to one side, then, the "genital" aspect of the dream and consider it in emotional or affective terms.

And we find, once more, repression – an intense desire for "union" with the mother. But the Oedipus complex is basically a *religious* complex (in the sense of *religare*: to reunite). To melt into the mother is to annihilate the self in a union with Life (the mother) and the universe. In this sense, no Oedipus complex can ever be wholly resolved. There will always remain a nostalgia – for lost innocence and passivity, for Paradise Lost.

## THE FREUDIAN APPROACH

Although Sigmund Freud was blessed with genius, he was cursed with adversity in similar proportions. He suffered physical and moral torments. Calamities seem to have pursued him. The First World War took two of his sons. Cancer of the throat afflicted him, but he continued to work, sustained by his thirst for knowledge, his devotion to his patients and the amount of love he bore. He was pilloried and venomously attacked through his adult life, because this man, for the first time in history, was able – and dared – to cast light on the secret motives for human behaviour, testing his every discovery on himself. He opened up whited sepulchres. He spoke frankly and scientifically about repressions and sexual taboos in infants as well as adults. He dared – and we must imagine just how momentous and shocking it must have been then – to speak and write about the Oedipus complex, that permanent spring and motivating force of human life.

Even today, there are many who consider Freud to have been a pure "materialist" or as someone obsessed with sexuality as the only human motivation.

The way in which this one man universalized instinct, however, made him almost as much a metaphysician as a physician. And it is too often forgotten that that "sexuality" is simply the immediate expression of emotional phenomena, whose principal end is always to try to unite the self with others – with the universe itself. When this is considered, it takes us a long way from the "pure materialism" so often attributed to Freud.

## Freud and the dream

Freud generally concentrates on the *personal* and *infantile-sexual* depths of the individual. For Freud, a dream reveals conflicts that were unresolved or badly resolved in childhood. A dream brings to the surface all kinds of repressions. It exposes denied and often unconscious desires.

For example, we frequently dream about the *death of loved ones*. To put it crudely, this means that, as a child, the dreamer desired the death of certain loved ones but repressed this desire as incompatible with morality.

Literalness, here, obscures rather than illuminates. We must remember that, as a child, the dreamer had no idea what death *is*. It merely signified, for the child, "elimination of something annoying". Freud believed that a death dream often has as its subject the parent of the same gender, so a son dreams about his father's death and the daughter dreams about her mother's. This is normal enough in relation to the Oedipus complex, in which the son wants his mother for himself alone, and the daughter desires her father's exclusive love. The rival is a nuisance, and in the dream the nuisance is quite simply eradicated. That is the logic.

When as *adults* we dream of the death of a loved one, however, it generally indicates (a) that we want that person to get out of our way for whatever reason, or (b) that we are in the process of making that person "die in us", that we are distancing ourselves from that person.

## The reductive interpretation

Generally, Freud considers the individual only and proceeds no further. He sticks to the personal. He does not interest himself in the wider context or the universal. Freudian interpretation is therefore "reductive". It makes the components of a dream converge towards a single point:

Freud believed that dreams are often about desires. Because, in sleep, we "let go", we liberate repressed desires in our dreaming. Remember here that the repression is totally unconscious. Any one of us may have repressed during the course of his or her life several thousand sensations or emotions without realizing it. We repress because this feeling, desire or memory would be unbearable and might dangerously threaten our equilibrium. Repression is an automatic defence mechanism.

This does not alter the fact that these repressed elements, highly charged with energy, prowl and growl away in the dark caverns of the unconscious and determine a large proportion of our actions. But during a dream our defences are down, the state of alert has been suspended. The trapdoor to the unconscious is raised, and repressions emerge, but always disguised as symbols.


# THE JUNGIAN APPROACH

With Carl Gustav Jung, the method of interpreting dreams was very largely modified. In Freudian analysis, the dreamer free-associates, but in the Jungian model there is much collaboration between the dreamer and the psychologist. The analyst asks questions. The associations are limited to the essential, and they are then amplified or enlarged upon. If a dream image seems important, analyst and dreamer return to it, then to another. The analyst's procedure from the outset is on the basis of knowing no more about the dream than does the dreamer. The interpretation is ferreted out by their joint efforts. In the Freudian model, the analyst would say, "Let your ideas run freely over this or that part of the dream." The Jungian analyst, on the other hand, would say, "What does this or that make you think of? What does this call up to you?"

In this way, the dream symbol becomes a starting-point, not a terminus.

## A dream with two interpretations

The dreamer is a man of thirty-five who is a chemical engineer. He has a sister three years older. He showed me a photograph of her taken when she was fifteen. She was a beautiful girl, worthy of a Botticelli.

This was his dream:

> I was gently strolling in a garden. There was an insect, a sort of enormous praying mantis, completely still on a tree. It was horrible and intriguing. I woke up twitching with anxiety.

That's all. So what can be extracted from this dream, which the man felt to be so important?

## Interpretation 1

This interpretation was made with almost no intervention from the analyst. The dreamer was simply invited to free-associate. It was, obviously, no problem for him to identify the principal elements.

*Garden.* I had a garden when I was twelve years old, at the time of the photograph. There were trees. Trees . . . I was frightened when night fell . . . but how pretty my sister was! More than pretty. How can I describe her? It was terrible, that insect . . . What the bloody hell was it doing in my garden? A praying mantis . . . death. Immobility. Nightmare.

*Praying mantis.* A beastly creature. Threatening. A sort of miniaturized crocodile. Unmoving, like death, then – bang! They're almost human in shape. I suppose that's where the mystery comes from. She kills her mate after sex. God, what a slut . . .

*Garden.* Oh, that garden! Stocks, phlox, sweet-william . . . scents of love and dreams. Quiet. Quiet meditation. Infinite, you know? I loved my sister infinitely. She's in the States now, since her marriage. I haven't seen her since. What would be the point? My garden was my secret place. That was where I had my childish dreams about love. My garden was like a woman. I . . . I waited for my sister there, for hours and hours. I'd have liked not to be a boy so that I could sleep in my sister's arms.

What is the extent of our harvest so far? Not much. At

twelve, the boy was in love with his sister. That is normal enough. Twelve is the age of infinite, ardent, unforgettable loves. Because, however, he fixed this love on his sister, the notion of incest crept in, with all the guilt which attached to it (especially since the dreamer was brought up according to strict puritan principles). On one hand, then, we see his "frenzied desire" (the dreamer's words) to be able to make love to his sister; on the other we see the incest taboo and the concept of a terrible monstrosity. Who could have told that feverish twelve-year-old that his feelings were perfectly normal, and in whom could he have confided so dark a secret?

In the end, we are looking at a sort of Oedipus complex; the mother here was replaced by the older sister – young enough to remain close to him, old enough to be, already, a woman.

So, this dream reflects (a) an incestuous love and (b) a desire for "castration" and punishment (the praying mantis, waiting in the garden of desires, and ready to annihilate him). I stress that these two conclusions were reached by the dreamer himself.

Well and good – but why should this dream crop up now, twenty-three years on? So far it has not led to anything very remarkable. The dreamer, incidentally, had never formed a close sexual relationship. Could this be the reason? Why was the dreamer constantly searching for his ideal woman, but never finding her?

Let's go further. I don't want the reader to think that dreams can be interpreted by quibbling away at random, but, given the impact which this dream had on this man, and given his own insistence that we press on without respite, we worried at it further.

## Interpretation 2

This time the associations were made in the context of the analyst's interventions.

> *Analyst.* Let's go back to the garden in your dreams. What does it make you think of?
>
> *Dreamer.* Of my garden, my childhood, my refuge, my sweet contentment, my sweet sister . . . Of the stillness of my soul then. I was like an alchemist. I was waiting for things to happen. I was sinking into time-lessness. I was taking part . . .
>
> *Analyst.* Taking part in what?
>
> *Dreamer.* In the world, in the universe. I was part of it all. Already I dreamed of becoming a chemist. I wanted to find out the secrets of things.
>
> *Analyst.* You seem to stress possession. You keep saying "my" – *my* garden, *my* refuge, etc?
>
> *Dreamer.* Yes, Yes, I hadn't realized. I think something from my childhood is blocked in me. My sister's at the centre of it, whatever it may be. She is all mixed up with my garden. I'm still deeply moved whenever I smell phlox or sweet-william. All my soul is there . . . That was my paradise, my love . . . my sister was my love.

Let us try to understand the essential factors which have emerged; and re-examine the dream's main symbols:

*The garden* is a symbol of earthly paradise, of Eden. It is the centre of the cosmos. It is also the universal image of heaven itself and of spiritual states. In Persia, for example, the garden is an essential and all-pervasive theme and works of music are dedicated to gardens. In Japan, the garden has a similar status as a spiritual centre and stimulus to thought and prayer. Finally, for the dreamer, the garden meant fraternal bliss, where the chosen one walks. Here, the chosen one is the favourite of his sister, for whom the garden stands as a symbol.

The dreamer himself quoted to me the verse from the Song of Songs: "A garden enclosed is my sister, my spouse; a spring shut up, a fountain sealed."

We are a long way from incest here. Of course the young boy is in love with his sister, but what does that mean? What does his sister symbolize?

*The sister* is generally the brother's double. She is his mirror. She often represents the brother's soul, his anima. A brother and sister with a close relationship form an indissoluble entity, greater than and distinct from the sum of its parts. It is yin and yang, the horizontal and the vertical, reconciled reunited. There can be deep loves between brothers and sisters, but the notion of incest is less strong. A sister is not a mother – which is why real-life sexual relations between siblings are so common. In our dreamer's case, the sister is the anima of his youth, with all the nostalgia of having lost it without ever having been able to re-integrate it in his personality – an unrequited love which prevented him from forming any other relationships.

*The praying mantis.* At one point, the dreamer said to me: "It's odd. I thought of a religious sister – a nun praying, you know."

This may seem far-fetched, but it does make sense.

Here there is a mixture of guilt (the devouring mantis) and of religion (the "sister"-nun who reunites him with the universe, according to his meaning of "religious").

"In this dream," he told me. "I felt that this mantis was an almost sacred creature – menacing, certainly, but priest-like, as if eternally fixed in religious tradition.

## What was the use of this dream?

This dream proved immensely useful. The man in question recognized something of which until that moment he had been totally unaware – that his endless search for the "ideal woman" was in fact due to an anima buried deep in a nostalgic past, that real women held no interest for him, that his sister, who was so much a part of him, had almost literally cut him in two by her marriage, and that, consumed by that anima and its relentless allure, he had totally neglected the masculine side of himself, thus becoming a typical man with a negative anima – capricious, effeminate, irritable, tyrannical, while maintaining an outward appearance of sweetness and charm. He could easily have sought refuge in homosexuality.

To sum up . . . For Freud, the unconscious is generally a dustbin, as it were, in which we pile our repressions and our unrequited or unavowed desires. This is true in many cases. We quickly forget that which makes us suffer – or, at least, we believe that we have forgotten it. But the risk is always there that one day, given certain circumstances, everything will once more come to the surface. What we have repressed far behind us awaits us far ahead.

For Freud, too, the unconscious is the depository for

the debris of our waking lives. A dream, then, is a surplus by-product of our personal lives. For Jung, however, human beings (and therefore their dreams) always aspire to additional spiritual dimensions beyond those of quotidian life, whose importance is often enormous.

# CHAPTER 10

## *In My Shadow is My Light*

I believe this chapter to be the most important in this book, because it touches the very core of human lives. The "shadow" contains incalculable energy which can liberate and enable the self to flower once the "I" or ego has been discovered in its total essence.

In general, the human being is no more than an assemblage of anxieties, yearnings, repressions, depressions and discontents – the very opposite of what he or she should be. For anxiety, depression and other dark forces do not make up the human being. Where inside us does it hide? Where is it waiting? Why and how does it hide?

It is not unreasonable to suppose that, if all these negative forces are apparent, it is our light and our freedom which are thus buried, forgotten and sometimes disdained. But instead we find ourselves wedged into systems where we waste our time behaving according to criteria imposed by others, who are themselves wrapped up in criteria that are not their own, and so on, right back to the dawn of time.

201

# BLACK SHADOWS

Shadow – the word inevitably conjures up association with obscurity, darkness, fear, menace, the secretive, the hidden potential, the invisible.

The concept of our own shadow is often associated with shame, the dark side we do not want to know. Our shadow contains repressed emotions unacknowledged needs, facets of our personalities which we have forgotten because they are "unworthy" of us. But is this true?

Consider a man who, on hearing a certain tune, bursts into tears. The conventional man who watches him shrugs his shoulders dismissively. "Childish senti-mental nonsense" would be the general consensus. Why does that first man cry? Regret? Nostalgia? Certainly, but nostalgia for what? Plainly he feels in some sense reunited by the music's trickery with something essential in himself, something aside from the "I" of his day-to-day life. Is he not, then, in such circumstances, many times more "normal" than the alienated man who reacts so dismissively?

## The conformist and the hippy

"What is your feeling about hippies or New Age travellers?"

"Disgusting!"

"Go on . . ."

"Well, they're dirty."

"Not necessarily. The true, old-fashioned hippy is perfectly clean, surely?"

202

"Maybe, but they have no sense of law or morals."

"What do you know about it? Do you actually know any of them?"

"No but . . . They have no structure to their lives. That's the whole point, isn't it? They share everything. They give up all individualism. They don't earn their living, so why do they deserve to live? They have no ideals, no purpose in their lives. They are nothing."

I could have asked this man: "OK, so *who* are you?" To which, no doubt, he would have responded by citing his occupation or profession. He would have identified himself with his job. But if I had gone on to ask, "Yes, but apart from your professional status *what* are you?", he would have been struck dumb.

We can bet, in the face of so strong a response, that the hippy represents this man's shadow. A few examples will show how this process works:

"I cannot stand that man. He represents what I would like to be, what I have never been able to become." This phrase could be spoken by 90 per cent of mankind, but we do not acknowledge that this is at the core of so many of our animosities.

We can use this, indeed, as a crude but effective starting point in the search for our shadows. For what or for whom do we feel animosity, resentment or fear without just cause?

While on the subject of hippies, here is a character-istic dream – that of a forty-year-old man – which will help us in applying this method of research:

*I was walking along a smart shopping-street of the Bond Street variety. Some sort of young layabout was singing*

*beside me. He irritated me. I wanted to chase him away;*
*he kept on singing, louder and louder. Then he started to*
*follow at my heels, like my shadow.*

No one prompted that final simile.

So who was this dreamer? A dry man, spick and span, well dressed, who had completed highly specialized studies.

But this noisy, irritating layabout was not only a part of the man; he was his principal part. The visible aspects of his personality were merely appearances. His true life was within himself. The young layabout represented the free, happy, careless part of him. He could not chase him away; he had been within him since childhood, but repressed by social rules inculcated by his education. The free "layabout", then, was the dreamer's shadow – or, rather, this "layabout" aspect has been carefully kept in the shadow, for fear of putting all the values on which the man's life was founded in question.

## *Revealing hostilities*

Let us turn to the method of detecting the shadow. Our dreamer hated all "layabouts" and free-and-easy types. But, at the same time, and without even realizing it, he would have given his life to have lived among them, thus rediscovering the central figure of his childhood.

Notwithstanding this yearning, this man scorned all adventurers, playboys, anyone who was spontaneous and unselfconscious. He had also given me a list of film stars of whom he could not stand the sight. The actors who had played James Bond were top of the list.

As we now realize, he was haunted by that part of himself which he had had to keep in the shadow, that part which he projected on to the "adventurers" and "layabouts" of life. In fact, he hated himself, for allowing himself to be wedged into a system with no way out. Then came the dream . . .

It is therefore always interesting to consider what we dislike in others, what we hate; to examine the people who irritate us – those of whom we say, "I would willingly strangle her" or "I can't stand the sight of him". It is instructive too to identify the criticisms of ourselves which cause our hackles to rise, the sort which make us say of the critics, "They're no better than I am. What right have they to criticize me?" For there is a good chance that, by this means, you will put your finger upon some aspect of your shadow . . . It is a first step.

## Some extracts from shadow dreams

### The footballer

*Mark dreams that he sees himself playing football. He is a spectator on the terraces. A medal is pinned to his shirt.*

Note first that Mark here is his own spectator. The game of football (incidentally a game which Mark, a civil servant, never played) represents a degree of extroversion which the dreamer had never attained in day-to-day life. From childhood, his had been a solitary and sedentary existence – not so much from choice as from obligation. He had become a civil servant, and he carried out life's duties. But now he has received a medal. He has done his bit, by following the procedures that have been imposed on him.

Mark, apparently self-absorbed and self-sufficient, had in fact become a pseudo-introvert. He had the natural means to have expressed himself fluently and to have been socially extrovert, but he had repressed these talents and natural proclivities, consigning them to the shadow. The football player, then, represents his shadow, a shadow which could have been his light. It is worth noting also that, as we might expect, Mark intensely disliked "sporty types", "rugger-buggers", "musclebound idiots" and so on.

## The scandal-monger

*Helen dreams that, caught up in a crowd, she is pursuing a woman who has done her great damage by spreading false scandals about her. She feels angry enough to kill her.*

Helen had this dream after seeing the classic Clouzot film, *Le Corbeau* ("The Crow"), which deals precisely with the subject of a woman accused of having written poison-pen letters.

In this dream, Helen is pursuing herself. She wants to kill a part of herself. Helen, incidentally, was no mean gossip. She could not stand this aspect of herself, but, at the same time, found herself unable to desist from her scandal-mongering, without realizing that the faults of which she accused others were none other than her own! Here we see a negative aspect of the shadow. (We

206

shall see further instances of this later.) Rather than looking squarely at our faults as revealed in the shadow, we project them on to others. Such projections also abound in commonplace malicious gossip.

## The African dancer

*Virginia dreams about a black African man. She is dancing with him. She experiences at one and the same time great pleasure and strong revulsion. The African is very affable, courteous and attentive. He dances "like a tropical creeper from the jungle".*

Virginia is blocked in behavioural stereotypes. She too has repressed her natural extroversion. Her mother permitted no self-expression, no manifestation of emotion. Fundamentally outgoing, Virginia was in reality an extremely "instinctive", impulsive woman who, but for her upbringing, could have overflowed with expressed feelings.

The dream reveals Virginia's shadow. The African, for her, represents the natural, instinctive life, close to nature and, because of his colour, he also symbolizes the shadow. One thing that is manifest here is that Virginia's shadow is by no means as repressed as she believes it to be. It (he) is close and courteous. With a little help, she can hope to recover it without too much difficulty.

## Apes in a forest

*John dreams that he is walking in a forest in pursuit of great apes which he wishes to tame.*

This is the same type of dream. John is searching in the forest (his unconscious) for a lost part of himself symbolized by the apes (instinct, the life of freedom). One excellent sign: he wants to tame these forces, to bring them close to him.

## The easygoing son

*Meg dreams about her son. She loads him with reproaches for his get-up, his long hair, his careless attitude towards life. At the same time, she shows her son photographs of herself as a child, telling him, "So you think that life was easy for me, do you?"*

A rapid translation: Meg is madly jealous of her son. Because she is jam-packed with repressions and terrors of life which have made her strait-laced and have caused her to justify her starchiness with rigid principles, her son, who is mildly rebellious, experimental, relaxed, is her shadow. With help she will recover the lost youthful, easygoing side of her nature which horrified her but which, in the end, represents the full and true potential of all human beings.

## The underground stream

Jung suggests the following image: when a stream is obliged to run underground, it inevitably carries in its current not just mud but also precious stones.

So too with the human personality. When we are compelled to repress feelings or sensations, this repression takes with it positive aspects of the personality as much as negative.

As an example, let us return to the dream discussed at the end of chapter 9. There, the repression of a sexual desire for the sister (a negative inclination) dragged with it the repression of the precious anima – the entire soul of the sufferer, containing his enthusiasms, joys and other creative energies. The repression of the positive factors hugely outweighed that of the negative.

# FROM TWILIGHT TO LIGHT

We have already established that the discovery of a part of the shadow may prove very beneficial. It unveils unknown or rejected aspects of oneself. It allows us to recover whole areas of our personality which, until now, have worked only for themselves, in the darkness of the unconscious, performing only "inside-out" functions, maintaining repressions and hostilities towards ourselves and those upon whom they are projected, even though these last possess none of the attributes ascribed to them.

Nine times out of ten, when the repression re-emerges from the shadows, it is found in reality to be something trivial, and although it has been kept in the shadows since childhood, it is actually no bigger than a pinhead.

Let us look at one example. A very docile man realizes that his shadow contains aggressive aspects or, indeed, that he is in fact an aggressive man. But what has in fact happened is that normal aggression – that of a quick-tempered child, say – has been presented to him as a major fault or vice. He has therefore consigned this essential part of himself to his shadow, where it keeps moving and using up his energy. Each time, then, that he feels a bit of anger arising within him, he prevents himself from showing it. His perfectionism demands that he remain calm at all costs. Docility, then, becomes his whole outward character. He needs to project his shadow self on to others, and hates angry or aggressive people – always taking care not to acknowledge that this hatred is in fact directed towards himself. Now, that aggression which was made out to him to be a grave sin is seen for what it always was, the essentially harmless aggression of a child with a quick temper, and he realizes that for all these years the mountain was in fact a molehill. To come face to face with one's real character – even if certain traits are undesirable – is always preferable to denying it, living a lie and storing up anxieties. If there is such a thing as a truly evil character it can be worked on. At least in those circumstances we are dealing with real traits, rather than living confined in a phantom, formulaic act.

Children, obviously, are always educated by others, not by themselves. It goes without saying that these others, these teachers, are not the children. Education, therefore, for all its unquestioned merits, never corresponds to the true nature of the child.

Education is the work of adults. Nine out of ten of such adults have lost touch with the Essential, which is the distinguishing property of the child. Adults are strongly "differentiated", professionally, socially and morally, from each other. They insist on their "individuality", while children are not yet separately determined and their predominant sensation is that of "being part of . . ." Children are rooted in the universal. They are each at one with all beings.

## All human beings have a great future behind them

This is not the paradox that it seems. Education consists in suppressing that universality in a child. It pushes him or her further and further into differentiation or alienation.

We could tell that child: "You are universal. You are of the same stock and the same substance as the rest of the universe. Your deepest essence is no different from that of others. Your essential being is that of your neighbour. Differences between beings are, of course, necessary in a social structure, but such differences are in large measure accidental and superimposed upon your undifferentiated essence. These differences, therefore, should be used merely as tools in communal life, but remember: the tool is not the same as the tool-user."

Instead, we tell our children: "You are radically different from your neighbour. You are unique. You are irreplaceable. You are very important. You must therefore cultivate those characteristics and talents which make you different from others, for these constitute your principal worth. Logically, since you differentiate yourself from others, you must become the best looking, the greatest, the most specialized, the most intelligent. You must become at all costs different from the Other."

211

In so teaching, we automatically separate the child from others, and from the world which he or she inhabits. In so differentiating, we commit a murder – that of the child's universal, participating essence. Automatically, in the process of differentiation, the Other becomes an enemy. It is an education in extreme paranoia, a Tower of Babel within everyone's reach.

Thus is there differentiation and dissociation in a universe where, in fact, nothing is ever separate. Such dissociation is therefore no more than an illusion which we studiously maintain. There is a permanent opposition therefore, between the essential being and the dissociated being, because of the necessity of never being at a disadvantage in relation to all the other separate adults.

So as children, in order to avoid being shamed and abandoned, we play the game of differentiation as instructed.

At this moment, our essential being descends into shadow, where it goes into hibernation – often for the rest of our life. This essential, potential being was the future of our being, but there, in shadow, we leave our future behind us.

We then proceed along routes delineated by others and according to the criteria of others, and, with our essential being stored in the shadow, we begin to live in a separate "me-I" role which is distinct, lonely and loveless – save for loves that are separate, codified, authorized or obligatory. We are shrunken things who once were vast. We are then forced into a narrow tube – that of permanent education. Our authentic ego or "I" is already far behind us, in the shadow, but it is arti-

212

ficially replaced by a social and moral "me" – whether middle-class, working-class, rich, poor, deserving, undeserving, rewarded, punished – which grows more and more alienated as the tube narrows further.

But the worst part of all this is that one day, emerging from the long and narrow tube of education at an age arbitrarily agreed to qualify us as adults, we can no longer retrieve our first, primal essence which lingers in our shadow. We have assumed the shape of the tube that produced us, and so we come out at the other end like sausages, but as fierce enemies of millions of other sausages.

And that is the murder of childhood.

Yet some, as they emerge from the sausage machine, spread out and stray a little. These are the poets. But, as they begin to participate and become less separate, they find themselves refused access to the separate territories, because separate individuals are hostile to all others.

It is in the shadow of childhood that the light of adulthood lies waiting, but adults do not know this. They live inside-out, as appearance only. But they feel the plea for recognition from the shadow which is their true self. It is a deep and indefinite plea, but its cries become more insistent and louder in depression, in sickness, in anxiety, in vague nostalgia, in apparently incomprehensible sadness.

Then, of course, most men and women harden their hearts and reinforce their dissociation and their otherness. They cannot bear to hear this plea. They are terrified of being defeated by this essential self that is theirs.

Torn between their apparent, dissociated self and their essence which lies neglected and in wait, alienated

213

men and women may experience deep depression and suicidal tendencies. It is not that they want to die; rather they want to recover that universal, participating, *belonging* being which once they were.

So how can this bright future behind us be recovered? Is there a magic spade with which we can dig behind us and exhume our lost essence?

This is perhaps the most difficult of tasks. To achieve it, one must first clear away everything that has been learned, all prejudices, preconceptions, ideals, religious doctrines, beliefs, and conventions. Everything must be swept away, and, even if some notions appear true, they will become false if they are found to be based on criteria imposed from outside oneself. One must then turn towards one's shadow and shine light on it, and only then take up what truly corresponds to oneself or reject what fits badly. Thereafter, one may play the game if necessary but never believe in it. Separations and differentiations then become instruments of adaptation, no more.

How, then, can we retrieve that first sensation of being at one with the universe? A man can do nothing unless his anima is freed from the influences of his mother, and unless that anima is restored in all its original power. A woman can do nothing until her soul too is liberated from all maternal control.

Dreams are essential in this process. They are milestones along the way. Above all, however, it is necessary for each individual to recognize that all that he or she has become is mere appearance compared to that which he or she is in reality. The seeker must recognize too that to live without one's shadow is to live in mourning for oneself. If this process recalls the Dark Night of the Soul where mystics such as St John of the Cross have sought the abnegation of self and total union with God, this is, I think, no coincidence.

In the process of this recovery, the "great dreams" will appear, as new links are established in the brain. As robotic habits cease, so new types of behaviour will manifest themselves. The great dreams turn towards those essentials which come closest to the absolute – music, poetry, astronomy, physics and, of course, metaphysics.

These, then, are the great dreams about *mandalas, numbers, geometric figures, illuminated labyrinths, stars, suns, wise men, crossings, infinite horizons*; dreams about dazzling freedom, music and gods . . .

This dream  – that of a forty-year-old man, comes from my files. Here is a résumé:

*He saw an absolutely circular sun of brilliant gold which slowly turned and threw out beams of light in all directions. The whole sky was filled with other suns, also revolving. Across these suns stretched an immense arch which gleamed like burnished metal. The dreamer moved slowly along it. He felt that he had once more left his childhood in order to arrive at his actual age, that he had become a unified entity, with no rifts. Laughing women accompanied him. There was music in the air.*

This man had entered analysis in order to "know himself" and to develop his potential. He had rapidly concluded that analysis served above all to identify *what he was not*, by pointing out and elucidating the various factors which prevented him from being what in truth he was. That he was something beyond these super-ego influences was clear, but what was that something else? Anxiety? He was something else, but not that. Fear? Something else, not that. A stunted, conformist creature, stuffed full of rules and preconceptions acquired from others? Something else, but certainly not that.

Bit by bit, as he cut away all those branches which were not truly his – or him – the negative shadow appeared. That too must be lopped away. At last, slowly, the positive shadow began to surface, and at that moment an enormous flash of awareness confused all his conceptions of life. From being a man rigidly constricted, like everyone, by guidelines, rules and regulations, he became, quite simply, a man at one with his universe. He was no longer alien in his own world because he had found his essential shadow. He was to found a commune, where he lives happily to this day.

I cannot overstress the point. To be deprived of one's shadow is to live in perpetual mourning for oneself.

# CHAPTER 11

## *Dreams in Colour*

Dreams in colour may not be more important than others, but they are unquestionably rarer.

All dreams are to do with sensory perception, be it auditory (hearing speech or music), visual (seeing things) or tactile (feeling a sense of touching).

Visual perception is by far the commonest in dreams. Auditory perception is rarer, and tactile the rarest of all.

The question of colour in dreams has proved of absorbing interest, and there has been much research into the subject. It is by no means easy to enumerate those dreams in which colour actually appears. Often we may claim to have dreamed in colour, only to admit, when questioned, that we are no longer certain of the precise colour, that we have forgotten, or that we have assumed rather than seen a particular colour. Often, too, in the great dreams, the very grandiosity of the dream seems to presuppose colour. One way or another, then, the actual number of dreams in colour is a matter of some doubt.

Some biologists think that colour is probably present

in all dreams, but that the colour element is not dominant or specific in its importance.

As already stated, dreams which evoke intense emotions are often said to have been dreamed in colour. Since the matter is still unresolved, the question to be answered should be: "Whether or not there was real colour, what was the dominant colour experienced or imagined in the dream, and what is the meaning of that colour?"

# COLOURS AND THEIR SYMBOLISM

Every colour possesses its own symbolism for every one of us. It is well known that colour has an important psycho-physiological role to play in our daytime lives. Even if we look at the moods which set designers, interior decorators and couturiers seek to convey with colours, we find a certain uniformity. Red, for example, is "exciting", while blue is cool or cold. Often a building is felt to be "hot" or "cold" simply on the basis of the prevalent colours and without regard to the temperature.

The importance of light and colour is increasingly recognized in the workplace, where millions of pounds have been devoted to finding the right balance of tones to induce the desired level of creative energy, activity and well-being deemed necessary in any particular field of work. Many people, moving into a new house, seek before all else to find the colours which will prove psychologically satisfying and reassuring. Many great cooks blend their ingredients by visualizing tastes as

colours, regardless of the actual colour of the ingredients, and many people make a spontaneous association
between colour and sound. Each colour conjures up the
sound of a particular musical instrument.

## Blue

Blue is a "cold" or cool, refreshing colour. It is, of
course, the colour of the sky. Blue evokes thoughts of
the sea, space and air. Blue extends and enlarges space. It
is the colour of horizons. It is also that of spirituality.

In the Christian world, blue is used in the festivals of
angels. In the Anglican Church, blue is the colour of
hope, love of God, piety. In heraldry, blue (cobalt, not
light blue) represents justice, fidelity, joy and nobility;
here it is known as azure. Blue also symbolizes eternal
happiness, constancy, chastity (it is the customary colour
of the Virgin Mary), gentleness and physical humility.

In dreams, blue most frequently signifies infinity. The
view extends into the blue distance. This colour is transparent and insubstantial. It melts naturally into brilliant
white. It is the colour of emptiness. In this sense, it may
be the colour of death (we have already seen dreams of
this kind). Blue is inaccessible, like the sky. Sometimes
it is frozen, like blue-tinged snow in winter. It can
symbolize sadness and melancholy ("the blues"). Many
find the endless blue skies of the Mediterranean somewhat intimidating and depressing. When the sky is
totally blue, there is nothing to hold on to: the view
above vanishes and the earth seems alone in infinite
space. Clouds give a kind of protection, surrounding us
and making us feel secure.

In dreams again, blue can be the colour of philosophical truth or of metaphysical speculation.

It is, as already stated, the colour of Mary, but it also symbolizes – whether by association or not – celestial, not terrestrial, fidelity, the peace of the soul in death and superhuman serenity.

In such a way, then, blue is the colour both of spiritual hope and of the death of the body. We yearn for the horizons, yet can attain them only when freed of our mortal shells.

In music, the colour blue is sometimes associated with the cool sublimity of the flute, as well as with jazz and the blues.

## Green

As it is a mixture, of course, of yellow and blue, there are countless shades of green. It is the colour of equilibrium and repose. It is found on billiard-tables, on board-room tables, on desk-top blotting-pads. The effects of green upon the blood pressure have been measured.

In ancient Egypt, green was the colour of hope. In the Christian world it also symbolizes hope and yearning for eternal life. In the Anglican tradition, it is the colour of faith, immortality, baptism and contemplation. In heraldry, green (or vert) is the colour of honour, courtesy, hope, joy and vigour. It also symbolizes love and abundance – green, of course, being the prevalent colour of the fertile lands.

In dreams, green is the colour of earth and the spring, rebirth and regeneration. It is associated with youth and innocence. It is also the colour of patience, waiting and real hope (as opposed to the metaphysical hope symbolized by blue).

It is nourishing (like vegetation) and maternal, but also has the freshness of young love, of lovers in springtime.

Green also has a bad side. It is the colour of deep waters, a silent threat of drowning. It is the colour too of decay, putrescence, madness, malice and jealousy. We think of the green eyes of Satan, of *femmes fatales* and of cats.

In music, green can be associated with the sound of the clarinet or the cor anglais.

## Red

Red is, of course, fire, heat, passion and ardent love. Red has many shades, from dark reddish brown to bright crimson or scarlet. It is the colour of blood and wounds, but also the bloom of good health. The archetypal hot colour, it is fierce, blatant, dynamic and irritating. It is a colour of war. It has a special place in the affections of many, being associated with high spirits and playfulness. Children particularly love red (you need merely look at the average toyshop), as do primitive peoples.

In the Christian world, red means the divine blood. It is worn for the feasts of the Holy Spirit, which ignite the flame of divine love. In the Anglican Church, it is the colour of martyrs for the faith, and of charity. In heraldry, red (gules) stands for love, courage, anger and cruelty. It can also symbolize Armageddon and the Last Judgement, when all is consumed by fire.

In dreams, red first and foremost evokes fire and energy. It symbolizes the vitality of energies and passions – sometimes consuming passions. It is the colour of strife, and extroversion. Purple–red is imperial.

On the other side of the coin, the colour of life-giving blood is also the symbol of violence, hatred, murder and carnage.

It is also a maternal colour, evoking the mother's womb, with all the anxiety which accompanies that concept.

In music, the trumpet is perhaps most often associated with red.

## Yellow

This is the colour of the sun or of clay, according to the context. In Christian tradition, yellow is the colour of humility; it is a reminder that our bodies are only made of clay and will turn to dust. In Anglican iconography, yellow has no great importance. In heraldry, it is replaced by gold.

In dreams, yellow is above all the colour of the sun, the colour of radiance, of brilliant minds and glowing hearts. It is the colour of the father. Pure yellow can appear in this context as blinding, harsh, tending towards dazzling white. When yellow reflects intense emotions, it is "warmer", like the inimitable yellows of El Greco. When it is pale it becomes a symbol of sorrow, sickness or deception. It is the colour too of cowardice and treachery.

Yellow is a "male" colour, dominant in its richness. Like gold, it symbolizes eternity and transcendent religiosity, but this colour's infinite nuances make it difficult to tie it down. Often, its significance can only be asserted by reference to its context and to the emotions which it evokes.

For yellow is also the colour of the ends of summers, of those glorious days which crown a year before winter usurps it; it is magnificence and splendour before death.

In music, bright yellow could be associated with the baroque trumpet or the bugle, warm yellow with the mellow sound of the horn.

## Orange

Orange symbolizes a warm welcome – the lights of home on a winter's evening – less fierce than red or yellow, softening both of them and blending them together. In heraldry, it indicates hypocrisy and dissimulation.

In dreams, orange is obviously a "solar" colour. It symbolizes the warmth of the hearth and of warm hearts. It is a colour which denotes activity, but is a little bit hybrid, even androgynous, in its nature. It is the colour of spiritual comfort, of deep tranquillity.

In music, orange can be associated with the horn played shrilly or the muted trumpet.

## Violet

Violet is rather a cold colour. In Christian tradition it represents penitence. In heraldry, violet (azure plus gules) stands for truth and loyalty. When it becomes amethyst or purple, it symbolizes temperance.

In dreams, violet often conveys feelings of sadness, spiritual penitence, even inner grieving. It is also a colour of passion (red, somewhat tempered by the blue of clarity and spirituality).

In music, violet can be associated with the viola, muted violins or the tenor saxophone.

## *Black*

Black absorbs colours rather than reflecting them. In the Christian tradition, black is the colour of waiting and mourning. In heraldry, black (sable) represents mourning, suffering, endurance of sadness, but also patience, prudence and wisdom.

In dreams, it represents mourning too, but above all it symbolizes the gloom of the undifferentiating, undifferentiated life of the shadow. Black is the colour of night, sleep and the unconscious.

There was "darkness on the face of the deep". It is the colour of potential and of symbolic waiting (absorbed colours can be restored). In this sense, in certain dreams, it can serve as a symbol of hope. It then becomes a symbol of gestation, of the unconscious at work, of primitive instinct which can be directed towards lofty achievements, because black indicates the shadow (see previous chapter). In this context, the human shadow is never death, but rather hope which one day can be realized.

In music, since black is a non-colour, drums and tympani, which make "non-sounds", are often associated. These instruments also represent mourning, but also expectation of what may happen next.

## *White*

A synthesis of all the colours, white can evoke moonlight as well as dazzling distance. It is the image of purity and light. For Christians, it represents innocence, joy and immortality. As argent, it has the same symbolic value in heraldic iconography.

In dreams, of course, white remains a symbol of purity and hope, but it can, like blue, symbolize the death of the self, the infinite horizons in which one loses oneself. In this sense, it becomes a colour of mourning. It is also the colour of snow, with its connotations of joy as well as desolation and death.

In music, we can relate white to nothing other than the synthesis of all the stringed instruments.

The symbolism of colours could be considerably expanded upon, particularly in relation to the world's many cultures and religions and their symbols. In dreams, the significance of colours is limited. Few dreams are in one colour, and if a dream is in several colours it is difficult to establish which, if any, is dominant. In any case, unless a particular colour evokes a distinct emotion in a dream, it should be disregarded and the dream should be analysed as if it were in black and white.

# CHAPTER 12

# *Dreams about Animals*

A nimals usually intervene only in important dreams. Among other things, they symbolize the deeper instincts and vital forces – often repressed. They may prove helpful or threatening. They may be friends from an earthly paradise or enemies intent upon our destruction. In dreams, they are precisely that which we make them, because they are projections of ourselves. They represent our passions, anxieties and fears. They can also be miraculous messengers, even guardians of our secret inner temple.

As well as being projections of ourselves, animals and other creatures also represent powerful people – our mother and father, for example. A "bad" mother may appear in the guise of a savage, runaway horse, or a crocodile, etc., while the "good" mother may appear as a lioness or a she-bear, among others.

Given the frequent appearance of certain creatures in dreams, let us try to establish their principal significance.

## The eagle

Emperor of the sky, the eagle is supposed to look at the sun face to face. It is a symbol of power and invincibility. A solar bird, it is often compared to lightning. The eagle swoops down on its prey, strikes, pierces and carries it away.

Eagles and other birds of prey frequently appear in dreams. They can symbolize inner spirituality or self-attainment, but, from the passive viewpoint, they can also represent anxiety at being "pierced" or torn apart – anxiety at castration and diminution of personality.

To be watched by an eagle, to be "spied on" by eagle eyes, often means that feelings of guilt give us a sense of being "seen through" by others, being unmasked, being watched by people we regard as superior to us.

There are dreams about an eagle being killed. This death symbolizes the destruction of an ideal or an illusion, or even the sense of having missed out on life.

## The spider

In Western civilization, spiders generally evoke only fear. Among other peoples, however, they have very positive significance. For example, in India spiders are important cosmological symbols. The shape of a spider's web recalls the sun which it reflects, and the spider secretes its thread as the sun "secretes" its rays. In certain African cultures, the spider is said to have made the stuff of human beings and to have created the sun, the moon and the stars. To the Ashanti, the spider is a primordial god which created man. From the fact that the spider weaves its web by drawing out of itself the necessary substance, takes on a positive role. It thus becomes privy to the secrets of life, the past and the future.

For us, however, the spider is generally thought of as negative in dreams, because we have had a dislike for spiders inculcated by our culture. We will later see, however, a "great dream" – a positive one, at that – in which the central character is a white spider.

## The negative spider

In dreams where the spider assumes its negative aspect, two factors are present – the web and the creature. It weaves its *snare*. It *lies in wait* for its victim. It entangles its prey. Although *immobile* at the centre of the web, the spider reacts with formidable *speed*.

Considered negatively, the spider becomes a symbol of the "bad" mother with a voracious, predatory nature, suffocating her child, grasping it to herself, keeping it to herself alone. The spider then represents the death of the personality. It frequently appears in this guise in the dreams of people suffering from the consequences of such a negative mother – above all, in the dreams of women thus afflicted. In this case then, the spider is another manifestation of the "wicked witch".

Again negatively, the spider is a symbol of the *femme fatale*, the fascinating, lethal, entrancing, blood-sucking woman. It appears in the dreams of men in whom the negative anima (see chapter 7) has remained a corrupting or malign force.

The spider can also be a symbol of oneself. In such cases it represents the over-narcissistic, over-introverted, self-absorbed aspects of a personality that is immobile and *self-centred*, like the spider in the web.

## The positive spider

Here is a dream experienced by a woman aged thirty-nine. It offers an unusual aspect of the spider's image in dreams.

> I dreamed about a spider. It was huge, and smooth as velvet. The strangest thing was that it was pure white. It was astonishingly beautiful. Even I could see that, although spiders terrify me. I don't know where it was. It was walking. Its web was further away – massive, and spangled with drops of water which glistened in all the colours of the rainbow. Then I could no longer see the spider.

The principal elements of this dream are: the *white* spider and the *water-drops* in the web.

We shall see presently how animals and other creatures in dreams can sometimes recall great myths and legends.

(a) *White spider*. The colour white here "defuses" the negative impact of the usual dark colour of a spider. It is remarkable, however, that in Islamic tradition it was a white spider who saved the life of the Prophet. In this dream whiteness denotes purity and the very *opposite* of menace.

(b) *Water-drops*. These shining multi-coloured drops are like jewels spangling the web (see the pages above devoted to precious stones). These drops of water recall irridescent *pearls*, which symbolize spiritual elevation and perfection. The web, furthermore makes one think of the similarly concentric form of the *mandala*.

## The deer

One merely has to think of the common associations which deer evoke and the epithets applied to them to arrive at their elementary symbolism. The deer's soft eyes ("doe-eyed") its grace, its shyness, its secretiveness all are bywords.

The deer (the hind or doe) is above all a feminine symbol and often appears in women's dreams. A deer then represents some part of the dreamer, but it is a femininity as yet underdeveloped and still identified with the mother. The deer represents a femininity that is too "pleasing", too "fearful". This femininity has not yet acquired the power which autonomy and detachment from the mother confers.

Here are two young women's dreams in summary form:

*Simone dreams that a deer is being pursued by masked hunters. She screams out, "Leave her in peace!"*

The hunted here represents the young woman herself, whereas the hunters are phallic men (hunters are generally equipped with rifles or knives). The hunters are masked. We are here drawn back to chapter 8 (on the animus). Note that there are *several* hunters, and recall that the negative animus often appears in the guise of *groups* of threatening or dangerous men. This dream means that Simone feels herself to be vulnerable to men.

She fears "rape" (of her personality). She is scared of expressing her self. Her animus (masked) is experienced as threatening. She projects it on men who, in consequence, are formidable creatures for her. Her scream in the dream could signify, "You – men – leave me with my mother! I don't want to throw myself into life. As for my animus, the masculine side of myself, I reject and repress it. I don't want to heed it, since it would oblige me to turn outward, to externalize, to create. In terms of any outward expression of myself, I feel as if I'm at bay."

> *Maureen dreams about a herd of deer scattered in all directions. The sky is overcast. There are rolls of thunder. Immediately afterwards a whole herd of bison pours out on to the plain.*

Maureen's femininity is anarchic, disorganized (the *scattered deer*). She feels threatened (thunder), but the most important element in this dream is the herd of bison, which sweep blindly and destructively on to the plain, devastating everything. This is the same symbolism as that of the horse pawing the ground. The bison here represent Maureen's mother, a "crushing" woman, who has left her daughter with a merely embryonic, frightened femininity. To summarize: "My femininity cracks up and splinters as soon as I am in the presence of my mother, who 'tramples' me and prevents me from going forward on to the plain (of life)."

232

## *The cat*

The symbolism of the cat oscillates between extremes. Sometimes hated, sometimes worshipped, the cat, like the snake, has always evoked violent passions in human beings. There are people who cringe from the very touch of the cat. Others like to live surrounded by whole colonies of cats.

These strong extremes of feeling and symbolism owe their existence to the cat's apparent character. Although it is supposed to be proud, independent, aloof, on the other hand it appears to be gentle, affectionate and loyal. Treachery and mysteriousness are ascribed to it, but also wisdom. In Cambodia the cat is credited with the ability to produce rain, and, of course, in ancient Egypt, the cat was venerated for its speed, agility and muscular strength.

Popular superstition has its own contribution to make to the cat's mystique. A black cat usually symbolizes good luck, but if a black cat crosses your path it is an omen of bad luck. Good fortune is presaged by a cat's miaowing at dawn, and so on. In many traditions, black cats symbolize death.

Dreams in which cats feature can also have widely different meanings, depending on the emotions which the dreamer projects on to the animal.

The feline and the feminine are often synonymous. The cat's mysteriousness, sinuosity, watchful eyes, savage and capricious release of tension are all attributes commonly ascribed to women, or femininity, usually pejoratively, in dreams.

## Some examples of cat dreams.

Here is a dream about a Siamese cat:

*A young woman dreams that she is crossing the street. A Siamese cat sits on a windowsill, gazing at her with half-closed eyes. The dreamer stumbles; people turn towards her.*

After free-association, we were able to establish that the Siamese cat represented those haughty, elegant, self-assured women before whom the dreamer "stumbled" and lost her footing in life.

The next dream involves sexual arousal:

*A woman dreams that a female cat approaches. The dreamer fondles the cat and awakes with sexual feelings.*

The principal associations drawn from this dream were: fur, softness, soft body, sinking into the warm, woman, shamelessness, waiting, revulsion, attraction. All these associations evoke woman. They are heavily tinged with sexuality. Latent homosexuality is perhaps involved.

Here is a man's dream about angry cats:

*A man dreams that a whole swarm of infuriated cats surround him, scratching him and letting out terrible raucous cries.*

These were the dreamer's principal associations: hell, blood, anger, insanity, laceration, breaking up, death and carnage.

This is an "infernal" dream of a somewhat pathological character. This man felt his inner life to be degenerating. He dreaded madness after a nervous breakdown. Paradoxically, however, this dream served to set him on the road to recovery. The dreamer recognized the extent to which he was the author of his own misfortunes, and how much he sought self-destruction (through alcohol, taking needless risks when driving, etc.). This dream made it possible for him to take positive action in his life.

These, then, are just some of the symbolic associations with cats, but we must not forget the cat's reputation for wisdom.

In interpreting dreams, therefore, it is necessary first to examine all the dreamer's feelings towards, and associations with, the cat, any personal superstitions, and, of course, the general context of the dream.

## The bat

The bat is like a defective bird, with its furry, mouse-like body, its membranous wings attached to its fingers and toes, its apparently hesitant flight (not forgetting its extraordinary sonic "radar"); but this silent flying creature of the night can symbolize the dark forces within us. It can represent anxiety, and difficulty in freeing oneself from a disturbed unconscious. It can also represent the dark seething of a soul shackled by fear and incapable of spiritual escape.

## *The horse*

'Horses frequently enter our dreams. The horse is an important symbol. Here we can only run through the principal meanings.

The horse jumps, gallops, paws the ground, charges, crushes and tramples. For many people, the horse is "the son of night". It brings life and death. It is also, however, a solar animal, and pulls Hyperion's chariot (the sun). The horse is ridden by warriors and gods. It is at the centre of the Apocalypse, destructive, but linked to the purifying fire. The horse carries on its back warrior-knight bringing justice as well as the ravaging hordes bringing death and destruction.

In dreams the horse is often a messenger of death, or the crushing of the personality – and, of course, its possible rebirth.

It is the dream image of instinct, wild or tamed. The horse is easily frightened, capricious, unpredictable, wild and often stupid. It is the animal that we try to "break" and "master".

In certain dreams, man and horse are an indissoluble unit – an image of accord between the conscious and the unconscious, an image of harmony in the personality.

Here, colour can be of particular importance. The black horse can be a messenger from hell and anguish; the white horse can allow us to ride towards our own rebirth.

As for the pony, it can represent the growing vital force, the potential for extroversion and *joie de vivre*.

## Some examples of horse dreams

The following concerns a horse that has grown wild;

*Anne dreams that her horse has become uncontrollable and now irresistibly bears her in a direction other than that which she has chosen.*

The interpretation of this dream is simple. There is disagreement between the unconscious impulses in Anne's mind and her conscious will. There is a "split" in her personality. In this case it is a warning dream. It tells her, "It is vital that you reconcile your real self or ego and your super-ego, your unconscious desires and your day-to-day life. Otherwise, you risk the anxiety which results from any disharmony in the personality.

In the next dream the horse is well behaved:

*Mark dreams that he is riding a white horse slowly (with the steps of haute-école dressage) towards a forest. He awakes in a state of enchantment.*

The horse's colour and the graceful trot are obviously positive signs. The dressage element indicates complete accord between horse and rider – and therefore harmony in Mark's personality. As for the forest, it stands for the dreamer's unconscious. He is setting off on an exploration of himself. The whole mood of this dream indicates the advent of great spirituality and the ineffable calm of the soul.

In the following dream the horse acts as a guide:

*Jackie dreams that she is allowing her horse to find its*

*way. She does not know where it is leading, but she trusts it.*

We find here the "horse-guide" figure, which bears the blind or wounded rider. Jackie feels here that she must trust to her instincts, "blinded" as she is by the contradictory demands of her everyday life. This is a very short dream, but none the less important for that.

Finally, here is a dream about threatening horses:

*Margaret has dreamed about horses for some years. The scenario is always the same. The horses are wild with anger, and the dreamer tries to find refuge wherever she can. Each of these dreams engenders panic.*

This is a common sort of dream. It would be intriguing to know just how many people have such a dream on any one night throughout the world. The characteristics of these dreams are (a) the sense of a blind, destructive force and (b) impotence in the face of that crushing force.

After such dreams each dreamer must ask, "Who is this horse?", "What does this great power represent?" and "By whom or by what do I feel, albeit unconsciously, threatened?" There is a strong likelihood that the horse here symbolizes the "bad" mother or, more rarely, the "bad" father. In any case, these dreams should always be given consideration, in view of their impact – especially if they recur.

## *The dog*

Usually, the dog is the attentive companion ("man's best friend"). It represents fidelity at all costs. The dog is instinct, but there is significance too in its capacity to track and trail, to experience things which are beyond our limited senses.

The dog's symbolism extends much further than these elementary characteristics suggest. The dog, of course, is a guardian – a guard-dog or the guardian at the gates of hell. It leads us through the darkness of death, as it leads the blind. Many mythologies associate the dog with the underworld, and with companionship beyond the grave. It is the guardian of sacred places. Among certain peoples, a dead man is always buried with his dog, which will lead its master to heaven.

The dog can be a solar – or even a maternal – symbol, but here is an interesting example of a canine dream – this one dreamed by a man of twenty-seven:

*I dreamed that I was approaching a huge mansion. The front door was at the top of a weird, surrealist sort of flight of steps. I was followed by two dogs, one white and one black. They were medium-sized dogs. Suddenly, the two dogs ran past me and took up their position at the top of the steps, facing me. I hesitated, but the dogs did not seem threatening, just severe, and very calm.*

According to the dreamer's free associations, we find:

*The house.* He felt this to be a residence which he had recently bought and to which he had not become accustomed. This house represented his ego or "I". This young man had in fact undertaken analysis and was beginning to discover in himself new potentialities as well as old blockages. The house, then, symbolizes the self to which he was not yet accustomed.

*The flight of steps.* Here, the staircase is also a threshold which must be crossed. The threshold here marks a "passage" towards an inner transformation.

*Two Dogs.* These were white and black, light and shadow: two opposites. The number two here symbolizes the "dualities" in a personality (good and bad, for example; see the symbolism of numbers in chapter 13).

*The dogs take up their position at the top of the steps.* They thus become the guardians of the house. Symbolically, they are "guardians of the threshold", the threshold which he must cross if he is to gain access to his inner being. The dogs are severe and calm but not intimidating. We can believe that the dreamer need only give proof of his identity – that is, to recognize that he is becoming increasingly in harmony with himself.

## The crow

Crows, ravens and rooks are popularly considered to be birds of all augury, presaging death and disaster. The crow's cry and colour can easily be associated with frustrated or anguished souls.

240

The crow is a social creature, noted for its social structures.

It can, in fact, be a bearer of excellent tidings. In Japan, the crow is the divine ambassador, and we need only recall that it was a crow or raven which, in Genesis, was sent out of the Ark by Noah to discover whether the earth had reappeared after the flood.

The crow is a perspicacious bird. Symbolically, it knows the secrets of life and death. It is the bird of witches and sorcerers. Among certain tribes (the Tlingit Indians, for example), the crow is itself the magician who organizes the world.

The crow is blessed with a vast catalogue of symbolic associations. In dreams, it can stand for voluntary solitude, spiritual retreat and hope; or, on the contrary, it can possess sinister qualities – as the announcer of impending inner troubles.

## A crow dream

*A woman aged thirty dreams about a large crow or raven. She is terrified by its abnormally hooked beak. She then dreams that she is being pursued.*

I cannot here afford this dream the deep analysis it deserves. I would need to rehearse, in the first place, the dreamer's entire history. Briefly, then, we note that it is a raven or large crow and, above all, that the beak recalls the classic hooked nose of the "wicked witch". The dreamer free-associated as follows:

"*Beak*. It excavates stomachs; it tears out entrails. Aunt Pauline . . ."

241

The beak is here a sort of phallic symbol, a weapon which disembowels. Why Aunt Pauline? Because she reared this young woman, forbidding her the slightest freedom or love. And the dreamer became almost certain that she was not in fact a woman, that she had no womb. The beak is therefore a "castration" symbol, associated with a phallic, dominant, absurdly masculine Aunt Pauline. At the end of the dream, the dreamer feels pursued by the whole world because of her feelings of guilt and anxiety induced by Aunt Pauline.

## The cuckoo

The cuckoo seems to appear very rarely in dreams. It can of course symbolize a sense that one is a parasite, that one is unwelcome or "in the way", that one has taken someone else's place etc. In such cases, the cuckoo signals guilt and feelings of inferiority. It can also serve as a symbol of possessiveness, with the agonizing jealousy which accompanies it.

## The crocodile

The crocodile is a far more frequent visitor to our dreams. It is an archaic symbol of the lower depths of our unconscious minds. The crocodile looks antediluvian, something from the mists of time. It is therefore not surprising that it can also represent ancestral wisdom. That is why, in certain cultures, it is credited with qualities of light or illumination.

Above all, however, the crocodile is the monster of silence and immobility, of brutal, lightning-fast attacks.

It is the crocodile that drags its prey to the bottom of the water, beyond help. It symbolizes the "evil eye" and "destiny".

The crocodile lurks, invisible, in its watery world. It resembles the dragon and other beasts that come to us from the depths of time. Capable of submerging and destroying – for it is a killer – it can symbolize the grand master of life and death.

Among Western people, at least, dreams featuring crocodiles almost never evoke agreeable sensations. We must always look into the great depths of the unconscious, and seek out those people whom the dreamer feels to be malign destroyers of his or her personality.

## A crocodile dream

*A woman dreams that a crocodile is breaking into her and her husband's bedroom. She fights with it, but the crocodile seems indestructible. The great open jaws of the beast bear down on her, and she wakes up screaming.*

Again, the question which must be asked is who or what does the crocodile represent? What is this "indestructible" power which dwells in the dreamer's unconscious and which breaks into her conjugal bedroom. Here, once more, and beyond doubt, the crocodile represents the "devouring" mother – a mother who reproached her daughter with abandoning her when she married; and these reproaches were only the culmination of twenty-eight years of repression and bullying. The guilt of the dreamer is manifest in that her mother entered her bedroom to lay hold of her once more and to drag her down into self-punishment and anxiety.

This, at least, was the dreamer's version . . .

## The owl

As a bird of the night, the owl has taken on symbolic overtones of solitude and melancholy. Superstition has intervened to make the owl a bearer of bad news. However, the owl can also be a symbol of higher knowledge: in certain dreams, the owl announces important changes in the dreamer's personality because it is thought to "know" the dark regions of the unconscious.

In other dreams, we find the owl acting as protector and guide (again in the night of the unconscious).

The owl also symbolizes wisdom, the "wise old owl" inside everyone. This may explain the popularity of owls as ornaments in so many modern houses.

## The wolf

Brer Wolf, the wolf in sheep's clothing, the wolf in Red Riding Hood, the Big Bad Wolf – why has this predator acquired such a daunting reputation in our mythology? It only needs one wolf to be on the prowl for shutters to be put up and people to tremble. It is not the supposed murderous tendencies of the wolf which provoke our fears; it is an almost sacred terror, an old dream deep in the collective consciousness.

It seems that this dream has to do with a supposed understanding between wolves and men in a long-lost paradise. The wolf is charged with a vast range of symbolic values, and the dreams in which it appears are always felt to be powerful and consequently important.

The wolf is perhaps purely "the beast", which appears from nowhere, wreaks devastation, and vanishes without trace, leaving carnage in its wake. In mythology, its role is sometimes benevolent, sometimes satanic. The wolf sees in the dark, so is symbolic of light and the sun. The wolf can be the solitary hero who defies the hunters. It is a symbol of intelligence and courage, but it is also the devourer of children, the werewolf, a demon from hell.

In our dreams, the wolf acquires the importance that we attribute to it. It is often a part of ourselves, positive or negative. It can represent solitude and self-absorption, and retreat from relations with others, but it can symbolize instinct, too – the instinct which certain people cannot externalize. The wolf can also, of course, represent a "devouring" character that we carry within ourselves – a father or mother, etc. It often represents a social character of this nature, for a man may be "a wolf" towards other men or women, but a wolf seldom behaves badly towards other wolves.

## Birds

Since birds belong to the realm of the sky, they often symbolize spirituality – particularly larks, swallows, songbirds or brightly coloured birds. Although they can represent the higher levels of consciousness, they can also serve as sexual symbols, or as symbols of the anima (see chapter 7).

Are your dream birds colourful, active, lifeless or solitary? Are they wounded? Obviously a crow and a humming-bird will have completely different symbolisms of their own. A bluebird is a symbol of hope, happiness and rebirth. A white bird represents simplification and internal harmony. The dove represents peace, and so on.

Everything depends on the context of the dream, but in general the symbolism of birds is fairly simple.

## Caged birds

*A young woman dreams that she weeps on seeing a cage in which some little birds flap and flutter desperately. She calls her father.*

Her free associations were simple: "That cage and those birds represented *me*. I am caged. My intelligence, my spirit and my freedom are all locked up inside me. My instincts are held in check by fear. I call my father so that he can open the cage and show me my way."

## A flock of birds

*A man dreams that a flock of birds, in many colours, is soaring vertically upward.*

His free associations were: "Joy and renewal. It's me who is going to fly up out of my constricted life. Joining in, participating . . . Those birds were like a huge living fountain of colour and song."

This is a dream marking an important inner

transformation, unquestionably an anima dream (see chapter 7).

## The bear

The bear is an endless source of fascination to children, because it seems good-natured and has a calm, paternal air. It is an important symbol, although it occurs rarely in nocturnal dreams. Certain tribes (the Saiates, for example), refer to the bear as the "Master of the Forest", the old black man. Others attribute wisdom to the bear. Above all, the bear symbolizes elemental strength, the power of the unconscious, but also the unforeseeable, the capricious violence and wildness which often constitute our negative shadows (see chapter 10). In children's dreams, the bear frequently stands for paternal authority (or maternal, of course, if it is a she-bear).

## Fish

Fish belong to the realms of water, as birds belong to the sky. If birds tend to symbolize the soul and the conscious mind, so fish often represent the unconscious, the inner, deeper life. They can also stand for that which we must "fish for" in ourselves, in order to bring the light of the conscious into the depths of the unconscious and dredge up all which has silted up there. Fish sometimes reflect the coloured light of rivers, but they also glide in the silent shadows of the ocean.

1 *A man dreams about a shoal of gleaming, very lively fish,*

*swimming in clear water.* This is a beautiful dream, closely akin to that of the soaring flock of birds (see above). Again, it speaks of inner beauty, of the unconscious being illuminated.

2 *A woman dreams about dead fish, floating on the surface of the water.* Is there any need for translation? This dream represents the dreamer's view of herself: depressed, desperate, living in a dark silence of the soul.

3 *A man dreams that some fish are flapping on the bank of a river.* The dreamer's free associations were as follows: "They are going to die; no more oxygen; I watch them but never think of putting them back into the water; I am paralyzed inside myself; I have no more vitality."

In fact, this man seemed to be very healthy. This dream translated his unconscious sensations. The dreamer had left the natural habitat of his essential being (like a fish out of water). He must urgently return to his proper element.

## Snakes

Here again is a creature loaded with multifarious symbols. In dreams, it represents whatever is dark and obscure in us. The snake or serpent belongs to the underground, invisible world. It dwells in crevices, in dark holes in the ground, but it darts out with lightning speed to strike. The snake can suffocate or poison its prey, swallow and digest it. Thus the snake is one of the most important archetypes in the human soul. Worshipped or hated, it has been represented thousands of times in art, and is the guardian of secrets and temples. The serpent is the great tempter, but it also represents knowledge and wisdom. It is the symbol of Western medicine. It is a universal sexual symbol, an erect and phallic image. Snakes will probably always retain their contradictory symbolism, exerting their fascination and provoking cries of fear and revulsion.

## A serpent guide

*A woman dreams that a blue serpent slithers in front of her as she goes along the road. They arrive at a river. The serpent slides into the water, and crosses over. The woman swims after the serpent.*

No one, surely, could see this as a negative dream. The dreamer's principal associations were: "Astonishingly blue; knowing where it was going; no fear; I followed it with confidence; it seemed to want to show me something; I had not got to the other side when I woke up."

Here we have a serpent guide, the serpent of knowledge. It wants to guide the young woman towards a greater knowledge of herself, by revealing a place which she does not yet know. There is also this "crossing" which symbolizes her passage from one inner state to another. Where would the serpent and the dreamer have ended up? At a temple? In a glade? A place where a sacred casket lay? Nobody will ever know, but, for all that, this dream released great energy.

## A phallic snake

*A woman dreams that a snake creeps into the room where she is lying. She screams and takes refuge in a wardrobe.*

249

This dream is phallic in the broadest sense. There is fear of rape (of the personality). The dreamer, moreover, felt that anyone who looked at her was "penetrating" her to the depths of her soul. She flees into a wardrobe, which is here a maternal symbol (enclosing, protecting, dark). Simply put, social life makes this woman anxious, so she seeks the protection of the maternal breast.

In the end, all dreams about snakes focus on the same themes: sexuality and phallic intrusion, menace within the unconscious, hidden "creeping" parts of ourselves; and also wisdom, arcane knowledge, guardianship of secrets and inner temples. In the latter aspects, the snake and the dog perform similar functions.

## The bull

The bull retains a significance almost as great as that which it enjoyed as the centre of many religions in the ancient world. Bulls are bound to life and to death. In most dreams, they are seen maddened, pawing the ground, snorting, insuperable. Then it is a devastating beast, and again we must discover whom or what it represents in this or that dream.

The bull also represents the animal nature in man – instinctive, bonded to the earth and the sun, virile, potent and with powerful senses. Jung, however, reminds us that "The sacrifice of the bull represents a desire for a spiritual life; such a life would allow a man to triumph over his primitive animal passions and thus, after an initiation ceremony, to attain enlightenment and peace." This symbolism, of course, is perpetuated in bullfights to this day. Love them or hate them, there is no doubting their fascination, with their matadors in embossed and sequinned suits shining with light, representing the triumph of mind over might, spirit over instinct. In dreams too, the killing of a bull can thus represent the need to eliminate "the beast" within us.

In other dreams, a bull can symbolize the angry father. Here we rediscover the Oedipus complex (see Dictionary). If, then, the bull is put to death, the son "kills" (eliminates) the father, and thus enjoys the exclusive love of his mother.

Sometimes, of course, the bull – the animal symbolizing instinct and strength, but also enjoyment of life and of nature – can represent the "shadow" (see chapter 10). In this case, it is highly likely that the bull serves not only as the shadow but also as the dreamer's "light", because his or her instinctive life has been repressed.

# CHAPTER 13

## *Numbers, Shapes and Directions*

Sometimes, but rarely, a specific number appears in a dream. For example, we read something in which a number seems of particular importance. More often, the number appears in a disguised form. We may dream of a triangle which is evidently composed of *three* angles and *three* sides. Equally a number 1 may appear as a single pillar; or some kind of pair may stand for the number 2.

The symbolism of numbers is, of course, very ancient and has been codified in many ages and many cultures. In general, dream numbers convey ideas, sensations and "lines of force" in the personality.

In so far as there have been studies of numbers and their symbolism through intellectual history, from Pythagoras to atomic science, it is unsurprising that there is great diversity in such studies. Here I can give a brief synthesis of the symbolism of the numbers 1 to 9 as they appear in dreams.

## Number 1

The number 1 is a starting-point, a *foundation*. Number 1 is the *unique*. In religious iconography, it represents the One God. In dreams, it is a symbol of *unification*, which is why it rarely occurs in its specific form.

Number 1 is vertical, upright, erect. It is thus a phallic symbol, and represents power.

We can dream about this number in different forms, for example, appearing as a *single* isolated object: *one* standing stone or monolith, *one* tower, *one* vertical pole, *one* upright mast, etc. I know a man who, at the end of a course of psychoanalysis, dreamed about an emerald-green serpent, which repeatedly formed a perfect 1 – a pure symbol of the unification of this man's personality.

The number 1 is also the sign of a beginning, an essential or primary element in oneself, a promise of continuity, an active and positive mind. It is the symbol of the masculine principle, sometimes, if it appears in a woman's dreams, of the animus. It is at once "yang" and father.

## Number 2

This is a beautiful symbolic number. It occurs frequently and is important in dreams, where it may appear in many forms, whether specific or hidden.

The number 2 represents the duality which exists in every human being – duality and, of course, often an opposition: the positive and the negative, the good and the bad, the real self (ego) and the imposed self (super-ego) the shadow and the light, and so on.

Sometimes there is agreement between the elements of this duality, but sometimes there is conflict and anxiety. It is also the number symbolizing *reciprocity*, reverse sides, love and hate, masculine and feminine.

Number 2 is thus the symbol of ambivalence within us, which, when revealed by dreams, warrants our urgent investigation.

The following is an example of a dream containing the number 2:

> *A man aged forty dreams that he is walking with his brother. The latter is his double. The dreamer is simultaneously delighted and filled with anxiety. He tells his brother. "I was born in 1922."*

First we should note that the dreamer has no brother. In this dream we are looking, then, at either a division of himself into two distinct parts, or a duality between himself and his "double", or else unification between these two parts within him. But the dreamer is simultaneously delighted and deeply anxious. This duality seems to indicate that the "brother" represents the dreamer's shadow (see chapter 10), which in turn would tend to prove that this man is "divided" or separated from his true self. As for the year of birth, 1922, here we have our confirmation. The dreamer was, in fact, born in 1927. The 2, however, is stressed by its twofold repetition in this date. It is as though the dreamer must stress and restress, confronted by himself, his consciousness of the duality, the schism within him. The evidence of radiant happiness on one side indicates that he is aware that inner peace depends upon the unification of this duality.

## Number 3 and the triangle

These are among the most fundamental universal symbols. Mathematically $3 = 2 + 1$. It is thus the union between the binary and unity. It is the trinity and the tri-unity. It is order and harmony; it is perfection. It symbolizes that which has been achieved, that which has attained its end.

In Pythagorean numerology, 3 is the perfect number expressing beginning, middle and end. Many religions, including Christianity, have a trinity of gods, or other supernatural beings – such as the Three Fates, the Three Graces, the Three Furies.

Here again, in dreams the number 3 occurs rarely in its specific form, but more commonly in the grouping of objects: we dream of three things, three people, or of an object composed of three parts – or else objects or people placed so as to form a triangle.

We may dream that we perform some feat or task which is divided into three parts. The third part then marks the accomplishment of that task.

The number 3 can also often symbolize the stages of life: – material life, intellectual life and the divine, the final achievement.

The triangle must be considered not only in relation to number 3 but also the geometric form itself. Equilateral triangles symbolize harmony, proportion and divinity. They are symbols too of fire, virility and the male principle. The masonic triangle is well known:

its base is duration; its two sides represent darkness and light; and perfection is achieved at its apex.

The number 3 and the triangle appear only in important dreams. It is worth noting that the third act or the third part of a dream is sometimes not accomplished, as in this example (illustrated in figure 1).

## A dream containing numbers 2 and 3

*A man (aged thirty-eight) dreams that he is standing motionless on a horizontal plane. Two oblique roads stretch from this plane into the distance, but never come together.*

Here is one interpretation, arrived at by means of the dreamer's free associations:

My left – that's my sad, my sombre side. My right – that's what I really am. Will the two roads one day join together? Will my past one day be integrated within me and become just one whole being, instead of being tugged this way and that between my super-ego and my free personality?

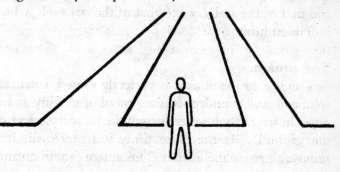

We observe in this dream:

(a) The numbers 2 and 3 are both present. There are two roads leaving a common base. They seem to run obliquely rather than in parallel, as if they must meet at some point and form a triangle (3). But this triangle remains unfulfilled. According to the symbolism of the number 3, if complete it would have marked an achievement, a perfection, a convergence. The dreamer therefore still remains in front of those two roads. He is torn between contradictory forces within him. But there is hope. It is a sort of unfinished symphony.

(b) We will see later the symbolism of left (darkness, the past) and the right (light, the future), of which the dreamer speaks in his associations. We should remember too the masonic triangle mentioned above. The left (shadow) and the right (light) should culminate at a point of unification and perfection.

## Number 4 and the square

The number 4 symbolizes fullness, solidity, totality, universality. Its symbolism is linked to that of the *square* and that of the *cross* (and to that of the *crossroads*, which is derived from it).

### The square.

The figure of the square is perfectly closed, balanced, solid and well rounded. It is a symbol of stability and of inner health. It symbolizes masculinity "with its feet on the ground". At the same time, it is enclosed, it is impossible to escape from it. The square can, in dreams, represent a mediocre stability which becomes a veritable emotional prison. The square opens on to nothing. It is the symbol of a stereotyped inner world. It represents a lack of suppleness and scope. It is not for nothing that we speak of "standing squarely" or "four-square", "square deals" and facing things "squarely". Why do we not behave in a "triangular" way?

## The cross

The cross is one of the most ancient symbols. It points in four different directions (the four points of the compass). It is therefore a symbol of internal orientation. Of course, Christianity has condensed the history of the Salvation into the one symbol. Representations of the cross have taken on countless forms throughout history. It represents "spatial totality" and the union of opposites. In dreams, it is a question of identifying the state attained in the dreamer's spiritual development, because while obviously it can represent suffering, it can equally signal spiritual attainment, or the unification of dualities. It can also, of course, stand for the crossroads.

## The crossroads

The crossroads has evident importance both in symbolism and in dreams. Banal clichés such as "a cross-roads in my life" abound. The crossroads symbolizes a confrontation with one's destiny. It involves making a choice and poses questions – forwards? backwards? right? left?

Every crossroads has a centre from which the *directions* radiate. In dreams, this point marks a *crucial* situation (the word "crucial" of course, tell its tale).

The crossroads can also symbolize the mandala with its centre and its radiating directions. Whenever it appears in a dream, it is always a highly important symbol, whatever its significance.

## Number 5

Rare in dreams, the number 5 is made up of 2 and 3, the first even and the first odd number. It generally symbolizes the active will and the creative personality. Geometrically, we are dealing with the five-pointed star, the pentagram, with its associations of magical protection.

## Number 6

This number is also rare in dreams. Equalling 2 × 3, it symbolizes two triangles. It represents contradictory situations, difficulties, struggles, trials. The two triangles when juxtaposed point in four different directions. Here is a difficult choice, oppression, even anxiety. It is often symbolic of a person tugged in different directions. It is a sort of closed crossroads.

## Number 7

This is the sacred number, the "magic number". There are seven days in the week, seven degrees of perfection, seven celestial degrees, seven petals of the rose, etc. etc.

The seventh day is the sacred day, the day of rest, after the creation of the world. It was a holy number in ancient China, Babylon and Egypt, and in Greek,

Hebrew, Islamic and Hindu traditions. In the Apocalypse, we find seven kings, seven thunderbolts, seven plagues, seven trumpets, seven stars and seven spirits from God. In Jewish traditions, there are the seven-branched candelabras and it took Solomon seven years to build the temple. There were seven wise and seven foolish virgins, etc. etc.

In dreams, the number 7 represents *accomplishment*, *perfection*, *totality*, *unification*. It can also symbolize the anxiety in the face of the unknown which marks renewal of an emotional cycle.

It is a symbol of dynamism. The number 7 represents work organized and directed to result in perfection. It is a symbol of initiation into the deeper life.

Once again, the number 7 rarely occurs in dreams as a graphic figure, although this does sometimes occur. The following dreams illustrate some of the disguises this number can adopt.

*Paul dreams that he buys six posts with the intention of fencing in a field – a huge property, "like something out of a western" (he says). The dealer tells him, "That's not much, for such a big property. Should I add an extra one? That will make seven." Paul agrees.*

Here we find 1, 6 and 7. We could translate the dream as follows (based, of course, on Paul's free associations): "You attain great emotional wealth – a great territory. You become master (owner) of yourself. But still you are struggling, still you have difficulties (number 6). You must go further if you want to manage yourself perfectly. You must add something else which will

261

signal your full flowering. Add unification (the number 1) to your accomplishments, and you will come to full fruition (number 7)."

Here is a curious and extremely interesting dream:

*Jane dreams that she is at the passport office. An employee is looking up her date of birth in order to give her an American visa. He tells her, "Ah, here we are. That's fine. You were born in 1717."*

This is an interpretation based on Jane's free associations: "I want inner freedom (America) but first I must have everything in order in my own eyes (the visa). The discovery of my date of birth means that I can now go (into freedom). I am, in other words sufficiently unified (the number 1 repeated twice) as well as being sufficiently developed after having worked on myself (the number 7 repeated).

## Number 8

This number is very rare in dreams. It is associated with the mariner's compass-card or compass-rose, drawn as a cross with four intermediate points. This figure also appears as the spokes of a wheel. It is also a cross (or crossroads) with the four other directions added.

As it possesses a centre and a total of eight directions, it can symbolize the mandala. It then becomes a symbol of wisdom, emotional stability and clarity of vision in relation to oneself. By means of its symmetry and balance, it becomes symbolic too of *justice*, *equity*, *tolerance* and *loyalty*.

## Number 9

Like the number 7, the number 9 plays an important role as a mystic number symbolizing full harmony and completion throughout the world. But it is of particular interest to us because it is the last of the digits 1–9. It is thus at once an end and a promise of continuation and renewal. In dreams it can indicate that one emotional or developmental cycle is coming to an end, and that it is necessary to go further when we reach number 9. New territories open up to us.

## The circle

Where the square is angular, the circle represents the world of curves. The circle speaks of perfection. It is the natural development of its central point. It is thus a mandala. It represents the celestial cycles and the revolution of all things in the universe, from electrons to planets, from stars to galaxies.

Circles also have a magical value. Anyone who is inside a circle (the magic circle, the circle of fire, etc.) is safe from attack. The circumference of a circle has neither beginning nor end.

In dreams, however, aside from these associations, to be inside a circle can represent an internal imprisonment. We also find dreams expressing anxiety at moving out of the "circle" in which one is living or to which one is emotionally attached (family circle, circle of friends, etc.).

The circle can also symbolize the encircling, sometimes imprisoning arms of the mother, in which one can remain blocked by anxiety. The circle then becomes like the centre of a crossroads where one finds oneself delayed by uncertainty about the right direction. Here, as elsewhere, then, we must examine the context of the dream, and the inner state of the dreamer.

Here is a splendid dream. The dreamer was a man who had been analysed.

*I dreamed that I was holding a very round apple. I cut into it and a bird emerged from the apple and flew away.*

The apple is a closed circle (sphere) from which one cannot get out. It is the image of a super-ego which holds the ego or real self in thrall. The dreamer performs a virile act (the cutting blade is a phallic symbol). He decides to slice open this super-ego or imposed self. A symbol of liberty bursts forth. His ego or real self, with its genuine emotions and sexuality, flies free.

# CHOOSING A DIRECTION

As we have already seen, at a crossroads a dreamer is forced to make a choice of direction. The crossroads symbolizes a confrontation with one's destiny. In our dreams we may be blocked at the centre of the cross-roads, unable to move in any direction.

Crossroads in dreams come in two forms (see figure): the horizontal giving a choice of forwards, backwards, left or right; and the vertical, in which case it is a cross, and the choices are to ascend, to descend, to go left or right. The symbolism of each is similar.

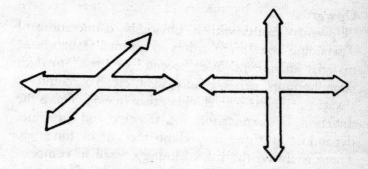

## *Forwards or upwards*

### Forwards

The significance of the forward direction is clear enough. In the dream we decide to pursue an end. We set off towards the horizon, sometimes at the risk, of course, of losing ourselves there, as everything diminishes to nothing at the horizon. We have already seen such a dream. In going straight ahead, we cut off our lines of retreat. It is rare indeed for the straight road to feature further byways which might turn back on themselves towards the road already travelled. We have cut our ties with the past. Only the end of the road, the culmination of the venture, now interests us. Sometimes the dreamer sees a point of light or someone waiting ahead. "Straight on" is generally a positive direction. It is sometimes chosen by those who are suffering from inferiority feelings or anxiety, who "leap forward" in order to escape their fears, without pausing to examine their capabilities at the moment of choice.

## Upwards

"Upwards" carries with it, obviously, connotations of "ascending" or "rising", thus of spiritual aspiration or material attainment. We "ascend" or "rise" towards fame, honours, riches, beauty, light, etc. To "climb" is always to climb to a level higher than oneself. This is the direction of purification, of serenity and of inner dynamism. But one may climb too fast or too high. There is always the risk of losing oneself in compensatory negative emotions, with all the risks of falling, so commonly found in dreams.

### Backwards or downwards

## Backwards

The dreamer retreats. When this happens in our dreams, we are returning towards our past or remaining in the neurotic security from which we dare not break free. Maybe then, we are regressing, or maybe we must pause and retrace our steps in order to collect what we need before we can move on.

Among the more frequent dreams: the dreamer slips backward (sometimes on foot, more often in a car) towards a precipice. Everything here depends upon the context of the dream. Often the car's brakes are working badly or are not working at all. This is an anxiety dream. The dreamer is afraid of "slipping back" into his or her unconscious, of falling back into pre-natal or infantile non-existence.

## Downwards

This is the direction of the descent into the self, be it positive or negative. It can be a descent into one's personal hell, a repression, an emotional or mental plummeting. It is the direction of violent and terrifying falls, but it can also signify introspection and a search for one's inner being. It can also represent restorative returns to childhood or an inner reconciliation with the figure of the mother.

Downward is also the direction of dishonour (debasement), decadence, darkness, sorrow, depression and all the shadowy caverns of the unconscious.

### To right or to left

*The right* is symbolically the direction of ascent. It signifies active work, order, truthfulness to oneself, honour and esteem.

*The left* has much the same significance as *backward*. It is the direction of the past, of childhood, of darkness and of the depths of the unconscious. In certain dreams it indicates shame and dishonour.

# CHAPTER 14

# *The Process of Maturing*

## THE GREAT LINEAGE

It is sometimes thought that dreams occur as if by chance – as if randomly placed, and isolated in one moment of time. It can also be maintained that dreams bear no strict relation to our daytime lives.

Both these claims are profoundly mistaken. Nothing is haphazard. Nothing is independent of its context. We can never consider any phenomenon, no matter what, as existing in and for itself and without relation to the universe from which it springs and which it affects.

Just as every fraction of every moment of our lives is intimately bound to every other fraction of every moment, making us tend towards a fully human condition of fulfilment, so every dream is part of a long lineage of other dreams from our birth to our death. We may see a zig-zag, but in fact there is a linear coherence running through our sleeping adventures.

Jung recognized that the totality of an individual's

dreams obey a general disposition, a characteristic orientation which he named *individuation*.

We know, of course, that dreams recur, but also that certain elements in our dreams recur, whether in the same symbolic guises or not, sometimes separated by several years. This may appear haphazard, but in fact an implacable continuity can be discerned when we analyse our dreams over a substantial period. As with so many facets of our lives, we see the parts, but are too close to the subject to see the whole.

Each of us is headed somewhere. Our ends, our purposes are ordained from the moment of our birth – even, perhaps, from the moment that the universe came into being. In all of our unconscious minds, there is a programmed directional tendency. This tendency is manifest in the process of continuous, progressive maturing, which follows a definite, if often imperceptible, plan.

Such maturing, which appears to us as a purely personal process, takes place within an infinitely vast context. The concept of man as the centre of the universe has been blown to pieces by modern science, but if we have lost our importance we have acquired a compensatory sense that, small cogs though we may be, each of us has a vital function to perform in the progress of the great machine which is the universe.

Just as many people keep an intimate diary so, in order to observe our psychological growth, it is indispensable for us to keep that "nightly" record of our dreams which, after some months, will be seen to be a saga, a serial rather than a set of unlinked "cameos".

For many people, anxiety springs from the conflict

between the real "me" and the imposed "me" which confines it (the ego and the super-ego). The chain of our dreams can show us how far we have moved in our attempts to liberate that inner self, the directions which we must take and the obstacles which we must surmount. Think of all those negative or anxious dreams which seem to insist, with, ever increasing urgency, that we give breathing space to a particular aspect of our personalities. Our unconscious minds are speaking to us. Can we afford to block our ears to what they have to say?

We can only undertake the process of "individuation" if we have taken stock of all that precedes it. We must acknowledge that the unconscious is a sort of gigantic mechanism whose function is to afford us balance at any given moment and help us to realize the fullness of our true natures. We must attempt to identify these false, imposed criteria, those prejudices, fears and resentments which prevent the unconscious from performing this function.

# CHILDREN'S DREAMS

Here is the dream of a little girl of seven. Its innocent, springlike quality is evident, even though it is the account of a nightmare. I reproduce her account using her own words and phrases.

*A little girl was walking with her parents in the forest. Suddenly she got lost. She was scared. Then suddenly she saw a great big giant who chased her. She started to say help, help, help! She was crying, and this man was panting, ah, ah, ah, but her mummy heard her and she came to the bed and said, what's happened? Then the little girl explained that she had had a nightmare.*

I also reproduce here the drawing which the young dreamer made of the scene. I never met this little girl. It is thanks to her father that I have this dream and this drawing (which he had the excellent idea of asking her to do). This drawing is obviously not an exact reproduction of the dream, but it gives us an idea of the childish atmosphere.

The *giant* is wearing a sombrero with a red pompom. The sombrero, I assume, comes from Mexican bandits on television, and the pompom is probably derived from sailors' hats (the little girl lived near a port). A tree represents the forest. A knife is being pointed, as well as another, indefinable object. But the giant is smiling. There is no trace of menace in his expression. The tree is painted in normal colours (green above, brown below). Without wishing to court accusations of seeing sexuality in everything, we could note that that tree closely resembles a phallus, and that the knife too might have phallic connotations. Why should the child dream about being pursued? Was she feeling any kind of guilt? Had she secretly observed her father in the nude, and had this caused the phallic images? Did the giant actually represent her father – or, transposed in the dream, her mother? In that case it would be a clear Oedipal dream (see the Dictionary).

The giant is symbolically an ugly creature with powerful instincts. He represents forces sprung from the earth.

Given her nascent sexuality, can we not assume that the little girl felt herself to be involved in a battle of the giants?

Here is another child's dream. The dreamer was an eight-year-old boy.

*Jim dreams that he is beneath a big apple tree bent low by its burden of fruit. He eats until he farts.*

This was how we spoke of the dream:

273

"Could you draw your dream for us? Do you remember it well enough?" I asked.

"Sure, I'll need black and green and bright red."

The boy drew rapidly. The apple-tree was enormous. Its branches covered the entire sheet of paper. The apples were big red blotches on the green. There was a little house on the horizon.

"But where are you, Jim?" I enquired.

"Me? Oh . . ." He pondered. "Oh, there. Under the branches, so you can't see me".

"But where had you come from, before you went to the apple-tree?"

"I don't know . . . From my house, there!" He pointed at the distant house. Then he started to weep.

"Do you like apple-trees?" I asked him.

"Apples? Oh yes!"

"No." I said do you like "*Apple-trees*?"

"They're beautiful, so lovely. There's shade, and all those apples . . ."

Listening to him, it became clear that the apple-tree represented a maternal gentleness which was denied him. This was symbolically stressed by the distancing of the house (which may not even have been in the dream itself). The apple-tree was like a broad, protective skirt under which he could slide.

The next example was dreamed by a twelve-year-old boy. The most surprising thing here was that this was a frequently recurring dream.

*In this type of dream, my mother is always at the wheel of the car. I'm lounging on cushions in the back, smoking a cigar. My mother's a sort of hired woman, a courtesan at my service. The car always drives past my father, who's standing still on the pavement. He's dirty and ragged. He's wearing torn clothes. I look at him with scorn while the car drives by.*

This was a child from a liberal, educated family. The father was young and good-looking. I therefore sought the source of this recurring dream. He was an intelligent child, well able to understand the overall concepts of the Oedipus complex. After I had spoken to him about this, he told me:

Yes. Deep down, I felt all that, without being able to define the feeling. Yes, that's it. But these dreams make me so anxious that I could never tell my parents about them, even though I usually tell them everything. But yes, I love Mum so much that I wish Dad would go off on a long journey for years and years. I'd like to be the only one that Mum loves. I suppose that I see my mother as being at my service because then she's more totally mine. She's at my mercy.

Let us note in passing the cigar, at once a stereotype of social success and a phallic symbol. This, together with the image of the wretched father, reduced to being a beggar on the pavement, constitutes a classic Oedipal dream.

## *The interpretation of children's dreams*

We can only rarely analyse children's dreams in the way in which we analyse those of adults by inviting them to free-associate on elements in the dreams. The child's collaboration is, however, indispensable, unless the dream is so clear that its meaning is obvious.

It is important that we understand just how important children's dreams are. They give us a direct line to their innermost selves. All their future conduct is already there in its potential state. We can compare a child to a small rubber balloon on which there are many small marks. These marks represent the potential components of the personality. For the moment, they are minute, but later, as the balloon is inflated, so these marks too will grow. What was condensed and potential will become large and all too real. It is necessary then, to detect the negative marks at the earliest moment so that we can erase them while they are still only superficial. A neurosis, after all, is no more than a failed attempt to adapt to the conditions of life. It is an inadequate exploration of the self. It is, in Jung's words, "the suffering of a soul in search of its meaning".

The first thing that the analyst must do is to ask the child to relate his or her dream. Sometimes this alone will prove sufficient to free the child of a great weight of anxiety, even if no further attempt is made to arrive at the dream's meaning. Above all, it is essential for us to establish whether a particular dream or type of dream has occurred before (as already stated, it is these recurrent dreams which keep up a persistent barrage throughout an individual's life). Such recurrence would indicate that the child is already sublimating or repressing fears or confusions which, while apparently trivial in themselves, may none the less develop out of all proportion as the child grows up.

If possible we should then invite the child to free-associate, either normally ("So what does this element of the dream make you think of?") or by means of a drawing. With young children, one can "act out" the dreams.

Of course, it would take a Salvador Dali to represent accurately the content of a dream in a drawing or painting. With children, as with many adults, we must often make do with very clumsy pictures, but the combination of the drawing and the child's comments is often sufficient to allow us to reach the depths of the dream.

## Understanding children's anxiety

Marian, aged nine, recounted the following dream:

> There was Mummy and Daddy. It was in the kitchen of their house. Mummy was making the dinner. Daddy wasn't doing anything. He was yelling at me. I was frightened, very, very frightened.

First of all, note that Marian referred to "their" house. I discovered the explanation in a separate investigation. After conversation with the dreamer's parents, it became apparent that, because of guilt (already!) for reasons which we cannot here explore, Marian felt that she lived not at "her home" but at "her parents' home".

This dream at first sight seems trivial enough, but Marian's parents had told me they had frequently heard cries of anxiety coming from the child's room, during the night.

I asked Marian, "Do you remember anything else about this dream?"

"No. Nothing," she replied. "I was afraid of Daddy, who was yelling. He was huge!"

"What was he doing in the kitchen?"

"Nothing. He was just yelling," she said.

"Very loud?"

"Yes. Very, very loud."

"Does your daddy often go to the kitchen to lend your mummy a hand?" I asked.

"No, never. He's always in his office. He works very hard, you know. He has responsibilities!" At this point Marian looked very solemn.

"And what about you, Marian? What were you doing in the kitchen?"

"Me . . . Well . . . Yes. I was holding Mummy's hand, because . . ."

"Because?"

"Well . . . to show Daddy. That's why. I hate him!"

"Are you sure?"

"Yes." Marian looked sulkily up at me. "I hate him. I hate him."

"OK, but why?" I asked.

"I don't know." The little girl's expression hardened. She cast a rather sly, spiteful glance my way.

"Could you draw your dream for me?" I suggested.

Marian painted. The kitchen was a yellow square. There was a woman in brilliant reds: the mother. Her contours were ample and reassuring. As for the father, he was depicted as far smaller than the mother. He was just a black scrawl with no colour to fill out the lines. Marian was sketched in by her mother's side. Her mouth was painted bright red.

I pointed out, "Your father is very small, but you said that he was huge in your dream."

"I'm cross with him."

"Why? What has he done?"

"I put lipstick on my mouth," she told me.

"Yes, but lots of women do that, don't they?"

"I know that. I know that." Marian's tone was patronizing. "But men like it, don't they?"

I nodded with as much seriousness as I could muster.

"But Daddy scolded *me* for doing it."

"Your daddy's nice though, isn't he?" I said. "Try drawing him normally when he's nice."

She took back her drawing. Her father's figure was made bigger. He too was coloured red.

"There. He's not glaring now." Marian became thoughtful. "But I'll put lipstick on again," she added.

It could be objected that Marian's dream was only a trivial part of the analysis, and so it was. However, it does illustrate the need for caution when dreams are translated by drawings. The "huge" father of the dream vanished in the second drawing.

The true basis of our analysis was Marian's nocturnal anxiety. She too saw herself engaged in a battle of "giants". As for the lipstick, it had indeed provoked unjustified anger in her father, who had failed to understand how normal it is for a little girl to make herself up "like Mummy" in hope of being noticed by her father as a woman. The father's anger provoked a retaliatory aggression in Marian. She became, in her mind's eye, her mother's ally against her father. The scene took place in a kitchen, the traditional maternal domain, where a father can be seen as useless or diminished.

It is sometimes difficult to know just what children actually dream. Particularly with very young children, memory fades fast. In general, we only learn of children's dreams when they spontaneously give accounts of them; fortunately, this happens quite often. It is then up to parents to take an interest in that dream if they have the time – and the courage.

A single dream generally affords us little to help our understanding. It is better by far for us to examine a series of dreams for common denominators which may give us an insight into the child's emotional world. One dream is good. A dossier of dreams is better.

Above all, we must avoid what I call "psychologism". Ours is an age of psychological meddling. Too often we seek to reduce human beings to their basic working parts, rather than trying to extend their scope to the heights and depths which we are all capable of attaining.

As already stated, it can be quite difficult to extract free-associations of ideas and images from children. Sometimes, even among young children, you will find "naturals" who readily and happily free-associate. Everything here depends upon the child's spontaneity and the extent of his or her imagination. Nevertheless we need a trained and cautious ear. It is not always easy to hear what is meant to be heard. Every childhood, after all, has its anxieties, but we must be careful not to miss the signs of an anxiety that could grow deeper and more significant.

## An example of unexpected association

Theresa, eleven, woke up screaming almost every night. She claimed that she never dreamed. This was all that she could offer:

> *I had one dream. It was a big house with big windows. The windows were shut. I was scared.*

That was it, but, one thing leading to another, she was able to tell me, "I'm scared in the street, afraid of people all the time. I want to hide."

But what did the house make her think of? Certainly there was nothing obviously frightening about the house; but what about those closed windows?

Again, bit by bit, it came out. Theresa's parents seemed to be a happy, united couple, but, after much gentle probing, she told me that the big house with its shut windows made her think of the prison where she "would be shut up one day soon".

Why did she have this conviction? Theresa, it turned out, had encountered (whether in reality or not) an exhibitionist, who had "flashed" at her for several seconds. She had told no one about the incident, for several months, but the fear of men, of the street and of people in general had developed along with a feeling of guilt. By the time that she came to talk about it, she had persuaded herself that she had somehow provoked the man to expose himself to her.

281

Had it not been for this apparently unremarkable dream, she would perhaps never have revealed this profound concern.

# THE MAIN TYPES OF CHILDREN'S DREAMS

The quality and complexity of dreams varies with the age of a child. The life of a young child is made up of a whole universe of sensations. He or she thus lives in a sort of full-time dream, divided between nocturnal fantasies and daydreams based upon a limitless imagination. Furthermore, a young child does not feel "separate" or "apart", although adults constantly encourage them to regard themselves as different from others (see chapter 10).

A child's actions are "religious", in that they reunite the child with the world and the universe. A young child, too, has not yet acquired a super-ego powerful enough to deform or repress the elements of a dream – even though adults are usually keen to help children acquire a super-ego that will impose rules and thereby limit their inner freedom.

But if a young child's dream does manifest "repressions" even these are generally expressed in sufficiently clear and disingenuous terms to be easily recognized. Children despite everything, do not distinguish between good and bad as unequivocally as adults. They therefore repress only those elements which they find excessive or unbearable.

It has often been observed that most children's

dreams fall into the following main categories:

(a) dreams which fulfil a desire repressed in waking life because of adult veto
(b) compensatory dreams
(c) dreams expressing fear or anxiety
(d) aggressive dreams
(e) dreams produced by the Oedipus complex
(f) dreams about identification with one or other parent

## Wish-fulfilment dreams

It is as though very young children have dreams in which they "avenge" a frustration experienced in waking life. Their dreams generally depict the situation as it is and without distortion, so one child will have a toy gun which he has been denied, another will gorge herself on sweets or lounge about in the garden, and so on. These, then, are dreams about desire in its simplest sense.

## Compensatory dreams

Dreams can offer enormous compensations. In dreams, children can see themselves as, for example, disproportionately strong, attractive, graceful, clever, victorious, rich or famous. These dreams will be all the more potent and exaggerated where, for whatever reason, the child has feelings of inferiority, impotence, rejection, desertion, and so on.

A child can also plunge into a sort of masochism

which is as pronounced as the compensation. One child is adopted by a tribe to whom he becomes a devoted slave. Another child sees herself alone, neglected and miserable. Another sees himself begging. Another weeps because she sees herself totally destitute. Here is a curious dream, dreamed by a nine-year-old boy:

> *He sees himself as an old man with a white beard. In this guise he administers justice.*

Talking to the little boy, I concluded that this dream (which frequently recurred) contained transpositions, substitutions of one person or thing for another. The old man was a recollection of the child's grandfather, who was both good and fair. The white beard is a well-known universal symbol of age and wisdom.

The boy told me, "I'd prefer to be very old. You don't have problems when you've become old and wise. You don't have to do anything any more. You don't have to account for yourself to anyone. You've got no more chores to do, no more teachers, nothing to humiliate and hassle you."

This then, was a simple compensation dream, but its frequency of occurrence was mildly disturbing.

Jimmy, another nine-year-old boy, often dreamed he was driving a Cadillac gleaming with chrome. His classmates watched him open-mouthed. Let's hope that this dream is not fulfilled.

## Aggressive dreams

I shall deal with anxiety dreams at the end of this section on types of childhood dreams, and turn now to the fourth type of dream.

Dreams displaying aggression are plentiful. They can be simple compensations for feelings of inferiority or weakness. They are "normal" in so far as the aggression does not become the mainstay of the child's personality. These dreams can also demonstrate nascent paranoia. Child paranoiacs will maintain that people are watching them in the street, that people are being nasty to them, that someone is listening to every word they say, etc. Such children therefore believe that they must always be first in everything, must never fail, must, in short, be superhuman, perfect in everything, and thus present others with no opportunity to criticize – a prospect which fills the paranoiac child with terror.

In these circumstances, the dreamer's associations must be minutely examined. "Perfectionism" is one of the greatest and commonest of traps of anxiety.

## Oedipal dreams

Dreams dealing with the Oedipus complex are probably the most frequent dreams by children, both boys and girls (though with girls, of course, it should properly be known as the Electra complex). The frequency of such dreams should not surprise us, since the Oedipal situation is the most powerful and problematic predicament in a human life.

## The father as pilgrim

*Michelle (aged eleven) sees herself carried in a pilgrim's arms. She tells her pilgrim, "I'm going to go with you all the way to Mecca." They quickly pass some veiled women.*

Michelle readily free-associated: "I don't know who the pilgrim was, but I trusted him completely, like God! I'd have gone anywhere with him, through fire if necessary."

I asked her what Mecca meant to her.

"Oh, well . . . I've seen it on television," she replied. "I think it's great, a faith that makes crowds of people all head for the same place. Mecca . . . it's something strong, something sort of, really inside you – you know what I mean?"

"Yes, I understand."

Michelle continued:

"Mecca . . . it's the end of the world. It's . . . it's another world, a forbidden world. A Christian can't go there, isn't that right? But with my pilgrim there was no danger. My pilgrim was invincible. It was very good, you know, life with him . . ."

"Have you ever seen veiled women?" I asked.

"Yes. Again on television. Oh, I wouldn't like to live among women like that. All these black eyes watching you, just slits in the clothes. How do you know what they're thinking? Whether they love you or hate you? In my dream, they seemed emotionless. I wasn't relaxed. Their eyes followed my pilgrim and me."

I think that, given Michelle's additional testimony, we can easily arrive at an interpretation of this dream.

The pilgrim was an idealized, symbolic father – "the father" in general. He is a version of the prince or knight who awakes Sleeping Beauty – that is, the man who draws her out of maternal identification so that she can lead an active and independent life.

The pilgrim is thus a *guide* with whom one would go "to the end of the world" with absolute confidence (in perfect unity or fusion with him). He is the "father" who shows the way to the centre of the personality (Mecca), who carries the traveller towards the dangers and the unknown in life (Mecca, the forbidden city).

As for the veiled women, they represent the Oedipal mother-figure. They are mysterious. The little girl does not know what her mother's reaction would be to the intimate union she desires with her father, but there is no guilt here – just a little disquiet.

This is a characteristic Oedipal situation, except that normally the child rejects the mother in order to possess the exclusive love of the father.

But we can go further. Probably this pilgrim represents Michelle's nascent animus (see chapter 8), with the curiosity, creativity and penchant for adventure which characterize the animus.

This is, then, a good, healthy dream of its type.

## The father as policeman

*Catherine (aged thirteen) dreams that she is at the police station. She has been arrested for stealing an apple from a woman stallholder who is giving evidence against her. The policeman makes the stallholder leave, then gives the little girl some food.*

This is a simple dream. The apple (Catherine acknowledged) is a version of the apple of Adam and Eve. The policeman is the father. The stallholder is the mother. The fact that the mother testifies against Catherine indicates that the mother has been robbed by the seduction which the girl works on her father in order to obtain his exclusive love and attention.

The father "eliminates" his wife (he makes the stallholder leave) – obviously a projection of the child's own desire.

## Identification dreams

Identification consists in adopting the manners, characteristics, gestures, style and words of a person who is generally admired or envied. It is also possible for a child to imitate the personality of someone whom he or she hates, and who in that case represents his or her "shadow" (see chapter 10).

### A simple identification with the mother

*Jill, aged eight, dreams she is in her parents' bedroom. Helped by her mother, she attends to her doll, puts her to bed and tucks her in. Then the little girl says to her mother, "There now. That way, you'll have a little sister!"*

We could suggest an endless variety of interpretations if we did not know that Jill is a very healthy girl whose parents are a genuinely happy couple. This could have been an aggressive compensation dream in which the girl was transformed into her mother and downgraded her mother to the rank of daughter. But here it is no more than a simple identification: Jill becomes a woman "like Mummy", and her dream gives her a child – her own mother, to whom the doll will be a sister.

## A simple identification with the father

*Philip (aged ten) dreams that he is out shooting with his father. Each owns an identical rifle and both are equally competent.*

The boy identifies with his father. He has the same weapon – a phallic symbol and a sign of virility. It has (at least probably) no Oedipal connotations, because normally in an Oedipal dream the boy would have "diminished" his father and eliminated him in order to enjoy his mother's exclusive love. The father would then have had a smaller weapon, and he would have been so clumsy that the boy would have despised him.

## *Anxiety dreams*

After a detour, I now return to the subject of dreams expressing fear and anxiety.

## Can childhood really be happy?

This is not a pessimistic question. We must, however, separate the child's conscious life – his or her family and play – from the depths of the child's unconscious.

The essential anxiety at the core of every human being is the fear of being abandoned. This anxiety goes back to early childhood. To be abandoned means to find oneself in absolute solitude and desolation on a hostile planet.

This is an enduring and powerful fear. We may even ask whether it governs and motivates most human deeds. Since the child comes out of pre-natal nothingness, the unconscious terror of returning to that nothingness is implicit from the outset. One person alone, through her very presence and her love, stands between the infant and a state of abandonment just one step short of nothingness – the mother.

There are of course many childhoods which are happy at a conscious level, but all must be permanently affected by this fear of annihilation and the fear of being abandoned that springs from it.

## Some anxiety symbols

In the dreams of children (aged from ten to fourteen) which I hold on file, abandonment and solitude are symbolized by *deserted houses*, *decaying houses*, *gardens in winter*, *silence*, *darkness*, *black abysses* and *roads which lead nowhere*.

As the mother is the only source of a sense of security, she can easily and rapidly be experienced as a "bad" mother (she who abandons). Here we find symbols such as *witches*, *dishevelled women* and *omnipotent women judges*. Again, the "bad" mother may take the form of an animal – a *savage dog*, a *werewolf*, a *crocodile*, a *gigantic horse* or some other animal felt by the child to be capable of devouring, trampling or killing. I have records of two dreams (by children of nine and ten) where a *shark* and a *stingray* perform this role.

There are also places such as *forests* where the child *gets lost* or *boarding-schools*, etc.

I also have dreams on file (from children aged between ten and fifteen) in which the child, having aimlessly wandered, is gathered up by *a united family*, by *bandits* or by *monks*.

We know, of course, how adults too have dreams of a similar nature.

When the father is thought of as menacing, the child can dream of *armed men*, *giants*, *gangsters*, etc. We also find dangerous "vertical" objects, *standing stones which are wobbly*, towers which threaten to *collapse on to the child*, and so on.

## DISTURBED CHILDREN

These are children whose emotional lives are deeply troubled, and their dreams must be very carefully examined. Think first of all of the children of couples in conflict, children caught in the crossfire of their parents' feuds, their tenuous security at every moment shaken by their parents' hostility and the threat of abandonment which that entails.

In the dreams of such disturbed children, we find considerable distortions. There is a feeling of an internal void.

Here is a dream of a child aged thirteen. It recurred frequently, and I quote it verbatim:

*All the people had their limbs all over the place. Their arms and legs weren't stuck to their bodies. Everything was moving about. It was dark. I was so terrified, as if I had been at the bottom of a big hole with the living dead.*

This dream translated a gravely disturbed emotional state – a schizoid state which needed serious attention. In this type of dream, people are "destroyed", there is a deep inner rift, loss of sense of reality, a drifting between the life and the death of the soul.

Other dreams of this kind show *apocalypses*, *catastrophes* and *tidal waves*. Sometimes the human figures are absurdly small. Here is a twelve-year-old's dream.

*I saw my father and my mother; there was lots of noise everywhere. They were like wires. They had no heads. They were separated by a thick wall. It was terrible.*

The couple in question were deeply divided and had frequent violent rows. The child then saw his parents as wire forms without real content, devoid of vital substance. His parents were becoming mere signs. *They were nothing more than symbols!* A lost child, in short, without guidance or guardians. And, to make matters worse, he had recently been placed – abandoned, we might say – in a boarding-school.

In the following account, the dreamer was an eleven-year-old.

*Jack frequently dreams about mountain ranges. They are extremely pointed and they block off the whole horizon. Barbed wire encloses the place where Jack stands.*

This child plainly feels his entire world to be "sharp", piercing, dangerous. On every side there is menace. Even the horizon – his future – is blocked off. His personal space is also shut off by sharp points. This dream reflects a deeply disturbed emotional state. Depression or schizoid behaviour lies in wait.

The same goes for this dream recounted by Anne, aged thirteen:

*Anne often dreams about people with tiny bodies, like larvae, but with huge heads. Their teeth are huge. These people are sometimes crawling. They shout or they snigger.*

Sometimes children's dreams are similar to those of adults. For example:

*Hannah (aged twelve) often dreams of excrement. The whole room is daubed with it. The little girl wakes trembling.*

This is a sort of dream also found among adults. It is a representation of a blocked "anal phase". Here the child was "retaining" her personality which she liberated only in occasional crises of aggression directed at everyone and everything.

A fourteen–year–old girl had the following recurring dream:

*Helen often dreams that her mouth if full of sand or cement or various objects, generally pointed – nails, drawing-pins, etc. She tries to pull out whatever is obstructing her mouth, but without success. She awakes "paralysed by fear."*

Again, this sort of dream is often found also among

adults. It represents the difficulty (or impossibility) of expressing oneself in language. It is found frequently in people prevented by mockery, humiliation or some other factor from speaking freely about their feelings. This generally ends in an anxiety-ridden inhibition of the entire personality – words, after all, being the fundamental tool of self-expression.

Other anxiety dreams include the following:

*Patrick (twelve) says that he always dreams in colour. The colours in question, however, are always washy and nebulous and invariably identical in all dreams – pastel pink and black.*

This sort of dream represents anxiety and inhibition, especially in that it is frequently recurrent. Everything is foggy and blurred. There are no bold or clearly defined tones – even if the boy actually dreamed in black and white and subsequently perceived his dreams as colour (see chapter 11).

And again:

*Annette (aged eleven) often dreams that she is knocking at the door of an unknown house where she expects a friendly welcome. She asks "humbly" if she may have something to eat.*

This recalls those dreams in which children see themselves looking for shelter and being "taken in". Are we dealing here with an exaggerated need for dependence because of anxiety at the prospect of being abandoned? A need to be loved at any cost because of lack of maternal affection? The parents should be trying to discover whether the child is perhaps constantly seeking signs of love, whether she perhaps tends to grow frantic at her mother's briefest absence, because this dream would seem to indicate incipient masochism or wilful misery. In any case, there is here an intense feeling of loneliness.

# PART II

# *Dictionary*

Consulting this dictionary may be a bit of a lottery, since no symbol has precisely the same meaning for everyone, and since I wish to eliminate any association with those "keys to dreams" that I discussed in chapter 1.

There are, however, in symbols, certain meanings which strike the same emotional chord in everyone. I have therefore tried to lay down here some "common denominators" in human emotions. This dictionary is of necessity limited to only those images which are most frequently found in dreams. It will, I trust, serve as a guide offering a few signposts to enable readers to get their bearings before attempting to analyse their own dreams.

The best approach will be to consult the dictionary in tandem with the contents page and the index, since many of the symbols defined and explored in the book are not included in this dictionary.

∞

# Abyss

An abyss or gulf generally symbolizes the unconscious, together with the instincts which lie within it. The abyss can also symbolize the mother, the maternal breast or the pre-natal nothingness.

Many people dream that they are standing on the edge of a vertiginous abyss. Their fear of falling is great. This can symbolize an unconscious invitation to descend into oneself in order to find the roots of one's problems. It can also symbolize the fear of knowing the repressed parts of one's nature.

In other dreams, a person leaps over a gulf or crevasse, or else a bridge spans the chasm. This is a sign of superficiality. One fears to look too deeply into oneself, for whatever reason.

Dreams of falling into the abyss are many. If this becomes a recurrent dream, it can be a sign of latent or impending depression or of an enduring anxiety.

∞

# Adventurers

For *men*, an adventurer in a dream may symbolize his *shadow* (see chapter 10). The dream unveils a hidden part of himself, still carefully maintained in the unconscious. This is particularly the case, for example, with men who have had to repress the free, extrovert part of their personality. Introverted and afraid of existence, they have locked up the adventurer, within them. Their dreams show such men what they really are, and what they might have been.

For *women*, an adventurer can often be the symbol of the *animus* (see chapter 8) which is about to achieve realization. The context of the dream will tell whether the adventurer is felt to be dangerous or not, and will thus demonstrate whether the animus of the woman in question is negative or becoming positive. In the latter case, harmonious creativity and balanced extroversion are on their way.

~∞~

# Aeroplanes

The symbolism of the aeroplane is basically that of the bird. It is linked to the symbolism of the air, freedom, climbing, the sky and heaven. Generally, being in an aeroplane in dreams signifies a spiritual search. The dreamer has left the limitations of the earth.

Aeroplane dreams (which are very common) come in nine distinct forms: (a) the dreamer is the pilot; (b) the aeroplane is being flown by someone else; (c) the dreamer is flying upwards or (d) descending; (e) the dreamer follows a determined route or (f) goes astray; (g) the aeroplane is stable and sound or (h) it is falling apart or (i) it is plummeting to the ground.

Dreaming that one is the pilot generally indicates that one is one's own master and that one is steering towards a spiritual domain. The dream will then indicate whether there are difficulties in piloting, whether the machine (oneself) encounters storms or whether, on the contrary, the flight is smooth, with no turbulence.

Dreaming that the aeroplane is being flown by someone else can signify that the ego or conscious "I" is being led by unconscious forces. Here, too, all will depend on the context of the dream.

I have an account of a dream in which the aeroplane's pilot is a man in a dark flying-suit. The aeroplane is buffeted by air-pockets and turns somersaults. The dreamer-passenger is terrified. The pilot remains cool and impassive. There is no sensation of danger, but rather a sense of questioning expectancy.

Obviously here the dreamer is "driven" by unconscious forces, but which? By complexes? Repressions? Anxieties? Or is this a representation of the dreamer's *shadow* (chapter 10). In fact, this last proved to be the case. His shadow, his unconscious "double", led him towards the light – the realization of himself – but with all the knocks and somersaults which that process entails.

Dreaming that one is flying upwards or descending is simply linked to the symbols of rising or descending, upward or downward motion, with which we have dealt earlier.

If, in a dream, the aeroplane follows its proper route or goes astray, we may readily deduce the meaning. The principle context to be considered is whether the dreamer is the pilot or a passenger (see above).

Again, the symbolism of a solid, sound aeroplane is self-evident. As for plummeting from the sky, we have already examined dreams about *falling*.

A thirty-year old man dreamt he was a passenger in an aeroplane. Suddenly the pilot turned into a dive towards the earth, deaf to the dreamer's cries. In this case, the dream told the man that he was flying too high, materially or spiritually, without first having done the groundwork for such aspiration. A temporary return to earth proved necessary. The pilot evidently symbolized the dreamer's unconscious. Once more, the internal "computer" which maintains order and stability had perfectly performed its warning function.

# Amputation

The most frequent amputation dreams concern arms and teeth. These dreams relate to anxiety at the prospect of mutilation, otherwise known as fear of castration. The dreamer believes his or her personality to be threatened or diminished. Such people experience the constant sense that others seek to mutilate, humiliate or reject them. These dreams represent the unconscious sense or fear of being weaker than others, of being ripped off by life's competititors. Put otherwise, they reflect fear of impotence in the broadest sense of the term. This sort of dream is always a sign of guilt or inferiority feelings.

# Angels

Angels generally symbolize inner transformation. In most dreams, an angel is the bearer of glad tidings (concerning oneself). In certain dreams, however, *black* angels appear. These dreams are very rare, but it is worth mentioning them. The black angel's symbolism links two important factors – the angel and the colour black (see chapter 11). It can be a sign of a negative judgement one has made about oneself; in any case it marks an important change of course, in consequence of a vital decision that the dreamer has taken, consciously or not.

I have records of two dreams in which an angel appears. In the first, a man aged forty dreams about a winged white angel sitting on the ground and smiling. The dreamer made associations with the "smiling angel" in Reims Cathedral. He saw the smile of the Reims angel as simultaneously welcoming and cruel. In this case we are dealing with a potent image of the dreamer's anima (chapter 7).

In the second dream, by a woman aged forty-three, the angel was felt to be masculine. He was nebulous and colourless, almost diaphanous – just an impassive presence. The dreamer made an association with ectoplasm. The angel said to her, "I really ought to take shape." In this case we find the animus (chapter 8) attempting to emerge and to be acknowledged, with all the creativity inherent in that element in a woman.

I must stress that the animus and anima are the most important elements within both women and men. If they are not set to rights and afforded their rightful place, no further realization of the self is possible.

# Army

An army basically symbolizes the struggle against the forces of evil – against the "dragons" and "monsters" which threaten us.

An army is a blind force, irresistible and invincible. It is an anonymous power. It can represent the forces of our emotions, and also our instincts as a whole.

Dreaming about an army almost always indicates that we are suffering from internal conflicts. An army on the march shows that we are running the risk of being outflanked and overwhelmed by our unconscious. When two armies fight during the course of a dream, it is clear that there are contradictory forces in conflict within the dreamer. There is a duality of position, emotional tension and, probably, anxiety.

Armies – and their weapons – are phallic symbols. Armies pierce, break through, penetrate, violate.

In a more positive sense, the army can represent the power of the father, yet this tends to be a despotic and castrating force.

In *women*, armies and arms can symbolize fear of rape (of the personality) and the fear of being "crushed" by others. An army dreamer must therefore examine the context of her dream. Is the army disciplined, friendly, threatening, or does it seem more like a band of outlaws, which would signify an animus "at the bottom of the ladder", still ill-defined and negative.

❧

# Ascension

In dreams, an ascension contains all the associations of *rising* or *climbing* (see chapter 13). Dream activity includes many types of ascent: mountains, steep roads, lifts, staircases, walls, etc. Ascents into the sky are by no means rare, whether the body rises on its own or as a passenger or pilot of an aeroplane. This almost always has to do with a spiritual quest, with its attendant risks. See *aeroplane* in this Dictionary.

❧

# Attics

Attics are common in dreams. Their general symbolism is part of that of the house as a whole. See *house* in this Dictionary.

❧

# Bandits

The symbolism here is much the same as that of the *adventurer* (see above).

*In a man*, the bandit can represent a part of himself of which he disapproves or despises. The bandit can also symbolize, however, an internal danger. As often as not, a bandit represents the dreamer's *shadow* (chapter 10). The context must be examined. Is the bandit dangerous or friendly, greedy or generous? Is he a terrible villain, or a free-and-easy Robin Hood character? In any case, the bandit symbolizes some part of oneself which has remained ignored in the shadow of the unconscious – or repressed.

*In a woman*, a bandit is generally a symbol of the animus (chapter 8). Here, too, the rest of the dream will set the dreamer on the right road and will indicate just how far she has got in her bid to free the animus, and to realize the full potential of her autonomous and authentic creativity.

# Baptism

See *water*.

# Bicycle

The bicycle affords autonomy and freedom. In dreams it can symbolize harmony between one's conscious behaviour and one's unconscious impulses: the rider and the bicycle are a single unit. It is in this context that dreams must be examined.

Bicycles appear frequently in dreams. For example: a man (aged thirty-seven) dreams he is clambering up a steep slope, pushing his creaking bicycle. This man is experiencing problems in real life. His path rises steeply. There is no harmony between his outer and inner lives (he is separated from his bicycle). He must "push himself" if he is to make progress. And his inner life creaks and groans . . .

In another example, a thirty-four-year-old woman is riding her bicycle along a country road; she is on her way to see a chemist. In fact the "chemist" of her dream stands for the psychoanalyst with whom she is making her inner journey. This woman also associates "chemist" with "alchemist". Her dream illustrates freedom and happiness, and the personal autonomy she is in the process of acquiring.

For men, the bicycle can sometimes symbolize their *anima* (see chapter 7).

# Blood

We have encountered this important symbol in the course of this book. Blood is inalienably linked to the concepts of life, vitality and physical warmth. In dreams, it is a potent symbol of energy. It is sometimes linked to fire, even to the sun.

Everything depends on the individual dream, for blood can also represent "castration", mutilation and the associated anxieties. In other dreams, blood represents a spiritual vehicle. The colour of blood means that it also contains the symbolism of the colour red (see chapter 11).

# Boats and ships

Boats often appear in dreams. For obvious reasons the boat symbolizes a *journey*, a *voyage*, *navigation*.

In dreams, a boat most frequently symbolizes a *crossing* (see chapter 6). It allows us to go from one point to another as we change and adapt in our inner being. A small boat is also a kind of *cradle* symbolizing the *maternal bosom* which gives us safety during a dangerous crossing. In this sense it is the mother's *womb* offering comfort and reassurance.

A boat can also symbolize the journey of the dead; this is the "solar" boat (like the sun's "chariot" in mythology), carrying the dead and following the sun across the ocean. This recalls the ancient Greek myth of Charon, the boatman who was paid to ferry the dead across the Styx.

Boat dreams are rarely insignificant. In interpreting dreams about small craft such as *rowing-boats*, *sailing-boats* or *motor boats*, etc., we should carefully examine the context. How is the crossing made? In what condition is the boat, and its oars, sails or engine? Do we know where we are going, or have we gone astray and got lost? What is the water like?

If we move from a small boat to a *big ship*, which is rocked by storms but remains solid, this reminds us of human beings tossed about by the events of life yet safe in our mother's arms, which have been internalized as feelings of confidence and hope. The larger boat or ship is thus a symbol of *the mother*, enclosing us within its secure and protective sides as we voyage through life.

Here is an example, dreamed by a woman aged thirty-five:

> *I was on board a huge ship which was headed for the Bermuda triangle. Way out at sea, I realized that there was no captain and no officers, just crewmen who ran, crazily, in all directions, while the ship steamed ahead at full speed . . . Then I woke up.*

Given the dreamer's free associations, it was clear that his dream indicated that she was undertaking a *crossing* to a place reputed to be mysterious and dangerous – in other words, that she wanted, at any cost, to know herself more truthfully. The danger sprang from the fact that she intended to question everything – absolutely everything – which had gone to make up her life and her personality to date. The Bermuda Triangle then symbolized this woman's deep-seated centre, but the ship was too big (again according to her associations). It represented too much security. It therefore represented the dreamer's mother, from whom she had never been able to detach herself and to whom she returned at the least sign of difficulty. This excessive security of the mother-ship was preventing the sailor from estimating the true size of any obstacles. She made the association with the *Titanic*, whose enormous safety had been much trumpeted so much so that the ship sank on its first voyage for lack of elementary safety precautions.

Furthermore, there is no captain − no responsible man on board the dreamer's boat. So: the masculine pole, the animus of the dreamer, has not developed. It is "scattered" − the disorderly sailors are running round in all directions.

The boat can also symbolize, *in a man*, the anima (see chapter 7). Many men are almost literally "married" to their boats. The boat also enables them to set off on adventures – in search of themselves. No wonder so many boats are given women's names.

❧

## Boxes

The box's symbolism is related to that of the *casket* or *chest*. A box contains things.

In dreams, boxes can symbolize mystery, but also the search for a secret about oneself, whose discovery will assist in one's personal and spiritual progress.

But a box can also have the same significance as the *cupboard*, in that it too encloses and can suffocate. In dreams, in that case, it can symbolize the stifling of the personality by the image of the mother (again, a box, because it closes, is a feminine symbol).

❧

## Castles

Castles are important symbols which frequently appear in dreams. They have many meanings. Childhood daydreams, of course, frequently include castles and palaces, princesses in danger, and fortifications that can be penetrated only by heroes. Here again is the symbolism of Sleeping Beauty and so many other classic tales. So, for children, castles and palaces signify noble deeds, difficult enterprise and nostalgia. When they appear in adult dreams in this sense, they represent the yearning for the Paradise Lost, for greatness that has gone astray, and the enduring regrets strewn across the paths of our everyday lives today.

In some dreams, however, a man "climbs up" towards a castle. The difficulties are many, the dangers enormous. It is not rare for us to find a dragon or vicious dog guarding the entrance, or the drawbridge raised. The outcome of his approach to the castle will demonstrate the dreamer's state of mind. Here is a dream recounted by a man aged forty-two:

*I was climbing towards a dark, turreted castle. The stones slithered beneath my feet, but I kept on climbing. There was no entrance to the castle. It was alone on top of a rock. I was going to save someone – a princess? a damsel in distress? I don't know. Whoever it was, in my dream, it was someone young. In front of the castle, there were these armed men with red hair. There was a battle, and then I was allowed to pass. I found myself in total darkness.*

It is clear that the dreamer is setting off in

search of himself – in search of his inner youth, probably the depths of his soul, his anima. But the difficulties are still great, and, before he can draw near, he must fight and then find himself, all alone, in the darkness of his unconscious.

The castle can have a different meaning, for instance as the "guardian" of a village or town. Overlooking its domains, it stands guard, ready to do battle to defend the territory which depends on it. Not just anyone, of course, can enter such a castle: a proof of identity is necessary. To dream of a castle thus perceived indicates that one is on the way to an "initiation" and to inner nobility, and that vigilance and spiritual strength must be installed within one's soul.

Again, because the castle is "isolated" from the everyday world, since it is situated "high up", it gives the illusion of having a magical, mysterious power. In dreams, it can therefore also symbolize the transcendence and increased spirituality of the personality.

∽

## Catastrophe

Dreams about various catastrophes are so frequent that they can only be understood by careful examination of the dreams context. Usually, such dreams are anxiety-centred. The catastrophe may be cosmic, universal – the earth might shake, the sea roll back, and so on. They can also indicate a deep emotional turmoil in the dreamer.

Other catastrophe dreams (train or car crashes, ships getting blown up, etc.) denote not just a deep-down anxiety but also fear of emotional impotence and waning vitality. We may feel that our journey will never end, that we have broken down on the way, that we are running the risk of losing our strength and our health. Such dreams must never be ignored; they can precede a state of depression.

∽

# Children

We have already encountered this symbol (see chapter 6). The appearance of a child in dreams is extremely common. We are expecting a child, we lose a child, we find a child, etc. Dreams about pregnancy are probably the most frequent. A child, in dreams, almost always indicates something essential in oneself which is about to be lost or is in the process of being lost.

# Church

In the Christian world a church contains all the symbols of the mother, even to the extent where the two things become confused ("Mother Church"). In consequence, even for unbelievers, the church becomes a centre of our personalities, our inner church, our place of peace and renewal. It thus represents the deep unconscious, the essence of our emotional life.

To *enter* a church generally means to attain a fusion with the mother and thus to examine, in the silence, one's authentic self. To enter a church can also mean a movement towards spirituality, and even a "crossing", for a church is a "vessel"; its symbolism is related to that of the *cradle* and the *boat*. This crossing allows us to pass from one spiritual "bank" to another.

To *come out* of a church signifies emerging after a renewal. It is a passage to a more adult, renewed spiritual state. We leave the revitalizing mother to set off once more into life.

# Cradle

I do not know how often cradles appear in dreams, but I do have one on my files, dreamed by a man of forty-eight.

> *He dreamed that he saw a little rowing-boat floating on the water, and was inside it. The rowing-boat drifted downstream on calm water. The dreamer woke up happy.*

Here we find a rowing-boat serving as a cradle. The dreamer is making an inner *voyage* and a *crossing*, for the child in the boat is himself, and the cradle-boat marks a return to the security of childhood. It is the mother, maternal warmth and the return to the essential. This man's dream symbolizes nostalgia for his childhood, which must be revisited and purged if the great journey to his profound authentic self is to be accomplished. This was a good dream. See also the shadow (chapter 10).

The symbolism of the cradle is that of the deep security it gives to a child; it is like an extension of the mother's arms.

# Crowds

Crowds often appear in dreams dominated by feelings of inferiority, loneliness or guilt. Often, too, we dream we are naked in a crowd. We have already read about a dream in which a woman saw herself opening her handbag in the middle of a crowd. We can also feel crushed in a crowd, which would indicate that we feel incapable of controlling our lives. Much the same sense is conveyed by those dreams in which we find ourselves being "swept along" by a crowd. Crowds in general represent blind power, and thus symbolize the forces of the unconscious.

In some dreams, the crowd is speciously reassuring. We get lost in a crowd; we melt into a crowd. This is a sort of suicide of the personality. In these dreams, the crowd is much the same as water when we allow ourselves to "go with the flow". It is a return to the unconscious, to maternal security. It is a regression to the irresponsibility of childhood.

# Cupboard

Cupboards (or wardrobes) enclose things. They represent dark "shelters". They can be seen as receptacles, in which case they serve as maternal symbols. A cupboard can be locked. It is thus related to the casket or chest in which treasures or secrets may be hidden. In certain dreams, someone hides in a cupboard to escape from some danger. Once again, we have a maternal symbol.

I have a record of a dream in which a man shuts himself, from the inside, in a cupboard; he sits and lights a feeble lamp; he feels he is waiting for something. This dream indicates that the man was retreating into himself, into the shadowy confines of his unconscious. The cupboard symbolized the centre of his personality.

Dreaming that one is locked into a cupboard (or any other place) indicates – according to Freud – that the dreamer is recalling pre-natal existence, in so far as he or she has remembered the experience. Some people dream that they are suffocating in a cupboard locked from the outside. They panic. This often reflects the sense of being stifled by a member of one's family or community (generally a female member, the cupboard being a feminine symbol) or of being a prisoner of one's own emotions or anxieties.

# Dancing

In dreams, dancing possesses a dual symbolism: sometimes sexual (erotic) and sometimes religious (in the broader sense of "reunifying"). In this latter, more frequent meaning the dreamer experiences the sensation of participation in events beyond his or her own "I" or ego. The dance thus reflects a deep accord with one's inner self. It is a ritual; it identifies the dancer with creation. It can demonstrate a growing spirituality, a liberation from internal constraints, the reconciliation of body and soul. In many dreams, dances appear at times of inner transformations.

A dance can also be an "orgy" in both the lowest and the highest senses (see chapter 4). Dreams in which dancing occurs are always important. They must be examined in their entirety.

# Dead leaves

Dead leaves, of course, are symbols of melancholy or sadness. They can represent a distant past. To see oneself sweeping up dead leaves is an excellent sign, in that one is getting rid of nostalgia or events that are over. I have records of dreams where the dreamer is buried up to the neck in dead leaves. This would seem to indicate that the person was suffocating, submerged by feelings of anxiety.

In certain dreams, dead leaves can represent suicidal tendencies and the death wish, which is as nostalgic as autumn.

# Decapitation

Dreams about decapitation are rare, but always powerful. These are evidently "castration" dreams. The head is cut off (or is threatened to be), which means that the dreamer feels cut off from his or her aspirations, reason and thoughts. This kind of dream appears at times of deep disappointments, or when feelings of guilt are linked to "the head" – that is, to one's way of thinking, speaking, putting forward ideas, and so on.

Dreams about decapitation can also be

sexual or can relate to the individual's strength;
they occur when there are feelings of sexual
impotence or of powerlessness in life.

# Departure

There are countless dreams involving departure, absence or exile, as well as countless
poems or works of music dedicated to absent
friends or lovers. Departure is surrounded by
a particular atmosphere of railway stations,
trains, and the ocean that separates people.
Even luggage is part of the atmosphere,
designed as it is for temporary or permanent

separations.

To dream of a person going away generally indicates that we cease to be "bound" to that individual, that he or she is leaving our inner life or that we are detaching ourselves from that person. We also find in dreams of departure that fear of being abandoned by the person who is going away. It is the theme of human loneliness.

In other dreams, seeing oneself departing can mean that one would like to leave something or someone. These are then dreams involving unconscious desires.

❧

## Exams

Our dreams positively teem with exams and tests, and therefore with examiners. In a

dream exam, we must show what we know and what we are. All exams constitute a form of judgement. In dreams, the examiner is a part of ourselves which judges another part. Exam dreams are therefore valuable because they let us know how we see ourselves.

∞

# Excrement

Symbolically, excrement represents the "vital force" of the creature which has produced it. It is thought of as a sign of power (or, in consequence, of weakness). Children – and many adults – give great importance to their excrement, not just for reasons of health, as some might believe, but also because of the symbolic value which excrement possesses. (In part, at least, this is because of the importance ascribed to it by impatient or expectant parents. It is the first gift which the infant can give which is his or hers and will gratify the mother or father. Equally, the child can win attention by refusing or withholding it.)

Dreams in which excrement feature, are exceptionally common. They almost (in Freudian terms) always relate to the "anal" state of the dreamers, that is to say, the way in which they either "retain" their "constipated" personality or give it freely.

In certain dreams (but this is rarer) excrement may be a sign of self-contempt. But it should be noted that "I am nothing more than a piece of excrement" is no different from concepts at the centre of the loftiest philosophical questions.

⌘

# Exercise book

Here is a dream in which the significance of the exercise book is clear enough:

> I dreamed that I was waiting for the bus to take me to the office. I was carrying my files and books from work under my arm, as well as a mysterious package. I opened the package on the bus. It contained exercise books from my primary school. I was filled with anxiety. I wanted to get off the bus.

Every Sunday evening, this man was anxiety-ridden (as are many others for the same reasons). It is the well-known "Monday-morning syndrome". This is a vestigial transposition of the child's anxiety at returning to school after a weekend spent in the security of the family. He will once more be forced to "account for" himself and to lay open his homework for judgement.

When exercise books appear in dreams,

they probably indicate that childhood anxieties have not yet evaporated, that we still experience the feeling of being abandoned by our mother to the mercies of our school. We project these anxieties on to our day-to-day work and, of course, on our bosses, who represent our childhood teachers.

## Festivals

Dreams about festivals or carnivals relate to those involving "orgies" (see chapter 4). There are numerous types of festivals, whether elevated or vulgar. A masked ball might indicate that every participant is hiding his or her personality from every other; in certain dreams, the anonymity provided by the mask makes the socially conditioned aspect of oneself cease to exist. In that case, there can be a sensation of participating in something much greater than oneself. This is the orgy theme, for the mask (in life as in dreams), suppresses the differences between personalities and the accompanying anxiety.

In a festival dream, then, we must ascertain whether all the participants are masked, or whether it is merely oneself – which would presuppose feelings of guilt or inferiority, provoking the fear of being "seen" or "unmasked" by others.

All types of festival are forms of "participation in the universe". In this sense festivals can sometimes appear in "great dreams" marking inner change. One's socially conditioned being is moving outward, towards ever greater dimensions. We should not forget that a festival is "religious" (in the sense of *religare* = to reconnect). Again we return to the symbols of the orgy.

∞

# Fire

Fire is, together with water, the greatest of the universal symbols. Everything about fire symbolizes ardour: its colour, its power, its heat, its brilliance. Fire is perhaps the least imperfect of the symbols of the divine. It purifies; but, on the other side of the coin, its smoke chokes and obscures, and fire burns and devours. The fires of passion, like real fires, destroy or give life.

If fire represents God, it can also symbolize the father. Here again, the symbol takes two directions. It can represent the admired father (ascendant, like the flame, which flickers upward towards life), but, as a destructive element, it can also be seen as the father who reduces and annihilates by his authoritarianism and tyranny.

Dreams about fire always represent energy, be it constructive or destructive. They often symbolize sexuality in a broad sense. Fire in dreams also shows impulses towards spirituality and towards the light of inner truths.

∝∞

## Flags

Strange as it may seem at first sight, a flag symbolizes the union of masculine and feminine. There is the "pole" which is an obvious erect, vertical, phallic symbol. At the same time, the piece of fabric is feminine; it symbolizes the material of the mother and of woman. The flag can also represent, in dreams as in life, a totality. Just as it symbolizes the combination of the men and women of one nation, so, in dreams, it represents the inner life as a whole – emotion and creativity, attraction and power.

To dream that one is erecting and planting a flag indicates that one is marking one's virile and emotional progress. To lower a flag to half-mast symbolizes, of course, an inner sorrow; we withdraw into ourselves, as the material is folded up.

∝∞

# Flying

Flight can mean space rockets and Concorde, or it can mean Icarus. In dreams, flying indicates a need to "rise" higher, a desire for the sublime – but, alas, flights in dreams too seldom end happily. Descent or falling are never far off. To fly in a dream generally signifies an attempt to rise above one's conflicts and difficulties. Contrary to what one might be tempted to believe, dream flights often demonstrate deep-seated feelings of impotence. We fly because we are anxious about finding ourselves on the ground. Flying is often a flight from oneself.

# Flying saucers

I have several dreams in my files in which UFOs or "flying saucers" appear. They are luminous and silent. They rotate at low altitudes, or they hover or land. In one of these dreams, a man emerges from a UFO. He seems very good. He is about to speak when the dreamer awakes.

Flying saucers in dreams are charged with hope or with terror – hope, in so far as everyone hopes that there might be a "better world". The occupants then represent bearers of glad tidings. They are the contemporary version of Christ. As for terrifying UFOs, they demonstrate the destructive anxiety which lies within the dreamer's soul. They become then the modern equivalents of the horsemen of the Apocalypse.

∞

# Fog or mist

"I am still in a fog, but I have a good compass": this is the gist of so many of my patients' testimonies when they are in analysis. I mention it because it exemplifies the whole symbolism of fog or mist.

Fog blurs or masks forms. It makes everything seem of one hazy substance. In dreams, a fog can often indicate a moment of change, the moment when the fog "lifts" or the mist "clears". Suddenly the sun appears and we can see where we are going.

Dreams about fog, then, almost always signify a change of direction. After wandering, confused, in a state of mind where everything looks vague, forms will become defined, the route will become clear. The important thing, of course, is to have a good compass – the self-knowledge which guides us through states of confusion or uncertainty.

∞

## Forests

Intuitively we know forests symbolize our unconscious lives, with their burgeoning fertility and their darkness, their dangers and their clear glades. Dream forests are peopled by friendly or hostile animals. Magical beasts, too, may appear – gryphons, dragons and such. Sometimes, especially in children's dreams, there are giants in the forest.

Whatever we seek in the forest, we seek within ourselves. Sometimes the dreamer will

head towards some secret place where a treasure lies waiting. This is clearly an image of the search for one's own centre, one's "jewel" or most valuable essence, after much wandering in the unconscious.

Sometimes in dreams we penetrate deep inside the forest. We are thus entering ourselves, where we hope to find clear waters and luminous glades.

Sometimes we leave the forest after our inner journey. In that case we have achieved a "crossing" (see chapter 6). This will probably be a "great dream" from which we will break forth more mature and better equipped.

In dreams, the "cathedral" of the forest may be the highpoint of a spiritual quest, despite the dangers concealed behind the tangle of trees and thickets.

## Fountains

Spurting, bubbling fountains, pure crystal springs . . . Fountains are joyful, "amorous", singing, bright. There is a fountain of life, a fountain of immortality and, of course, a fountain of youth. Symbolically, drinking at a fountain affords longevity. The meaning of a fountain will depend upon its context. There are powerful fountains which symbolize emotional and sexual vitality, but there are also dried-up or muddy springs which appear in dreams involving anxiety and lack of self-esteem.

In men, the fountain can stand for the anima (chapter 7). Here, too, the context of the dream must be carefully examined.

See also *water* in this Dictionary.

〜∞〜

## Heroes

Dreams about heroes (others or oneself) show that one identifies with a person considered heroic and brave (the father, for example).

Other dreams are compensatory: we see ourselves performing brave deeds and emerging unscathed. Some heroic dreams, however, are indications of an inner achievement or a profound change. See the section on "Heroic dreams" in chapter 6.

❦

## Hospitals

Dreaming about hospitals can be due to fear of illness, anxiety concerning the advent of old age or fear of accidents. On a deeper level, some dreams about hospitals indicate a desire to be taken into the care of others, to give up all competition and struggle and to abandon one's responsibilities. Hospitals then become symbolic mothers, who cherish, nourish, calm and shelter. In such a case, to dream of hospitals marks a regression to infancy or even to pre-natal non-existence.

Hospitals can also appear in dreams when there is fear of castration of the personality (see chapter 3). In these circumstances, the operating-theatre appears most often.

❦

# Hotels

This symbol can stand for many states of mind in dreams. The first thing to establish is the category of the hotel. Here are some examples, chosen from the many dreams in my files:

> *I was in a grand hotel. I was checking the bill when suddenly I realized that I had no money. They sent me off to work in the kitchens.*

This is an obvious inferiority dream. The dreamer (a man aged forty-eight) feels that he is aiming too high, that he is an impostor, and that any admiration he receives has no real object. This is yet another man who cannot find reason to love himself.

> *I was in a little hotel. It was a bit shabby, but it was a family hotel. I felt good there. I never went out.*

We have already seen a dream of this kind. This dream (a twenty-nine-year-old man) shows comparable sensations of fear in the face of life, as well as the conviction that the dreamer has no right to an easy life. He sets out to be miserable. He needs to put himself down. This self-imposed misery gives him a sense of security, since it is a "family" hotel.

> *I was in a enormous hotel in America. I*

*didn't have a telephone, and I'd given a false name.*

It would seem that the dreamer (a man aged forty) is running away from his existence. The fact that he is totally anonymous (the false name) and that no one could find him (there is no telephone) gives him a sense of security. Note that this might have been a "crossing" dream (see chapter 6), in which case the dreamer would have *crossed* the ocean from one side to the other, thus marking an important transformation in his inner life. He would have changed his name (that is, he would have abandoned his "I" or ego for a far greater, more transcendant personality). But this was not in fact the case here.

The hotel can also be a maternal symbol (as, for example, with the hospital). Here, too, one is cared for, one need merely exist. As with the hospital, again, the hotel then symbolizes a regression towards childhood.

Hotels can also, of course, represent an inner dislocation (travelling around) or uncommitted life.

❧

# Houses

Houses in dreams symbolize both social appearances and one's inner being.

*Appearances* are represented by the *outside* or *façade* of the house, and, as with many people, the most beautiful façade may conceal the most dreadful hovel within the personality. The façade is not the house, just as fine feathers do not make fine birds. Often in dreams we find gleaming façades, but the door opens on to a filthy corridor, just as a humble exterior may open on to sunny rooms.

*Shutters* in dreams are part of the house's "mask". Most of us keep our shutters firmly closed in order to keep out prying eyes.

*The door and the threshold* are symbols of *passage* towards our own interiors. We know already the significance of the threshold where we must show our credentials before being admitted. We must ascertain, then, who it is who welcomes us or who bars our way. This can refer to the imposed self or super-ego which prevents us from being at one with ourselves.

What are the *windows* of the house like? These are generally important because they represent our receptiveness to the outside world and the amount of light which is allowed in.

The *interior* of the house obviously symbolizes the centre. It represents our own interiors, our spiritual lives. The interior of a house is also conventionally the domain of women, of mothers. In dreams, then, it represents the "feminine pole". In a man, therefore, if often signifies the anima (chapter 7). The dream in this case would illustrate the condition of the anima – whether harmonious, orderly, undifferentiated, miserable, expectant, etc.

The different *levels* or *storeys* of the house represent either different parts of the body or different levels of the persona.

The *cellar* is the cavern of the unconscious, the foundation of the personality.

The *kitchen* is often important in dreams. It is the place where culinary transformations are wrought – that is, mutations of the personality. It is comparable to the workplace where the alchemist constantly attempts to transform the soul from "base" to precious and pure.

The *attic* symbolizes the past, childhood and memories, but also the inner "debris" of which we cannot rid ourselves. The attic can also represent the elevation of the soul in solitude. It is the highest level of the house. It looks out on heaven. We must climb if we are to reach it.

The *staircase*, whose symbolism is discussed separately in this Dictionary, links the different levels of the house. It represents therefore the emotional link between the different parts of oneself, conscious and unconscious.

In dreams, then, we must examine not only the general appearance of the house but also every part in which dreamers may find themselves. The surroundings, including the garden, are important. Here is a dream from my files (dreamed by a man aged thirty-nine):

> *I was walking through all the rooms of a house which was very simple but beautiful. Avenues stretched from the house in every direction, like a star.*

This is a good dream. The house has here become the centre of a mandala.

343

# Hunting

Hunting almost always has a sexual significance. It is, traditionally and historically, a characteristically and almost exclusively masculine pursuit. Dreams of hunting (and hunting itself) often exhibit emotional and sexual inhibition – the need to watch, to trail, to surprise and to kill. In certain dreams, a deer pursued may symbolize woman. This sort of dream may reflect a repressed sadism in the man, or homosexual tendencies in a woman. Hunting weapons are obviously phallic. In so-called "sporting" men, hunting dreams often denote a desire for vengeance on women, which they project on to the prey.

# Islands

Generally, an island symbolizes a refuge, an earthly paradise, a "centre".

Islands are the theme of countless poems and songs. Many people dream of going to live on a desert island as a way of seeking refuge or a paradise. Dreams about islands are also about autonomy. On an island, one is left to oneself. One is left alone to fight against hunger, sickness and the assault of the sea.

In certain dreams, islands are comparable with gardens.

In some "great dreams", an island becomes a "centre", from which innumerable directions radiate. The island then symbolizes a mandala. Here is a dream of this kind:

> *I was on an island. I did not know how I had come there. I was alone. It was a luxuriant, fertile island. As I looked at the wide horizons I thought how round the earth was.*

This is a "great dream", dreamed by a man aged fifty-three. Here we certainly have a mandala. The earth is circular. The island is the centre of an immense circumference. This is a dream which marked a vitally important transformation in the dreamer – the more so because the dreamer's arrival on the island had, obviously, been preceded by a "crossing" over the water.

# Jewels

Jewels appear generally only in "great dreams": those which mark our major transformations or movements towards the energizing "centring" of our personality. These are the dreams which demonstrate that one's alienated, codified social being has released its stranglehold. Jewels share their symbolism with fire (see above) because of their brilliance and their radiant warmth.

(See "Precious stones" at the end of chapter 6.)

⁘

# Kings and queens

Kings and queens often symbolize the father and mother in the spiritual sense of the terms. Many have died (and many still would die) for their king or their queen, but would think more than twice before dying for the president of a republic. Monarchs stand outside time. They are permanent. Individual monarchs may come and go, but their office possesses immortal mythic power.

The king is the radiant guide. It is he who watches over and centralizes the powers that be. In dreams, he becomes the "centre" of

our emotional forces. He represents the totality of our ego or being, much as he represents the totality of a nation. The queen, meanwhile, is messenger and mediatrix. She is the link between our unconscious minds and the king – that is, our higher consciousness.

The queen can also symbolize the anima (chapter 7) in a man, just as the king may symbolize the dominant animus in a woman. In these guises, kings and queens appear only in "great dreams".

∞

## Marriage

Marriage occurs often in dreams. It represents any form of union or alliance between self and self or between self and the outside world. In dreams, marriage often indicates that a bond is being created between the unconscious and the conscious, between our deep emotional structure and our reason.

*In a man*, a dream marriage between himself and a woman (but only when it occurs in "great dreams") means that he is preparing to unite with his anima. These are dreams of the first importance.

*In a woman*, some dreams take the same form and have the same meaning. She marries an unknown man, for example, who is the symbol of her animus, that is, her creative and social extroversion.

Dream marriages can go still further. They can be the sign of sacramental union between the self and the universe.

⚬

## Mist

See *fog or mist*.

⚬

## Motor car

The symbolism, albeit terrestrial, is much the same as that of various aeroplane dreams. The same questions apply.

If one is the *driver* of the car, the quality or otherwise of one's driving will reflect the manner in which one feels that one is managing day-to-day life. The dream will thus show what one really is, in depth.

If one is being *driven* by someone else, the dream demonstrates the way in which unconscious forces are "driving" the personality.

If one finds oneself in a car belonging to someone else, there is duality in the personality. The car generally symbolizes the "I" or ego in its entirety. One may dream, for example, that one finds oneself in a fine car to which one has no right. The dreamer probably suffers from a feeling of being an imposter in life, of having no right to others' regard or toleration. It's as if the dream were saying, "This car is too good for you." It is the same symbolism as that of the dream in which one travels first-class while holding only a second-class ticket.

The *bodywork,* the *tyres,* the *brakes,* the *carburettor,* the *steering,* etc., all have fairly precise significance in dreams. The analyst will usually find that their meaning becomes clear as he or she relates the dream to everyday life.

Here are some examples:

*I dreamed that I was driving but that the steering would not respond. The car was running towards a precipice.*

This indicates that the dreamer (a fifty-year-old man) was failing to "direct himself" in life. His behaviour was unrelated to his deeper desires and needs. He had reached an age when his inner life, for so long repressed or ignored because of professional duties and concerns, was demanding its right to exist. This man was becoming profoundly unhappy. Tension existed between his deepest being and his social behaviour. His "steering" pulled him this way and that. As for his "I" (the car), it was rolling straight towards the precipice of depression and resignation.

Another example:

*I dreamed that my carburettor broke down on a deserted road.*

The significance is clear. The dreamer lacks inner vitality. He is not "nourished" by his emotional centre. And the road is deserted: it is time for him to attend to his personal development, for the landmarks are already beginning to disappear.

Again:

*I dreamed that my car was toiling along, with all the brakes jammed down.*

An easy interpretation: there is inner "braking", inhibition, blockage. This man's need for freedom is "braked" by anxiety and, probably, difficulty in tolerating himself.

A final example, came from a forty-two-year-old man:

> *I dreamed that I was driving a car and that its bodywork was all damaged. Layers of paint-work kept falling off.*

The dreamer is beginning to realize that fine feathers do not make fine birds and that appearances are of no significance if there is nothing inside.

There are similar dreams in which tyres are punctured, the fan belt is broken, the brakes fail at a crucial moment, the bodywork gleams while the car's interior is shabby, or the car crashes into an obstacle.

We should remember too that the car is a phallic symbol in so far as it can smash, breach, break and kill.

# Mud

Mud, marshes, swamps, and so on, often appear in dreams. Inferiority feelings often give rise to dreams in which one is struggling to wade through a sea of mud. Other dreams include those in which people slowly sink into mire until they are in danger of suffocating. Here we find ourselves dealing once more with the symbolism of all that engulfs, buries or swallows – that is, women perceived (rightly or wrongly) as stifling, despotic, inescapable, etc. This can also indicate, however, that the dreamer is becoming embroiled in the inextricable mess of his or her inner life as it appears negative, anxiety-ridden and destructive.

◯∞◯

# Nudity

Nudity is common in dreams (see chapter 3). To see oneself naked usually signifies a sense of inferiority. We feel we are being "undressed" by others; we believe that other people's eyes are "stripping us bare" or "seeing right through us". These are the dreams of people who feel inner deprivation or inadequacy.

At the same time, nudity in dreams can symbolize a sloughing off and a vital step towards one's reunion with one's inner self. We remove our useless social "clothing" because we have acquired emotional security and stability.

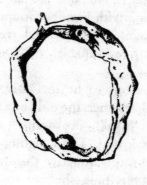

# Oedipus

The Oedipus complex is probably the most potent, the most famous and the most misunderstood. It was first identified and described by Sigmund Freud, and many have not forgiven him to this day. In fact, it is logical enough. The Oedipal situation is the essential core, the nucleus of human life about which countless emotional situations revolve. Given this, it is hardly surprising that this complex manifests itself in many dreams.

Let us briefly recall the details of the classic Oedipus complex.

*The boy* desires his mother's exclusive, absolute love. For this reason, he wants to "eliminate" his father, his rival for that love. He tries to do so by becoming stronger and more handsome, etc., than his father, but also by identifying with him, becoming a copy of him, necessarily younger and therefore, he believes, more capable of winning his mother's love.

*The girl* wants to be the only one to be noticed by her father, the only one to be loved by him. Her "rival" – her mother – must therefore be eliminated. The daughter tries to be prettier and more attractive than her mother. She does everything she can to attract her father's attention (clothes, make-up, etc.); or she may identify with him, attempting to imitate him or to beat him on his own ground. She then becomes a failed boy – with the grave risk of ending up as a failed girl.

In order to understand the symbolism of the more basic Oedipal situation, we must remember that the essential need which supersedes all others in a human being is to feel "connected" to all that surrounds us. Our permanent impulse is to rediscover the lost sensation of melting into the universe. This desire lies at the roots of what I term "masochism" and of all forms of orgy (see chapter 4).

For such a "religious" (from *religare* = to reconnect) quest, the Oedipal situation, particularly for boys, is ideal. Imagine that a boy had his heart's desire, that he had his mother entirely at his disposal, that he was indeed the only creature in her world, that she saw no other boy or man. There would be total fusion then – not, in fact, with his own mother, but with what the mother symbolically represents: absolute acceptance, total security and the sense of being at one with woman, the ultimate symbol of life.

This boy would know, then, a "paradise" in which he stood at the centre, but that paradise must rapidly become a paradise lost, because of the taboos which prevent any absolute union – even emotional – with the mother.

Any paradise lost will engender intense nostalgia, not, here, for the boy's own mother, but for the sense of universal oneness which she has come to represent. One can say that an Oedipus complex, in this regard, can never truly be resolved.

The boy, then the man, will always retain this nostalgia for a lost union, but the very existence of such nostalgia impels him to become "a man", to know "women" in short, to take on the conventional "masculine" role.

On the other hand, should a man remain too attached to his mother or to her symbol, he will always be a little boy. He will idealize women and will dream of grandiose platonic loves. He will do anything not to cause displeasure, although he may become fiercely aggressive. He will seek to charm and to seduce, not in order to love a woman but to *be loved* by her. It is hardly necessary to say that his anima will become unsteady, bringing all the negative dreams which spring from such a situation (see chapter 7).

The unresolved Oedipus complex will manifest itself in dreams about ideal and unapproachable women, great betrayed loves, men who appear as dangerous potential castrators. Enough Oedipal dreams have been reproduced in this book to give some idea of the range and nature of images which represent this universal complex. See also the symbolism of the mother and the father in chapter 6.

∽

# Princes and princesses

Princes and princesses generally symbolize changes in the personality brought about by love. They represent reconciliation with oneself, because princes and princesses are the focus for all eyes. They are centre of attraction and curiosity. In dreams, their appearance shows that emotional efforts are converging towards the unification of the personality. In certain 'great dreams', a royal couple will signify the harmonization of the masculine and feminine poles which are present in all human beings. Princes and princesses are thus symbols of inner youth and spirituality.

## Rags and tatters

To see oneself dressed in rags often denotes a wounded spirit. These are dreams involving anxiety, fear, sorrow, and feelings of inferiority and impotence. Rags may, however, also be symbols of inner wisdom (gurus, hermits, etc.), indicating the insignificance of outward appearances.

# Rainbows

Relatively rare in dreams, the rainbow symbolizes a bond, a union, a connection. It is a *bridge* drawn in the sky. It is always an excellent symbol in dreams. It is often linked to the symbolism of the *crossing*, indicating important inner changes (see chapter 6). The rainbow is also a *ring*; it is then the symbol of a union and of new relations with oneself.

# Rings

A ring, of course, is a symbol or sign of attachment and fidelity. To wear a ring means that one is "bound" to another person. We need think only of the wedding-ring or the bishop's ring. Dreaming about a ring generally means that one is making a connection with oneself, that one is taking oneself in hand after deciding to realize one's unity. The ring being circular, it has within it all the symbolism of the circle.

Here is a dream dreamed by a thirty-year-old man. He dreamed he removed a ring from his finger and placed it on the ground. The ring grew and grew to an enormous size, but then he saw that the ring was flawed. A part of its circumference was missing.

In the case of this man, this dream meant that the union which he had contrived to make with his self extended far further than this personal ego or "I". The great ring also involved the lives of others. Further, the ring left a passage so that he could go still further, instead of enclosing him within the limits of its circumference, however vast that might be. This dream came after another in which the dreamer sailed across a sea. See the section on "The crossing" in chapter 6.

❧

## Rivers

A river is an image of life springing from its source, flowing irreversibly onward, and dying as it blends into the infinite. To go into a river evokes the idea of bathing and baptism. Rivers thus represent purification and spirituality. See also *water* in this Dictionary.

❧

# Roses

The rose, of course, symbolizes beauty, but also perfection in the promise of the bud, the glory of the bloom. It is a feminine symbol, and may be related to the jewel (see above) or the anima (see chapter 7).

# Secrets

In some dreams, in which one is told a secret, passes on a secret, keeps a secret or shares a secret, there are overtones of initiation or participation.

For example, I have an account of a dream which was dreamed by a thirty-year-old woman. She was in a great colonnaded hall. A man came up to her and handed her a round polished stone. The man put his index finger against his lips in a hushing gesture, then walked away.

This was a "great dream". It marked an important inner transformation. Given the dreamer's associations, we were able to arrive at this interpretation: the vast colonnaded hall was a temple, a symbol of initiation, knowledge and truth. Those who foregathered in this temple shared the same secret or revelation. The round polished stone was a "jewel" representing the centre of the personality (see above in this Dictionary). The man was probably the creative part of the dreamer, her animus, the extension of herself outwards towards external life. The man demanded silence. He passed on a secret. Now, since a secret deep inside of us confers power, a secret is in itself a centre. Being given a secret, then, the dreamer had been entrusted with a privilege. She was now among the elect, and here the secret is linked to the idea of treasure.

This dream, then, can be translated as follows. If you become yourself, the centre of your personality will be like a jewel which will enable you to face existence with strength. You will become your own secret; and keep quiet. Do not share yourself with anyone except those who are capable of keeping your secret. The fact of becoming profoundly that which you are affords you entrance into a new state of freedom and, in consequence, solitude, as well as participation with those who share the same secrets.

∞

## Ships

See *boats and ships*.

∞

## Shoes

As we know that the foot has phallic connotations and that the shoe must fit the foot, it becomes clear that the shoe is symbolically feminine.

We may dream that we are walking comfortably in new shoes, or sometimes the shoes are shabby, with holes letting in water. The meaning here is clear: the dreamer either is relaxed on life's roads or suffers feelings of inferiority. If the shoe does not fit the dreamer, we must suppose that the dreamer is no longer in harmony with him or herself.

In many men's dreams, the appearance of women's shoes can reveal a fetishistic tendency (shoe fetishism and fetishism in

relation to women's feet are both common forms).

A shoe can also be a symbol of wealth or authority. To remove one's shoes in a dream is to perform an act of humility or self-abasement (recall that the ancient world considered the shoe as a sign of freedom; slaves went barefoot).

## Spears

A spear is a *stick* (see below) and shares its symbolism. A spear is phallic and masculine. In dreams, it can stand for men, fathers, power, strength or honour. It can also stand for the fear of being "pierced", "impaled", raped in one's personality; it is then a sign of castration anxiety.

∞

## Stables

Stables seem to appear rarely in dreams. They are among the negative representations of our instincts. To see oneself sweeping or washing down a stable signifies one's desire to put oneself in order. Sometimes, too, we find stables being swept by a tidal wave or destroyed by fire. These are anxiety dreams. They indicate that we feel our inner world to be seriously threatened.

∞

## Staircases

A staircase allows us to climb up or descend; we have discussed the symbolism of both these directions (see chapter 13). A rising staircase represents a change of level. The dreamer is climbing, moving higher. It is the symbolism of the *ascent*.

*Climbing a staircase* signifies emotional and spiritual search. It is an act of inner purification. We sometimes find dreams in which the top of the staircase is guarded by humans or animals. We are back here with the *guardians of the threshold*, to whom we must show our credentials if we are to be allowed to move to a higher level and to initiation into life.

*Descending a staircase* generally signifies voyaging into one's own interior, towards one's instincts and one's unconscious.

A staircase also joins two storeys in a *house* (see above, in Dictionary).

The staircase also symbolizes the fear of the vertical. We have to go up or down it. The dreamer is imprisoned in a single dimension. It allows no rest, other than temporary (a "landing"). In this way it represents human uprightness, merciless effort, lack of rest and the absence of any reassuring horizontals.

❧

# Sticks

The significance of sticks is linked to that of weapons. The stick is phallic. In dreams, its meaning depends – as always – on context. We often find broken sticks in dreams, or people fighting with sticks or truncheons (especially in Oedipal dreams where the boy attempts to eliminate his father by showing himself to be more virile. Sometimes a big stick is suddenly reduced to the size of a wand, etc. Generally, the meaning can readily be deduced.

Sticks, of course, also support walkers, shepherds, pilgrims, the blind (the pilgrim of darkness). They are props and means of defence because they can be turned into weapons.

As a sceptre or a soldier's baton, the stick becomes a sign of power and authority. It can also be the shepherd's crook or the bishop's crozier. As a magic wand, it allows inner transformations.

# Trains

We have already encountered this symbol in chapter 3, but it is necessary to return to the subject here, given the frequency of its occurrence in dreams.

The interpretation of train dreams is relatively easy. It is often enough simply to "transpose". A *station*, for example, is a point of departure or arrival. One can evidently set off in any number of directions in life, or arrive at a stopping-place or a halt. We must then examine the context of the station. Is the station from which the dreamer departs a big one? Is it teeming with people and full of trains? If so, it symbolizes significant inner potential. Again, if it is disused and deserted, it represents an inner life which is emptied of vital possibilities. The station where one arrives should be similarly examined.

The *train* itself represents our evolution. It is the vehicle of our mental and emotional journey. It also symbolizes social and collective life. Sometimes we dream about a runaway train, or a broken-down engine, or incompetent driver. This means that we are committed, notwithstanding our conscious will, to "journeys" which could be ill-omened.

*Delays* and *mistakes* are very frequent in these dreams. We arrive late, we miss the train or take the wrong one, sit down in a carriage to which our tickets do not entitle us, and so on. These dreams indicate feelings of impotence, inferiority or guilt. They can also show to how great an extent we allow life's opportunities to pass us by.

*Ticket collectors* also regularly turn up in dreams. They demand a reckoning, and so represent a form of imposed "self" or superego.

*Overcrowded* trains often appear. This can be interpreted as indicating difficulty in social integration. If the dreamer cannot get on to the train for lack of space, it might mean that the dreamer too willingly drops back in the face of competition.

The train, then, marks our successes, our failures, our constraints and our anxieties. It is the modern version of the dragon.

# Tramps

I personally possess transcriptions of forty dreams in which the male dreamers saw themselves as tramps. A tramp may pass as a free spirit, going where he will, living or dying at the pleasure of the passing seasons. Largely replaced today by the "hippy" or "new-age traveller", he often represents the shadow (chapter 10) of the dreamer. He is his double, his hidden brother, whom he envies but whom he has hidden deep within himself. This interpretation is likely only in important dreams.

In lesser dreams, the tramp can represent the contempt which the dreamer feels for himself, the sensation of having missed out on life, remaining only a tramp, wandering hither and yon through life. These are dreams of disappointment and anxiety in the face of an uncertain future.

In women, it is not uncommon that a dirty, hairy tramp represents a masculine pole which yet needs to be uncovered, an animus (chapter 8) still in its unrefined state.

⁂

# Trees

The tree is a universal symbol. It is the sign of permanence and vital evolution, even eternity. It links earth and sky. It symbolizes rebirth and immortality – which is well understood by those who have planted a tree, knowing that their purpose lies beyond their own graves. Lovers too understand this. How many have carved their initials and interlaced hearts upon a tree-trunk, so that their love may stand recorded for the tree's life, or for ever?

Upright and phallic, generally vertical and powerful, the tree is a common symbol of masculinity and of the father. By contrast, where a tree is luxuriant, covered in leaves and laden with fruit, etc., it can stand for refuge, welcome and shelter from the blazing of the sun – the mother, in short.

In dreams, the tree can also symbolize inner vitality or else the aridity of the self, depending on whether the tree is flourishing and green, or wizened and leafless.

I have records of many dreams about trees. For example, one man, aged forty-five, said: "I dreamed about a mighty oak. I tried to gather its acorns, but I could not manage." This was an indication that the dreamer had developed to an exaggerated extent his apparent strength, to the detriment of an emotional life which might have produced "fruit".

Another person dreamed about "a big red

tree in an orchard. It had three very green branches which looked as if they had just sprouted there." The big tree here symbolizes the dreamer's inner vitality. The colour red also indicates energy, which here gives birth to new shoots. Vitality, in short, is growing and regenerating. The number 3, of course, as already stated, is the sign of perfection and of perfect harmony between the unconscious and the conscious (see chapter 13).

As a *phallic symbol*, the tree becomes a symbol of sexuality. Dreams where one falls from trees are common. They can indicate a fear of impotence. They must be linked with dreams about *falling* (see chapter 3). Some adolescents dream they are felling a tree. These dreams are linked to the Oedipus complex. The boy "cuts down" his father, in order to gain his mother's exclusive love.

Other dreams present the tree as a symbol of *castration*. Branches hang or are torn off (the same symbol as teeth falling out). In women, emotional sterility or frigidity are often symbolized by trees with wilted flowers.

In analysis, it is important that all four principal parts of the tree be envisaged (roots, trunk, branches and foliage, and fruit). Often dreamers report that they have scrabbled and dug at the soil in order to extricate and separate entangled or recalcitrant roots. This is an excellent sign of profound searching within the psyche.

The *roots*, then, symbolize the "planting" of the personality; they are the original, emotional, unconscious life which nourishes the conscious.

The *trunk* is the vertical element, symbol of the "upright" or erect personality, and also of the outwardly apparent or social part of oneself. As we have seen, the trunk can represent one's view of one's own sexuality.

*Branches* and *foliage* can take on many guises and demand close attention from the analyst. Foliage can be compact or expansive, round or pointed, healthy or diseased. Branches may be upright, leaning, dead, wrenched off, withered or, on the contrary, sprouting with promise. These many aspects must be carefully examined.

# Valleys

In many dreams, valleys are symbols of emotional riches. Thanks to the combination of sun and water, it is in valleys open to the sky that the earth is made fecund. In dreams as in life, there are green valleys and valleys of death. The fertile valley is a symbol of spirituality, inner transformation and contemplation. Such a valley can be drawn into the symbolism of a large garden. An arid valley in which the water has dried up is a symbol of death.

A valley also possesses the symbolism of the number 2 (see chapter 13). This is because the sun (fire) plunges into the valley to be united with its opposite, water. Fire and water, a duality of apparent incompatibles, marry and have issue in the fruitful soil and harvests.

In a man, the valley can sometimes symbolize the anima (chapter 7). We have already encountered a happy dream of this variety in chapter 6.

❦

# War

Many dreams about war spring from memories, or anxiety about the future. Most of them, however, deal with internal battles –

moral or emotional conflicts. The interpretation of such dreams is easy enough. As ever, the context of the dream is of the first importance.

**Water**

Water has no shape, but takes on those which we give it. It is thus perfectly supple. Water has no colour, yet it reflects all colours. It is thus a perfect mirror.

Equally, water represents fertility. It "marries" and has union with the sun to propagate life on earth. Water contains infinite menace, infinite potential, infinite promise. It irrigates, it washes, it purifies, it engulfs, it drowns, it floods, and it breaks into waves and foam.

The appearance of water in our dreams is always an important sign.

Dreams about *bathing* are frequent. They can mean that we are "washing" our souls; they thus symbolize *baptism*, with the inner purification which that rite presupposes.

*Swimming* also features often in our dreams. The context of the dream will reveal whether we are at ease or in difficulties, whether we allow ourselves to be carried along by the water or whether we must struggle against it (that is, the unconscious). In this last case, water can symbolize the mother, whose influence is the current.

We have to examine in what form water appears in a dream. Is it a calm lake – an image of serene emotion – or a wild ocean? A stagnant pond? A swelling sea, announcing a tidal wave?

Whatever the case, water is almost always a *feminine* symbol. It can represent the mother, the wife or the anima in man. In this last case, it appears in the guise of streams, lakes, fountains, rivers, springs, waterfalls or oceans. The dreamer must look at the totality of the dream. Is this anima peaceful, iridescent, spurting, threatening, stagnant or black?

Dreams of being *engulfed* by water often occur. These are anxiety dreams, which demonstrate that the unconscious is negative and stifling. As often as not, the central image at work in such an unconscious is probably that of the mother.

In dreams as in life, water can be attractive and bewitching. It often produces unconscious suicidal desires. It is also a symbol of pre-natal peace, such as we knew in the "maternal waters" of the womb.

But if by chance you should dream about ice, beware. Your soul is frozen, your emotions are in danger of dying, you are drawing close to psychic stagnation. Better by far to dream of warm and shimmering waters.

# Window

A window is an opening on to light and the outside world. Generally, the dreamer is inside a room and is looking out. That means that the dreamer is situated in the present (the room which is not as light as the outside) observing the *future* (the light, the expanses, everything that spreads out from the room where the dreamer is standing).

We may find then, any number of situations. Is the future (the outside) clear and sunny? Is the glass in the window murky or rain-streaked? Is the street out there animated, or does the window give out on to an icy waste? What, if there is one, does the horizon tell us? And what of the room in which the dreamer is located? Does the dreamer want to leave and to head for the future, or would he or she prefer to remain in the safety of the present?

A window, however, can also symbolize *receptiveness* towards the external world. From beyond a window, after all, we receive the messages of human life, the life of light separated from our own.